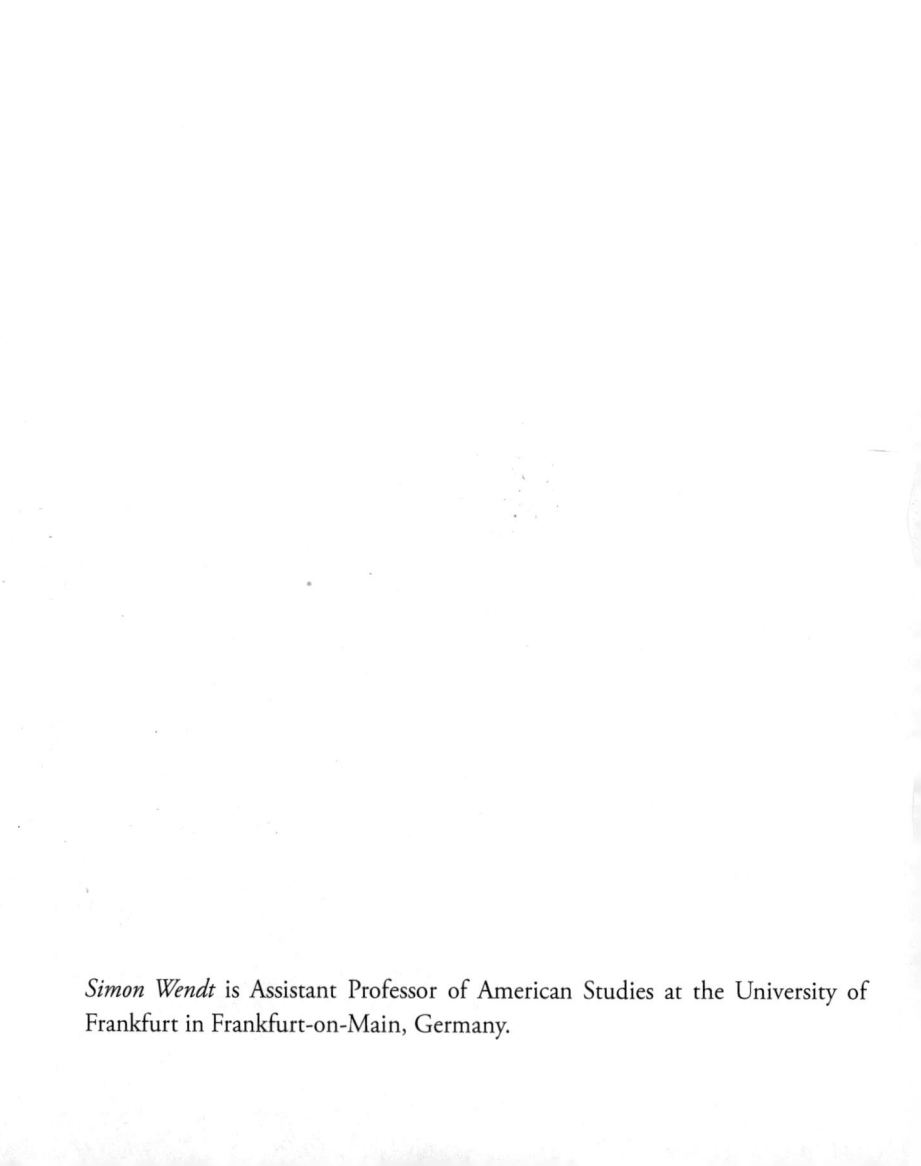

Simon Wendt is Assistant Professor of American Studies at the University of Frankfurt in Frankfurt-on-Main, Germany.

Simon Wendt (ed.)

Extraordinary Ordinariness

Everyday Heroism in the United States, Germany, and Britain, 1800–2015

Campus Verlag
Frankfurt/New York

The editor gratefully acknowledges the financial support of the Fritz Thyssen Foundation.

Parts of Janice Hume's essay "Narratives of Feminine Heroism: Gender Values and Memory in the American Press in the Nineteenth and Twentieth Centuries" have previously appeared in the following publications: Janice Hume, "Press, Published History, and Regional Lore: Shaping the Public Memory of a Revolutionary War Heroine," *Journalism History* 30, no. 4 (2005): 200–209; Janice Hume, "Saloon Smashing Fanatic, Corn-Fed Joan of Arc: The Changing Memory of Carry Nation in Twentieth-Century American Magazines," *Journalism History* 28, no. 1 (2002): 38–47; Janice Hume, *Obituaries in American Culture* (Jackson: University Press of Mississippi, 2000); Janice Hume, "Changing Characteristics of Heroic Women in Mid-Century Mainstream Media," *Journal of Popular Culture* 34, no. 1 (2000): 9–29; Janice Hume, "Defining the Historic American Heroine: Changing Characteristics of Heroic Women in Nineteenth-Century Media," *Journal of Popular Culture* 31, no. 1 (1997): 1–21.

Distribution throughout the world except Germany, Austria and Switzerland by
The University of Chicago Press
1427 East 60th Street
Chicago, IL 60637

ISBN 978-3-593-50617-3 Print
ISBN 978-3-593-43519-0 E-Book (PDF)

All rights reserved. No part of this book may be reproduced or transmitted in any form or by any means, electronic or mechanical, including photocopying, recording, or by any information storage and retrieval system, without permission in writing from the publishers.
Copyright © 2016 Campus Verlag GmbH, Frankfurt-on-Main
Cover design: Campus Verlag GmbH, Frankfurt-on-Main
Cover illustration: "With the Greatest Difficulty They Reached the Boat" © Frank Mundell, *Heroines of Daily Life* (London: Sunday School Union, 1896), 49.
Printing office and bookbinder: CPI buchbücher.de, Birkach
Printed on acid free paper.
Printed in Germany

For further information:
www.campus.de
www.press.uchicago.edu

Table of Contents

Introduction: Studying Everyday Heroism in Western Societies
Simon Wendt 7

"Our Heroes of To-day": The Royal Humane Society and
the Creation of Heroes in Victorian Britain
Craig Barclay 25

Everyday Heroism for the Victorian Industrial Classes:
The British Workman and *The British Workwoman*, 1855–1880
Christiane Hadamitzky and Barbara Korte 53

Everyday Heroism in Britain, 1850–1939
John Price 79

Volunteers and Professionals: Everyday Heroism and
the Fire Service in Nineteenth-Century America
Wolfgang Hochbruck 109

Narratives of Feminine Heroism: Gender Values and Memory
in the American Press in the Nineteenth and Twentieth Centuries
Janice Hume 139

Heroic Ordinariness after Cavell and Capra: Hollywood Cinema and
Everyday Heroism in the Interwar Period and World War II
Matthias Grotkopp 167

Everyday Socialist Heroes and Hegemonic Masculinity in the
German Democratic Republic, 1949–1989
Sylka Scholz 185

Everyday Heroes in Germany: Perspectives from
Cultural Anthropology
Silke Meyer 217

After Watergate and Vietnam: Politics, Community, and
the Ordinary American Hero, 1975–2015
William Graebner 235

"It Must Have Been Cold There In My Shadow":
Everyday Heroism in Superhero Narratives
Michael Goodrum 249

After the Working-Class Hero: Popular Music and Everyday
Heroism in the United States in the Twenty-First Century
Martin Lüthe 271

Notes on Contributors 291

Introduction: Studying Everyday Heroism in Western Societies

Simon Wendt

In April 1906, in the small town of Midway, Kentucky, a retired blacksmith named Rufus K. Combs saved Richard Godson, a local lawyer whom he utterly disliked. Despite their enmity, Combs jumped into a gas-filled vault to rescue Godson, who had fallen into the pit when inspecting a leaking gas tank. Americans would probably never have heard about Combs's courageous act if it had not been for the newly established Carnegie Hero Fund Commission, which honored Combs by granting him a silver medal and $1,500. Subsequently, newspapers across the country reported about this astonishing case of altruism. Journalists lauded Combs's unselfish bravery and noted approvingly that other Carnegie awardees had similarly risked their lives to save those of others.[1] To the editors of the *Washington Post*, for instance, such noble acts represented "a pleasing record for the encouragement of our faith that the heroic impulse still greatly moves the hearts of men to courageous acts of self-sacrifice."[2]

In November 2014, more than 100 years after the Carnegie Hero Fund Commission paid tribute to Richard Combs, Tuğçe Albayrak, a young German woman of Turkish descent, tried to protect two teenage girls who had been harassed by three young men in front of a McDonald's restaurant in Offenbach, a town near Frankfurt. During a subsequent altercation, one of the young men punched Tuğçe, who fell on her head and died a few days later. After her death, many commentators lauded what they called Albayrak's civic courage, and some even called her a heroine. One of those comments appeared in the *Süddeutsche Zeitung*, a center-left newspaper from

---

1 "Note and Comment," *Daily Springfield Republican*, October 20, 1906, 8; "Stories of Heroism," *Anaconda Standard*, November 18, 1906, 17; "His Enemy Fights Fair," *Duluth News Tribune*, December 2, 1906, 1; "Too Good To Lose," *Grand Forks Daily Herald*, July 17, 1907, 3; "Too Good To Lose," *Morning Olympian*, July 13, 1907, 3.
2 "Brave Acts of Humble Heroes," *Washington Post*, October 13, 1907, 3.

Bavaria. In December 2014, the paper published a long article on the case, in which the author stated: "What those people who dared to oppose the murderous system of Nazi Germany did, from the ... Communist workers who smuggled comrades out of the country, to the resistance of July 20– for that, the word civic courage is too weak a word anyway. Even if the term has so often been misused: it was something that one can call heroism. ... Tuğçe will now also be celebrated as a heroine and as an idol."³

These two examples occurred in different countries and in very different historical contexts. Yet in both cases, ordinary people's courageous behavior was regarded not only as praiseworthy, but as heroic. More importantly, their deeds were infused with particular meanings that reveal much about the societies in which they occurred. In the case of the United States, praise for ordinary citizens' heroism around 1900 reflected people's hope that the greedy selfishness that was believed to characterize American society had not yet destroyed altruistic self-sacrifice. In the case of Germany, the praise for Tuğçe Albayrak's "heroism" revolved around a particular understanding of democratic civic-mindedness, which many deem essential to post-1945 German identity and which is inextricably intertwined with anti-Fascism.

This volume probes the complex history of such examples of everyday heroism (*Alltagsheldentum* in German). On a general level, everyday heroes and heroines can be defined as ordinary men, women, and children who are honored for actual or imagined feats that are considered heroic by their contemporaries or by succeeding generations. Scholars have devoted countless pages to war heroes, heroic leaders, and superheroes as well as to the blurring distinctions between heroes and celebrities, but they have said little about the meaning and impact of ordinary citizens' heroism.⁴ For this

---

3 "Tochter Courage," *Süddeutsche Zeitung*, December 6–7, 2014, 49 (my translation).

4 On the history of heroism in the three countries that this volume examines, see, for example, Sidney Hook, *The Hero in History: A Study in Limitation and Possibility* (1945, reprint; New Brunswick: Transaction Publishers, 1992); Orrin E. Klapp, *Heroes, Villains, and Fools: The Changing American Character* (Englewood Cliffs, NJ: Prentice-Hall, 1962); Harold Lubin, ed., *Heroes and Anti-Heroes: A Reader in Depth* (San Francisco, CA: Chandler, 1968); Marshall Fishwick, *The Hero, American Style: Changing Ideas of Greatness from John Smith to John Kennedy* (New York: David McKay Company, 1969); Theodore P. Greene, *America's Heroes: The Changing Models of Success in American Magazines* (New York: Oxford University Press, 1970); Mark Gerzon, *A Choice of Heroes: The Changing Faces of American Manhood* (Boston: Houghton Mifflin, 1982); Edward Tabor Linenthal, *Changing Images of the Warrior Hero in America: A History of Popular Symbolism* (New York: Edwin Mellen Press, 1982); Barry Schwartz, "George Washington and the Whig Conception of

publication, the few scholars who have studied everyday heroism kindly agreed to elaborate on their previous research, while a number of other contributors probe hitherto unknown aspects of the topic.[5] This book thus constitutes the first comparative effort to bridge the historiographical gap that continues to characterize scholarship on heroism. Comparing the United States, Germany, and Britain from a multidisciplinary perspective, it asks when and how everyday heroism emerged, how it changed, and how it was discussed and depicted in public discourse, mass media, film, and other forms of popular culture between 1800 and the early twenty-first century. It also draws attention to the various social, cultural, and political functions that this new hero type served, including the norms, values, and collective identities ordinary heroes were believed to embody. Focusing on

---

Heroic Leadership," *American Sociological Review* 48, no. 1 (1983): 18–33; Susan J. Drucker and Robert S. Cathcart, eds. *American Heroes in a Media Age* (Cresskill, NJ: Hampton Press, 1994); René Schilling, *"Kriegshelden": Deutungsmuster heroischer Männlichkeit in Deutschland, 1813–1945* (Paderborn: Ferdinand Schöningh, 2002); Anuschka Albertz: *Exemplarisches Heldentum: Die Rezeptionsgeschichte der Schlacht an den Thermopylen von der Antike bis zur Gegenwart* (München: Oldenbourg, 2006); Susan J. Drucker and Gary Gumpert, eds., *Heroes in a Global World* (Cresskill, NJ: Hampton Press, 2008); Barry Schwartz, *Abraham Lincoln in the Post-Heroic Era: History and Memory in Late Twentieth-Century America* (Chicago: University of Chicago Press, 2008); Andrew J. Huebner, *The Warrior Image: Soldiers in American Culture from the Second World War to the Vietnam Era* (Chapel Hill: University of North Carolina Press, 2008); Melvin Smith, *Awarded for Valour: A History of the Victoria Cross and the Evolution of British Heroism* (New York: Palgrave Macmillan, 2008); Larry Tye, *Superman: The High-Flying History of America's Most Enduring Hero* (New York: Random House, 2012); Jason, Dittmer, *Captain America and the Nationalist Superhero: Metaphors, Narratives, and Geopolitics* (Philadelphia: Temple University Press, 2013). On the tensions between heroism and celebrity, see, for example, Daniel J. Boorstin, *The Image: A Guide to Pseudo-Events in America* (1961, reprint; New York: Vintage Books, 1992); Ray B. Browne and Marshall W. Fishwick, eds., *The Hero in Transition* (Bowling Green, OH: Bowling Green University Popular Press, 1983); Joshua Gamson, "The Assembly Line of Greatness: Celebrity in Twentieth-Century America," *Critical Studies in Mass Communication* 9, no. 1 (1992): 1–24; Charles L. Ponce De Leon, *Self-Exposure: Human-Interest Journalism and the Emergence of Celebrity in America, 1890–1940* (Chapel Hill: University of North Carolina Press, 2002).

5 There are only three scholars who have explicitly addressed everyday heroism in the United States, Britain, and Germany, and all three have kindly agreed to contribute essays to this volume. See John Price, *Everyday Heroism: Victorian Constructions of the Heroic Civilian* (London: Bloomsbury, 2014); William Graebner, "'The Man in the Water': The Politics of the American Hero, 1970–1985," *Historian* 75, no. 3 (2013): 517–543; Silke Meyer, "Helden des Alltags: Von der Transformation des Besonderen," in *Die Helden-Maschine: Zur Aktualität und Tradition von Heldenbildern*, ed. LWL-Industriemuseum (Essen: Klartext-Verlag, 2010), 28–40.

this long-neglected phenomenon, the following essays shed fresh light not only on heroism, but also on the history of everyday life in Western societies.

Defining heroism – let alone everyday heroism – constitutes a major challenge for those trying to study its history, and there are two main strategies that scholars can employ to tackle this vexing problem. One strategy would be to focus on the myriad functions that heroes and heroines serve in Western societies. In general, they tend to embody the norms, values, and beliefs of particular social groups. They also contribute to the formation of collective identities and become role models that people seek to emulate. As symbols of dominant norms and identities, they constitute central sources of authority and are used to legitimize social, political, cultural, and racial hierarchies. Yet, although heroism tends to be a stabilizing force in society, it is a social and cultural construction that is subject to constant debate, reevaluation, and revision. As people's norms and values change over time, so do heroes' attributes and the functions they serve.[6] Relying solely on this strategy, however, can be frustrating, since it can be applied to a multitude of illustrious figures, whom contemporaries might or might not regard as heroes or heroines. The second strategy, proposed by anthropologist Silke Meyer – who is among the very few scholars who have examined everyday heroism in Germany – could therefore be the more fruitful one. Meyer rightfully laments the arbitrariness of universal definitions of heroism and suggests that methodological insights from cultural anthropology might offer a solution. Rather than utilizing universally applicable concepts, cultural anthropologists take seriously the terms that are used by the ordinary people they study. When viewed from this perspective, people themselves define what heroism is, by employing such terms as "hero," "everyday hero," and "ordinary hero," or

---

6 Orrin Klapp, "The Creation of Popular Heroes," *American Journal of Sociology* 54, no. 2 (1948): 135–141; Janice Hume, "Changing Characteristics of Heroic Women in Midcentury Mainstream Media," *Journal of Popular Culture* 34, no. 2 (2000): 9; Susan J. Drucker and Robert S. Cathcart, "The Hero as a Communication Phenomenon," in *American Heroes in a Media Age*, 3–5; Tristram Potter Coffin and Hennig Cohen, "Introduction," in *The Parade of Heroes: Legendary Figures in American Lore*, ed. Tristram Potter Coffin and Hennig Cohen (Garden City, NY: Anchor Press, 1978), xxiii; Lance Strate, "Heroes: A Communication Perspective," in *American Heroes in a Media Age*, 15; Lance Strate, "Heroes and/as Communication," in *Heroes in a Global World*, 19; Roger R. Rollin, "The Lone Ranger and Lenny Skutnik," in *The Hero in Transition*, 30–34; William J. Goode, *The Celebration of Heroes: Prestige as a Control System* (Berkeley: University of California Press, 1978), 7–8, 151–152.

by labeling ordinary citizens' behavior as "heroic."[7] For scholars of everyday heroism, such an approach not only makes it easier to identify what Western societies considered examples of "ordinary extraordinariness," but also allows us to trace the idea of the heroic and how it has changed over time. Ultimately, however, it will be necessary to use a combination of these two strategies to fully understand heroism and its multiple meanings and uses in Western societies.

As suggested by cultural anthropology's usefulness in defining heroism, only multidisciplinary or interdisciplinary approaches will lead to scholars developing a methodological toolbox that allows them to fully probe the complexities of everyday heroism. Media studies and communication studies probably provide some of the most important methodological insights. Already in their 1994 introduction to the edited volume *American Heroes in a Media Age*, Susan Drucker and Robert S. Cathcart emphasized that heroes and heroines are "communication phenomena," meaning that studying heroism primarily entails studying communication about those persons society deems heroic.[8] In the same publication, Lance Strate pointed out that "different kinds of communication will result in different kinds of heroes," reminding us that the construction and impact of what he calls "oral," "typographic," and "electronic" heroes differ significantly and, therefore, require analyses that take into account these differences.[9] While such a communication perspective is crucial to enhancing our understanding of how information about everyday heroism was interpreted and disseminated in different media, historians of everyday life caution us not to forget that heroism is more than merely discourse. In fact, as John Price has pointed out in his comprehensive study of everyday heroism in Victorian Britain, media accounts that celebrate the exploits of ordinary citizens provide important glimpses into the lives of people who tended to leave no written sources for scholars to consider.[10] Psychologists can also add much to our understanding of ordinary people's heroism. By focusing on questions such as why some people risk their lives to save those of others, or what role gender plays in their decision to do so, psychological research not only directs our attention to those individuals who are hailed

---

7 Meyer, "Helden des Alltags," 34.
8 Drucker and Cathcart, "The Hero as a Communication Phenomenon," 5.
9 Lance Strate, "Heroes: a Communication Perspective," in *American Heroes in a Media Age*, 15.
10 Price, *Everyday Heroism*, 11.

as heroes and heroines, but also suggests new ways of understanding the interrelationship between their motivation to act "heroically" and the norms and values that society sees confirmed or strengthened in those actions.[11] This volume's contributors – who include historians, literary scholars, media scholars, film scholars, sociologists, cultural anthropo-logists, and Americanists – utilize these and other methodological ap-proaches to provide crucial insights into ordinary people's heroism in the past and the present.

While the various case studies that are assembled here do not constitute a definitive history of everyday heroism in Western societies, they suggest at least partial answers to the questions this volume seeks to answer. With regard to its origins, the idea that ordinary citizens were capable of heroic behavior appears to have emerged around 1800, at least in the case of Britain, and became more widespread and accepted over the course of the nineteenth century. A cursory look at press coverage of everyday heroism in the American print media after 1865 suggests that the development in the United States closely mirrored that in Britain, reflecting a general democratization of heroism in the nineteenth century.[12] Significantly, only pro-social behavior elevated ordinary people to heroic status and, thus, clearly distinguished everyday heroism from entrenched traditions of warrior heroism. Especially those kinds of rescues that were daring, and in which people risked their lives to save those of others were called "everyday heroism" in the nineteenth century, although even simply enduring the tribulations of everyday life could be enough to earn the label of hero or heroine. In general, it appears that use of the designations "everyday hero" or "ordinary hero" underwent an increasingly inflationary

---

11 See, for example, Selwyn W. Becker and Alice H. Eagly, "The Heroism of Women and Men," *American Psychologist* 59, no. 3 (2004): 163–178; Douglas M. Stenstrom and Matthew Curtis, "Heroism and Risk of Harm," *Psychology* 3, no. 12 (2012): 1085–1090; Philip G. Zimbardo, James N. Breckenridge, and Fathali M. Moghaddam, "'Exclusive' and 'Inclusive' Visions of Heroism and Democracy," *Current Psychology* 32 (2013): 221–233; K. J. Jonas and V. Brandstätter, "Zivilcourage: Definition, Befunde und Handlungsempfehlungen," *Zeitschrift für Sozialpsychologie* 45 (2004): 185–200.

12 See, for example, "Rewards for Bravery," *Boston Daily Globe*, April 2, 1875, 3; "Burned to Death," *New York Times*, September 27, 1875, 10; "A Horrible Holocaust," *Boston Daily Globe*, November 16, 1878, 1; "Two Brave Farmer Boys," *New York Times*, October 10, 1881, 2; "A Father's Heroism," *New York Times*, July 3, 1883, 1; "A Boy's Heroism," *Chicago Daily Tribune*, May 14, 1885, 1; "Bishop Whipple's Bravery," *New York Times*, October 29, 1886, 1; "Johnnie Curley's Heroic Act," *Boston Daily Globe*, June 7, 1888, 1; "Out of the Jaws of Death," *New York Times*, August 8, 1890, 8.

growth in the nineteenth and twentieth centuries and, ultimately, came to encompass a wide range of pro-social behavior by the beginning of the twenty-first century.

During the second half of the nineteenth century, the mass media – followed by radio and film in the twentieth century, and the internet in the twenty-first – became the main "hero makers," praising ordinary citizens' exploits and familiarizing readers with their heroic deeds. However, philanthropic organizations, local communities, as well as national governments also recognized civilians' feats as heroic, and did much to spread the idea that common people's actions could be as praiseworthy as those of valiant soldiers. In light of the fact that so many different groups and people helped disseminate stories about everyday heroes, it is not surprising that such stories served a number of different functions at different points in time. For the mass media – and that holds true for the nineteenth as well as the twentieth century – the thrilling stories drawn from everyday life became a journalistic technique of storytelling that helped sell newspapers and magazines. For middle-class organizations and the state, by contrast, the idolization of everyday heroism around 1900 was primarily intended as a means of social control, since they presented working-class people thus honored as virtuous citizens who neither intended to challenge social inequality nor questioned the authority of the state. If heroes tend to be a stabilizing force in society, this appears to have been particularly true for everyday heroes. In general, ordinary heroes and heroines were especially in vogue during times of perceived crises, when societies seemed to lack the type of social solidarity that was believed to have characterized them in the past. Perhaps even more so than in the case of traditional hero types such as military heroes and political leader heroes, everyday heroes tended to become both reflections of people's anxieties about a perceived lack of unity, as well as a sign of hope that not all was lost, since incidents of heroic rescues were interpreted as evidence that the nation's citizens still cared for one another. In fact, praise for and the popularity of everyday heroes and heroines at particular moments in time appear to have been inextricably intertwined with longings for a sense of community. If heroic civilians generally reflected dominant social and political norms, they were also frequently utilized to strengthen traditions of gender difference – at least in the nineteenth and early twentieth century. While women could attain heroic status, their heroism was depicted as gender specific and became a means to highlight accepted notions of femininity that revolved around passivity and submissiveness. The example of the German Democratic Republic, whose ordinary "heroes of labor" were mostly male, suggests that such forms of gender discrimination continued well into the twentieth century.

If the following essays allow us to draw at least a few generalized conclusions, each case study offers additional insights into the complexities of everyday heroism in Western societies. The first three chapters shed light on various aspects of its history in Britain. In "'Our Heroes of To-day': The Royal Humane Society and the Creation of Heroes in Victorian Britain," Craig Barclay discusses an organization that became crucial to the dissemination of the idea of everyday heroism in Britain in the nineteenth century. Founded in 1774 by private citizens and supported by the British Crown, it primarily honored ordinary citizens who had rescued others in life-threatening situations, mostly on rivers and at sea. Initially, the Royal Humane Society awarded most of its medals to the upper echelons of the British nation but, over the course of nineteenth century, an increasing number of working-class citizens were also recognized as heroes. Since medals of distinction had traditionally been bestowed only upon the country's nobility, the organization's recognition of the bravery of the lower rungs of society by awarding medals resulted in considerable social status for their wearers. In general, however, the Society's upper middle-class leaders, as well as Victorian writers who used its awardees to pen riveting stories about ordinary heroism in everyday life, intended their work to encourage working-class citizens to adopt and refrain from challenging middle-class norms and values. In addition, the organization perpetuated class distinctions by reserving most of its silver medals for members of the upper class, while laborers not only tended to receive primarily bronze medals but also needed eyewitnesses of social standing to corroborate their accounts. Thus, although the Royal Humane Society sought to stimulate pro-social behavior and contributed to a public discourse that valued such behavior, its work can also be interpreted as a form of social control that sought to ensure society's stability in the face of class tensions and social unrest.

In the second chapter, "Everyday Heroism for the Victorian Industrial Classes: *The British Workman* and *The British Workwoman* (1855–1880)," Christiane Hadamitzky and Barbara Korte provide additional evidence that Britain's upper classes considered the idea of everyday heroism a discursive means of social control during the second half of the nineteenth century.

Focusing on two popular educational monthlies that were created by middle-class editors, but aimed to reach a working-class readership, Hadamitzky and Korte show that while these publications reflect an increasing democratization of heroism, they were also intended to foster class harmony by constructing exemplars of moral and social responsibility who shunned political agitation intent on challenging economic and political inequality. As part of this attempt to prevent social unrest, *The British Workman* and *The British Workwoman* honored the same types of heroic rescues that the Royal Humane Society deemed praiseworthy, but they also introduced the new category of "moral heroism," which was used especially for describing women's brave and selfless efforts to protect the domestic sphere and to encourage their men to lead a morally unblemished life. The two magazines thus also sought to influence working-class people's ideas about gender by stressing middle-class notions of femininity that revolved around women's "silent," "restrained," and largely passive "heroic love," while generally neglecting war heroes, sports heroes, and famous labor activists, since such traditional heroic figures were believed to incite working-class men toward violent upheaval. In many ways, the type of everyday heroism lauded by these two periodicals reflected a sense of social crisis among middle-class citizens rather than a genuine belief in the ubiquity of heroic qualities in all strata of society.

The following chapter, John Price's "Everyday Heroism in Britain, 1850–1939," shows that such efforts to honor ordinary citizens for what people deemed heroic behavior were far from exceptional in the British Isles in the nineteenth and twentieth centuries. Indeed, "everyday heroism" was a widely used term – generally connoting daring rescues undertaken by civilians in everyday life – with numerous organizations, communities, as well as the state recognizing such exploits, rewarding rescuers, and commemorating their deeds. Reflecting a gradually growing democratization of heroism in the nineteenth century, news media widely reported about everyday heroes and heroines. In addition to inspiring poets, writers, and artists, these people also became the subjects of intellectual debates about what heroism actually stood for. Price identifies three specific contexts in which ordinary citizens' life-risking behavior was praised as heroic and the different purposes each served. In what he calls the "establishment context," it was primarily the state that championed a version of heroism revolving around civilian pro-social bravery that was intended to strengthen citizens' allegiance to the nation and the British

Crown. In the "organizational context," philanthropic organizations such as the Society for the Protection of Life from Fire also heaped praise on intrepid rescuers and publicized their stories because such public recognition was believed to help make people aware of, and possibly teach them how to prevent, the many perils with which modern British society was confronted around 1900. Finally, progressively-minded individuals and organizations who operated in a "radical context" deemed civilian heroism important because its public recognition might help improve working class people's lives and provide exemplars of morally upright and respectable behavior that laborers could emulate – not only to improve their lives as individuals, but also to foster a more deeply-felt class consciousness within the context of economic inequality. Price argues that this group of reformers, writers, and artists was radical because they proposed alternatives to those state-sanctioned and educational hero-making efforts that did not challenge traditional notions of heroism because they were intended to promote social and political stability. The "radicals," by contrast, called into question such entrenched traditions by highlighting working class heroes' contributions to the welfare of the nation and by introducing pacifist ideas that were at odds with military heroism. Significantly, Price suggests that World War I, while generally believed to mark the decline of the ideal of heroism in Britain because of the conflict's shocking carnage, did not tarnish the idea of everyday heroism. In all three contexts described by Price, ordinary citizens' heroic exploits continued to be widely recognized in the interwar period.

In chapter four, "Volunteers and Professionals: Everyday Heroism and the Fire Service in Nineteenth-Century America," Wolfgang Hochbruck examines what can be regarded as the most visible civilian hero of the nineteenth century: the firefighter. Hochbruck sheds light on the gradual shift from volunteer to professional firefighting and on what this process reveals about the discourse of everyday heroism in the United States before and after the American Civil War. As was the case in Britain and other countries, U.S. firemen were widely admired for bravely facing the blaze while selflessly risking their lives to rescue men, women, and children from the flames. However, in the case of volunteer companies, their heroic status was undermined in the 1850s and 1860s by media reports about these firemen's unruly behavior and purported inefficiency. Hochbruck argues that this temporary fall from grace can be explained, at least in part, by the growing influence of working-class volunteers who tended to join fire companies because of their interest in male fraternity rather than in protecting their home communities. Ultimately, however, despite the fact that firefighting became less "everyday" due to its growing professionalization, the heroic image of both volunteer and professional firefighters endured, as can be seen in the immense popularity of lithographs that depicted firefighters and their heroic struggle against the flames in American cities in the 1850s and 1860s. Even the increasing use of technology – such as steam pumpers – did not erode firefighters' heroic status in U.S. society, which remained intact throughout the twentieth century and experienced a new boost at the beginning of the twenty-first century.

The fifth chapter, Janice Hume's "Narratives of Feminine Heroism: Gender Values and Memory in the American Press in the Nineteenth and Twentieth Centuries," examines the multifaceted ways in which journalists covered women's everyday heroism in the United States in the nineteenth and twentieth centuries, focusing on the intricate interrelationship of the memory of heroism and dominant gender norms in the American press. Hume explains that the emergence of mass media and new journalistic techniques in the post-1850 period fostered the increasing coverage of ordinary people and their "heroic" deeds. Although heroism thus became more egalitarian, those heroic figures that the press primarily wrote about were white men whom journalists portrayed as symbols of American nationalism. Yet, some women and their exploits did find their way onto the pages of U.S. newspapers and magazines, and journalists' stories about them reveal important connections between changing interpretations of femininity and the depictions of American heroines. Throughout the nineteenth century, mirroring the coverage in *The British Workwoman*, American publications such as the *Lady's Book* confined the label of heroism to those women who had selflessly and silently suffered hardships as faithful wives and mothers, notwithstanding the first stirrings of women's activism in the 1840s. By the mid-twentieth century, the heroic qualities attributed to women had changed considerably, albeit some continuities remained in place. In the 1950s, female heroism and wifehood or motherhood continued to be inextricably linked in the women's magazine *Ladies' Home Journal*, and only in the wake of second-wave feminism in the 1970s did the publication allow for a larger number of independent heroines that were noted because of their intellect outside the home. Nevertheless, heroic wives and mothers remained a staple of the magazine's gendered heroism discourse. In general, then, female heroes were rarely acknowledged publicly, and their heroism tended to be associated with the private sphere and female submissiveness. Only through obituaries did stories about women's "heroic" lives reach a wider audience, although the term "heroine" was rarely used to describe the deceased. As Hume shows, this form of commemoration reflected the same norms and values that were perpetuated by newspaper reports about living heroes and heroines. In the nineteenth century, the few women thus remembered were commended for qualities that tended to be associated with traditional notions of femininity, including patience, obedience, piety, and tenderness. Only in the early twentieth century did obituaries begin to list character traits normally associated with men, including their business acumen and wealth. In general, however, obituaries reflected and preserved entrenched gender dichotomies, reminding us that the media expresses dominant norms and values when reporting about ordinary heroes and heroines while simultaneously shaping and reinforcing them.

Chapter 6, Matthias Grotkopp's "Heroic Ordinariness after Cavell and Capra: Hollywood Cinema and Everyday Heroism in the Interwar Period and World War II," complicates our understanding of the interrelationship of the ordinary or the everyday and the idea of heroism in the United States in the 1930s and early 1940s. Relying on Stanley Cavell's philosophy of moral perfectionism as a point of departure, Grotkopp defines everyday heroism as behavior that aims to create or uphold a certain moral ideal in everyday life. This ideal revolves around efforts to preserve both democracy and a sense of community in Western societies, which, according to Grotkopp, are prone to subvert their own idea of egalitarian freedom. Grotkopp regards American director Frank Capra's films of the interwar period, in particular *John Doe*, which was released in 1941, as prime examples of the ways in which this notion of everyday heroism was interpreted in U.S. culture. In Capra's interwar films, ordinary citizens initially fall prey to corrupt elites who seek to use them for attaining their dubious goals but, then, ultimately reject their evil overtures. Grotkopp argues that their struggles can be read as lessons of Cavell's philosophy and the idea of everyday heroism in American society, but he also emphasizes that the dialectic of the ordinary and the heroic tends to be a conservative means to preserve the social status quo.

Chapters 7 and 8 turn to the history of everyday heroism in Germany in the twentieth and twenty-first centuries. In "Everyday Socialist Heroes and Hegemonic Masculinity in the German Democratic Republic, 1949–

1989," Sylka Scholz examines how post-World War II East Germany utilized so-called "heroes of labor" and other heroic, but otherwise ordinary figures to strengthen people's allegiance to the socialist nation, to legitimize its authority, and to present socialist role models that East Germans were expected to emulate. Given that most of these heroes were men, Scholz argues that the concept of hegemonic masculinity helps to understand how the idea of the socialist everyday hero served not only political ends, but also perpetuated entrenched gender inequalities, the emancipatory rhetoric of socialist elites notwithstanding. Since the defeat of Nazi Germany had largely discredited military heroes and heroic political leaders, seemingly ordinary heroic figures, especially workers, took on a particular significance in post-war East Germany in the second half of the 1940s – the attempt being made to portray them as epitomizing the egalitarian vision of socialism. Solely constructed by the state, this idea of ordinary socialist heroism also informed the country's film industry, which was encouraged to depict strong and resourceful men and women in everyday life. Despite the fact that the "heroes of labor" were no longer in vogue by the 1950s and had not necessarily enjoyed widespread popularity to begin with, the German Democratic Republic's leaders continued to give awards to those workers who had proved particularly resourceful until the regime's collapse in 1989. By the 1970s, the socialist hero in general and the socialist everyday hero in particular were in crisis, and despite the fact that the GDR's successful athletes briefly rekindled people's heroic imagination, East German authorities were unable to produce new heroic figures that would help them revive people's trust in and support for the socialist nation.

Silke Meyer's "Everyday Heroes in Germany: Perspectives from Cultural Anthropology" focuses on West Germany, pointing out that the terms "hero" and "heroism" are omnipresent in twenty-first-century German popular and everyday culture. Echoing Sylka Scholz's observation that World War II marked a fundamental break with long-standing traditions of military heroism, Meyer argues that the void that the absence of such traditional hero figures created was filled by various forms of what was regarded as civic heroism, including such behavior as helping fellow citizens in need of assistance and engaging in similar tasks deemed beneficial for society in general and local communities in particular. But not only such forms of pro-social behavior were regarded as heroic by German society in the twentieth and twenty-first centuries. Simply being able to endure and cope with the daily struggles of everyday life elevated many to the status of hero or heroine. Interviews with German teenagers revealed that the label hero is applied rather loosely today, since interviewees named athletes as well as family members when asked to name heroes they admire. Their answers also complicate our understanding of the character traits people deem heroic, since especially male adolescents considered "coolness" a noteworthy attribute that they said was part of athletes' heroism. Paradoxically, then, everyday heroism could stand for seemingly conflicting qualities: pro-social behavior that benefits society, as well as an artificial pose that professes distance from and seeming indifference to society. Since ordinary heroes and heroines permeate contemporary German culture, they reflect a growing heroic pluralism and a certain ambivalence with regard to the norms and values they seem to represent. At the same time, such character traits as endurance, perseverance, loyalty, morality, and fair play tend to dominate in contemporary debates on, and media representations of, everyday heroism, suggesting that the pro-social elements of what people regard as heroic behavior continue to reign supreme in twenty-first-century Germany.

The last three chapters return to the United States and examine the political and cultural dimensions of everyday heroism between the 1970s and the present. In "After Watergate and Vietnam: Politics, Community, and the Ordinary American Hero, 1975–2015," William Graebner probes the politics of the everyday hero in the post-Vietnam War era, showing that ordinary heroes became ubiquitous in political discourse as part of a longing for traditional values and a sense of community in the face of military defeat, the ascendancy of liberalism and hedonism, as well as the highly visible cultural and ethnic pluralism of the post-civil rights era. Especially conservative pundits and politicians lamented the seeming disappearance of traditional heroes and utilized the ordinary hero discourse to convince white working-class men to support the Republican Party in their attempts to fend off the fundamental social changes brought about by the social movements of the 1960s. Significantly, this American embrace of everyday heroism continues to the present day, although it has become more inclusive in terms of race, ethnicity, and gender. Despite the flexibility of the concept of ordinary heroism – which could include hero types ranging from everyman rescuers to police officers and firefighters – as well as the changes that this discourse has undergone since the 1980s, it continues to reflect a deeply felt concern about what many observers regarded as the fragmentation of America's social fabric. Through their praise of the heroic exploits of ordinary citizens, numerous journalists, politicians, and other commentators criticized the lack of social solidarity that they said had characterized U.S. communities in the past, while simultaneously offering a reason for hope and a potential solution to this predicament in the present.

The tenth chapter, Michael Goodrum's "'It Must Have Been Cold There In My Shadow': Everyday Heroism in Superhero Narratives," offers important insights into the interrelationships between everyday heroism and super heroism, focusing on fictional stories offered in comics and Hollywood movies in the late twentieth and early twenty-first centuries. Although superheroes outshine almost everybody else in these narratives, Goodrum shows that other seemingly ordinary protagonists are shown as being capable of heroism as well. In doing so, he introduces the important conceptual differentiation between heroic conduct and heroic goals, but also identifies two major "flows of everyday heroism" in the narratives he analyzed. Through "in-flows," real-life examples of ordinary citizens' exploits are integrated into superhero stories, while "out-flows" refer to the fact that flesh-and-blood people draw inspiration from these narratives and engage in heroic behavior in the real world. This observation is significant because such flows are not necessarily confined to the U.S. context in which most superhero narratives are created. Rather, they become part of a globalized notion of heroism that attracts and inspires readers around the world. Ultimately, superhero narratives limit the range of behavior deemed to be heroic and tend to serve a regulatory function that aims to preserve the social and political status quo. However, as Goodrum shows, they also allow for considerable heroic pluralism, which reveals that super heroism and everyday heroism frequently operate in tandem and in tension in twenty-first century popular culture.

In the final chapter, "After the Working-Class Hero: Popular Music and Everyday Heroism in the United States in the Twenty-First Century," Martin Lüthe examines the ways in which notions of everyday heroism permeate popular music in twenty-first-century America, arguing that it is characterized by a reappearance of a particular working-class folk hero type that had first emerged in the post-World War II era and was most conspicuous in the 1960s. According to Lüthe, the combination of a new form of capitalism, the changing ways in which popular music is produced and consumed, and the impact of the terrorist attacks of

September 11, 2001 prompted many musicians to praise and highlight the exploits of white working-class people who not only played a crucial role in the rescue operations during 9/11, but also contributed to U.S. society through hard, manual labor. Using the singers Bruce Springsteen and P!nk as examples, Lüthe's essay shows that song lyrics, as well as artists' performances of particular songs, reveal much about the manifold ways in which ordinary people were elevated to heroic stature in the post-9/11 United States.

Addressing a vast array of topics in three different countries, this collection of essays makes an important contribution to the study of heroism by shedding light on the long-neglected history of everyday heroism. However, this volume makes no claim to geographical or topical comprehensiveness and raises as many questions as it answers. Indeed, there are a number of important aspects of the topic that future research could and should address. First and foremost, this volume reveals that there are a number of time periods that still await scholarly attention. Even though we appear to have a fairly good idea of the emergence and significance of everyday heroism around 1900 in Britain, for instance, we know only little about its history in the United States during the same time period and virtually nothing about it in Germany. This last point exposes a surprising blind spot that calls for a thorough historical examination of ordinary heroism in the nineteenth and early twentieth centuries. The immediate post-World War II period and the 1960s also constitute a historiographical lacuna that should be of interest to historians and other humanities scholars. For example, although we know that the Cold War influenced East Germany's decision to use "heroes of labor" to legitimize the ideal of a socialist nation, there is no research on the reactions of West Germany, Britain, and the United States to such uses and interpretations of ordinary heroism, nor are there studies on alternative constructions of heroic civilians in these three countries during the 1950s and 1960s.

There are also a number of additional analytical perspectives that would help us better understand the genesis and the various functions of everyday heroism in Western societies. What role, for instance, did religion play in the evolution and growing popularity of ordinary heroes and heroines in the nineteenth century? Could ordinary people who risked their lives to save other human beings become heroic only after 1800 because such rescues had previously been believed to be God's providence, and did Enlightenment thought help legitimize the idea that the agency of ordinary

Christians was praiseworthy? And how did traditions of Christian compassion influence people's interpretations of everyday heroism? Another analytical lens that a few of this volume's contributors only hinted at is race. How was everyday heroism used to make the case that ethnic and racial minorities could be heroic as well? Or was it rather employed to confirm people's beliefs about white superiority and help legitimize entrenched racial hierarchies?

Finally, historians need to go beyond mere comparisons and probe the transnational dimensions of everyday heroism to fully understand its complexities. How, for instance, did British interpretations of heroic civilians influence the United States and Germany in the nineteenth century? Or was it rather the United States that shaped European representations of ordinary heroes and the efforts to honor them? The Carnegie Hero Fund Commission, which was mentioned at the very beginning of this introduction, suggests possible transatlantic connections. Founded in 1904 by American steel magnate Andrew Carnegie, the Commission honored ordinary people who risked their own lives to save those of fellow citizens. Encouraged by the lavish praise that the Hero Fund Commission received in the United States during the first three years of its existence, Carnegie decided to set up similar Hero Funds in Europe. Beginning with the United Kingdom in 1908, he offered generous endowments to several European nations to provide them with the means to organize commissions that would emulate the example of the American Hero Fund. European governments and rulers reacted enthusiastically to the proposition and gladly assisted in the organization of such institutions in their respective countries. By the beginning of World War I, Carnegie Hero Funds had been established in ten European countries, including Great Britain, Germany, France, Italy, Sweden, and Switzerland.[13] While historians, among them John Price, have begun to examine the Hero Fund's history in Britain and Germany, much remains to be learned about its impact in Europe as well as the similarities and differences between the meaning of civilian heroism in the United States and other parts of the

---

13 "New Carnegie Hero Fund," *New York Times*, September 25, 1908, 6; "Adds to Long Reward Roll," *Boston Daily Globe*, June 4, 1909, 4; "German Carnegie Fund," *Baltimore American*, April 9, 1911, 45; Carnegie Endowment for International Peace, *A Manual of the Public Benefactions of Andrew Carnegie* (Washington, DC: Rumford Press, 1919), 124.

world.[14] Examining the work of philanthropic organizations such as the Carnegie Hero Fund could help historians to discern the transnational intellectual and organizational processes of exchange that shaped Western interpretations of everyday heroism. Related to this need for transnational perspectives on the topic, scholars should also examine whether and how non-Western societies praised ordinary people as heroes and heroines, and what functions such adulations served. Was there – as suggested by Michael Goodrum in this volume – such as thing as a global idea of everyday heroism, and what role did colonial conquest, trade, and globalized transfers of knowledge play in its dissemination? It is to be hoped that this volume's findings, as well as the blind spots it has revealed, will prod scholars to delve deeper into a topic that promises to help us to better understand the history of heroism and its interrelationship with everyday life.

---

14 See Price, *Everyday Heroism*, 125–165; Olaf Wittenberg, "Die deutsche Carnegie Stiftung für Lebensretter: Auszeichnungen, Anerkennungen, Beihilfen," *Militaria* 30, no. 3 (2007): 84–97.

"Our Heroes of To-day"[1]: The Royal Humane Society and the Creation of Heroes in Victorian Britain

Craig Barclay

Medals that preach with beams of sterling truth
Acts of true greatness to our gallant youth
And telling plain the noble exploits raise
In noble hearts the highest tide of praise,
Their young souls brace and fortify to and steel
To dare great deeds with death-defying zeal.[2]

The nineteenth century was an age of heroes. Statues and other monuments commemorating the brave deeds of the Empire's gallant sons were to be found in almost every city in Britain. With few exceptions, these commemorated the lives and deeds of the nation's leading men – sailors, soldiers and politicians – whilst the bravery of the less exalted members of society went un-remarked and unrecorded. An exception to this general rule is to be found in London, where the Watts Memorial to Heroic Self Sacrifice in Postman's Park records the deeds of those from all walks of life who gave up their own lives in an effort to save others.[3] The memorial was the brainchild of the artist George Frederick Watts, who had recognized the need to create a monument that could act both as focus for national celebration and as a source of inspiration for others, explaining in the *Times* of September 5, 1887 that "The character of a nation as a people of great deeds is one, it seems to me, that should never be lost sight of. … The material prosperity of a nation is not an abiding possession; the deeds

---

1 Title of poem by W.C. Bennett, *Penny Illustrated Paper*, February 1, 1873, 73.
2 Edward Dalton, "The Sea," originally published in Edward Dalton, *The Sea, the Railway Journey and Other Poems* (London: Dalton & Lucy, 1866). Reprinted in J. Cumming & C. Vince (eds.), *The Life-boat in Verse* (London: Hodder & Stoughton, 1938), 23–24.
3 John Price, "'Heroism in Everyday Life': the Watts Memorial for Heroic Self Sacrifice," *History Workshop Journal*, 63, no. 1 (2007): 254–278; John Price, *Heroes of Postman's Park: Heroic Self-Sacrifice in Victorian London* (Stroud: History Press, 2015).

of its people are."[4] In choosing to commemorate the deeds of those who sacrificed their lives to save others, Watts envisaged a new type of inspirational public memorial that celebrated worthy heroic individuals, irrespective of their social background. Even as Watts' memorial was being constructed however, the medals of the Royal Humane Society[5] were already performing a similar purpose: celebrating and memorializing brave deeds performed by individuals drawn from across the spectra of class, age, gender and race.

This essay explores how the work of the Royal Humane Society and its kindred organizations fitted into the broader cultural framework of Victorian Britain. In particular, it examines how the process of celebrating the deeds of lifesavers morphed with time to mirror wider changes in class relations and how – building upon the practices pioneered by the Royal Humane Society – the systematic granting of medals as a visible means of recognizing bravery (both in the civil and military spheres) came to be widely accepted both by the state and the public. It also throws light upon the processes whereby the priorities of the Royal Humane Society shifted over the course of the nineteenth century from solely rewarding members of the middle and upper classes towards establishing systems that also allowed for the recognition of members of the lower social orders. Parallel to this, it examines the motivations and backgrounds not only of those who recommended, validated and approved the granting of rewards, but also of the men and women who exploited and embellished tales of "Every-day heroes" as tools for encouraging "worthy" behaviors and social compliance in the aspirational working classes.

The Royal Humane Society

The Royal Humane Society was established in 1774[6] as a result of the work of two English doctors, Dr. William Hawes and Dr. Thomas Cogan, who

---

4 G. F. Watts, "Another Jubilee Suggestion," *Times*, September 5, 1887, 14; reprinted in John Price, *Postman's Park: G.F. Watts' Memorial to Heroic Self Sacrifice* (Compton: Watts Gallery, 2008), 9.

5 Craig Barclay, *The Medals of the Royal Humane Society* (London: Royal Humane Society, 1998).

6 P. J. Bishop, *A Short History of the Royal Humane Society* (London: Royal Humane Society, 1974), 4.

drew their inspiration from the Amsterdamse Maatschappij tot Redding van Drenkelingen, which had been established in 1767 with the aims of publishing guides for treating people who had apparently drowned and awarding prizes to lifesavers.[7] The Humane Society proved an immediate success, swiftly attracting the support not only of non-conformists such as Cogan and Hawes, but also leading members of the London elite, including both the Lord Mayor and the Bishop of London. The Society's star rose even further in 1783 when King George III became its patron. In 1787, the organization was formally renamed the Royal Humane Society (RHS).

Although the saving of life was a core driving force behind the Society's activities, it was not its sole motive. During its formative years, the saving of souls – and money – were likewise deemed by the Society to be of paramount importance. Accidents could place a great burden upon the state and society, depriving employers of valued labor and leaving grieving wives and children dependent upon the parish for support. These risks were recognized by the RHS which, as a patriotic body, made it very clear that,

> it is our duty as well as interest to replace the industrious poor in their sphere of usefulness, that they may again work for their wives and families; whereby they are snatched from misery and want, and the community relieved from a troublesome and expensive burden. These are a part of the important benefits to the publick, (sic) by the establishment of the Humane Society.[8]

The saving of souls was also recognized as a priority with W. Poutney, for example, celebrating in verse his successful resuscitation of an "industrious man with numerous family":

> Ours is the joy, the heartfelt joy, to save
> Friend, lover, parent, from th' untimely grave
> To snatch from death the victims of despair,
> And give the means of penitence, peace and prayer.[9]

From the outset, the Royal Humane Society recognized the desirability of establishing a framework of rewards to recognize the efforts of those who had contributed to the achievement of its aims. Building upon the practice

---

7 K. Hines, "The Royal Humane Society," *Pre-Hospital Immediate Care* 3 (1999): 38.
8 Royal Humane Society *Annual Report* 1785–1786, 82.
9 Letter sent by W. Poutney to W. Hawes (Treasurer of the RHS) on February 28, 1803, *Gentleman's Magazine*, January–July 1803, 222.

of the Amsterdam Society that had served as the role model for its foundation, the RHS established a medal with which to reward those who contributed to the success of its activities. The medals, often bearing the words "Go Thou and Do Likewise" inscribed on their edge, were intended to be desirable and to inspire emulation. The RHS was in full agreement with Napoleon Bonaparte, who noted that "I defy you to show me an ancient or modern republic in which there are no distinctions: You may call these baubles, well, it is with baubles that men are led."[10]

The wearability of the Society's medals was of paramount importance. At the time of their inception, no outward badges of distinction were available to those who did not occupy the very uppermost strata of civil or military society. The association with royal patronage imbued these rewards with a rare aura of status and respectability, and ensured that they would be desired and coveted. To possess and to wear such a medal was to mark a man out as a person of virtue and significance. In the society's early years, these silver medals were presented primarily to doctors and medical assistants to recognize successful resuscitations, whilst members of the working classes who recovered bodies or rescued drowning individuals were granted monetary rewards. As the eighteenth century progressed, however, the medal of the RHS came to be used more commonly to recognize acts of individual bravery and, by the early nineteenth century, had effectively evolved into a device used exclusively for recognizing courage. An early example of the award of a RHS medal granted for bravery is provided by an account of the presentation of a silver medal to Mr. Peter Quibilingo of the Royal Marines, in recognition of his having saved no fewer than eight seamen from drowning in a rescue that resulted in his own hospitalization. The medal was most definitely intended to be worn and displayed since, as the description noted: "A silver chain has been added, apprehensive that so fine a Medal would risque (sic) being lost, if suspended only from a ribbon."[11]

Class boundaries were further broken down following the introduction of a cheaper and more widely awarded bronze medal in 1837. Thus, although in its earliest years the RHS had restricted the granting of its

---

10 Speech of Bonaparte to Council of State, May 4, 1802. Quoted in Colonel Vache, *Napoleon at Work*, trans. G. F. Lees (Stroud: Nonsuch, 2007), 118.
11 See A. J. Henderson, "The Presentation of Medals," *Orders & Medals Research Society Journal* 33, no. 2 (1994): 122–125; J. Wilson, "Peter Quibilingo – An Early RHS Medallist," *Orders & Medals Research Society Journal* 35, no. 3 (1996): 208–211.

medals to its more respectable supporters and sponsors, by the latter part of the century this was certainly not the case. The Society's awards were widely distributed and had gained a status and desirability that extended far beyond the borders of Britain. Indeed, even an American writer such as Mark Twain could write with some justification of "that reward which a sailor prizes and covets above all other distinctions, the Royal Humane Society's medal."[12] Thus, the RHS had come to be inextricably associated with the rewarding of courage and the celebration of bravery.

There is ample evidence to support the conjecture that, during the nineteenth century, lifesaving awards were held in high regard by the general public. Popular poetry recorded the gallantry of lifesavers, whose bravery was readily and favorably compared with that of the soldiers who defended Britain's Empire. For example, Clement Scott's *The Lay of the Lifeboat* (1880) proclaimed:

They talk of battles and rank and file;
they call the roll, count cannon and loss,
And Tom he wears a Corporal's stripe,
and brave little Jim the Victoria Cross.
They march to the front with fife and drum,
and follow the beat of the regiment's band;
They see their flag as it waves,
and hear the jolly old Colonel's clear command.
But there's never a sound in the battle at sea,
but the howling storm and the scream afar;
And it's only duty points the way when
the ships break up on the harbour bar.[13]

The medals received – and proudly worn – by rescuers were likewise specifically referred to in verse:

Praise to the men whose well-earned medals rest
On many a storm-scarred brave and manly breast,
And tell the tale of noble efforts made,
Of hard brought succour and triumphant aid,

---

12 Mark Twain, "Perils at Sea," *The New York Times*, November 26, 1872, 1. Reproduces letter written by Twain to the RHS on November 20, 1872, highlighting the gallantry of several seamen of the Cunard steamship *Batavia* who had risked their lives to rescue the crew of a sinking ship in mid-Atlantic.
13 Reprinted in Cumming & Vince (eds.), *The Life-boat in Verse*, 13–15.

Trophies more precious than laurelled bays,
The brazen plaudits or venal praise.[14]

Whilst these verses both refer specifically to the bravery of lifeboat-men, the heroic deeds of fireman,[15] engine-drivers[16] and members of the general public[17] were likewise celebrated in print. Such bravery was frequently recognized by the RHS, which granted medals in recognition of acts of bravery on land, in rivers and at sea. It is clear from the accounts printed in the Society's *Annual Reports* and contemporary journals that the bulk of the medals given during the eighteenth and early nineteenth centuries were awarded to members of the professional classes, with the Society's own medical assistants (who frequently composed their own recommendations) being especially regularly rewarded. This in part reflects the primary role of the Society's medals: the rewarding of those who advanced the organization's core aim of "affording immediate relief of persons apparently dead from drowning".[18]

Indeed, many of the earliest medals recognized successful resuscitations rather than brave rescues. In the majority of cases involving members of the lower social orders, rewards took the form of cash payments rather than medals; the Society taking the view that these would be more appreciated and would serve as a greater stimulus to action. This situation did not last indefinitely however and, by 1830, it was very much the exception rather than the rule, with the Society awarding almost all of its medals in recognition of acts of bravery which had been brought to its attention by third parties. These reporters were often private individuals (albeit generally drawn from the professional classes) or representatives of larger organizations, whilst numerous recommendations were also received via the commanders or officers of naval or merchant vessels.

A survey of the status or occupations of those who received the Society's silver medal between 1830 and 1914 confirms a tendency to reward those at the higher end of the social spectrum. Unsurprisingly, awards to those employed at sea dominate, and of these a disproportionate

---

14 Dalton, "The Sea," originally published in Dalton, *The Sea, the Railway Journey and Other Poems*, Reprinted in Cumming & Vince (eds.), *The Life-boat in Verse*, 23–25.
15 F. Mundell, *Stories of the Fire Brigade* (London: Sunday School Union, c. 1895).
16 M. Reynolds, *Engine-Driving Life, or Stirring Adventures and Incidents in the Lives of Locomotive Engine-Drivers* (London: Crosby, Lockwood & Co., 1881).
17 Laura M. Lane, *Heroes of Everyday Life*, 2nd Edition (London: Cassell, 1896).
18 RHS *Annual Report*, 1774, frontispiece.

number were given to officers, particularly during the period up to 1880 when awards to officers markedly exceeded those given to ratings[19]. Indeed, it was until the period 1890–1909 that awards to ratings came significantly to outnumber those to officers; although, even then, the proportions of medals granted did not come close to mirroring the numbers of men serving in each of the two groups. An almost identical pattern can be observed in the awards granted to military personnel: those holding commissioned rank being proportionately far more likely to receive silver medals than non-commissioned officers or other ranks.

RHS Silver Medals: Status/Occupation of Recipient (Percentage of Awards)[20]

	1830-1839	1840-1849	1850-1859	1860-1869	1870-1879	1880-1889	1890-1899	1900-1909	1910-1914
Naval Officer/Mercantile Marine Officer	35.7	26.1	33.3	35.9	29.6	16.4	11.7	10.8	28.6
Army Officer/Cadet	3.5	3.8	5.1	3.9	8.2	8.2	7.5	5.4	2.4
Aristocracy/Gentry/Farmers	6.3	5.7	4.1	5.5	4.1	3.7	5.8	2.7	-
Clerical/Professional/Managerial/Academic	8.4	9.6	7.7	4.7	7.1	8.9	5.8	6.3	9.5
Police	0.7	2.5	1.5	0.8	2.0	5.2	4.2	3.6	2.4
Foreman/Supervisor/Skilled Labor	3.5	1.9	2.1	-	3.1	9.7	5.8	2.7	4.8
Pilot/Harbor Master	1.4	0.6	1.0	0.8	-	-	-	-	-
Sailor/Boatman/Fisherman/etc.	9.1	17.2	15.4	23.4	18.4	17.9	21.7	28.8	26.2
Army NCO/Other Rank	3.5	1.9	4.1	3.9	5.1	5.2	14.2	7.2	-
Domestic Service	-	1.3	1.0	0.8	-	-	0.8	-	-
Unskilled/Manual Labor	0.7	1.3	1.5	-	4.1	15.7	15.9	27.0	23.8
School Pupil/Youth	6.3	6.4	5.1	1.6	8.2	3.0	1.7	-	2.4
Unspecified	21.0	21.7	17.9	18.7	19.2	6.0	5.0	5.4	-
TOTAL AWARDS	143	157	195	128	98	134	120	111	42

---

19 Non-commissioned sailors.
20 See RHS *Annual Reports*; Lambton Young *Acts of Gallantry* (London: Sampson Low, Marston Low & Searle, 1876); and William H. Fevyer, *Acts of Gallantry* 2 (Chippenham, Naval & Military Press: 1996).

Indeed, it is only when the numbers of silver medals awarded to unskilled and manual laborers are considered that we can map a developing trend towards a more liberal distribution of rewards to the lower orders of society, with the percentage of medals granted rising from a negligible 0.7 percent of the total for 1830–1839 to a far more respectable 27 percent during the first decade of the twentieth century.

The Society's introduction of a bronze version of its lifesaving medal in 1837 offered the organization the means greatly to increase the number of awards bestowed. The Society's *Annual Report* for 1838 records that, in its first year of existence, the bronze medal was awarded on a modest 22 occasions (including 3 medals presented by the Society's Brighton branch).[21] During that same year, the silver medal was voted to 14 rescuers. Recipients included Lieutenant Archibald Macdonald of the Bengal Army who, along with five coastguard boatmen, had crewed a small rowing boat which went to the assistance of a fishing boat in distress off the Cork coast. Significantly, whilst a silver medal was given to the officer, the coastguards each received only a bronze medal in recognition of their efforts. Indeed, these men are all but invisible, and are not even individually named in the *Annual Report*, which merely records that "The SILVER MEDAL awarded to Lieut. Macdonald and a BRONZE MEDAL to each boatman."[22] Nevertheless, by offering such recognition, the RHS was pioneering the rewarding of working class bravery and helping to establish a pool of "working class heroes" which others would be able to draw upon and exploit.

RHS: Rewards Voted 1837[23]

Reward	Number Voted	Percentage of Awards
Silver Medal	14	7.6 %
Bronze Medal	22	11.9 %
Testimonial on Vellum	3	1.6 %
Pecuniary Award	146	78.9 %
TOTAL	185	

---

21 RHS *Annual Report* 1838, 11, 18–29.
22 RHS *Annual Report* 1838, 14, 24.
23 Table derived from data in RHS *Annual Report* 1838, 11, 18–29.

The vast majority of awards made in 1837 took the form of pecuniary rewards,[24] given to individuals who had placed themselves in some danger by entering rivers, ponds, canals and locks in order to affect rescues.[25] Generally their names – unlike those of Lieutenant Archibald's boatmen – were recorded, although in one instance the rescuer was described simply as "A Dumb Pauper."[26]

By the latter part of the nineteenth century, the bronze medal was being distributed far more lavishly, with its distribution reflecting a substantial increase in the Society's activities. In 1838 the Society was able to report that it had considered cases resulting in the restoration of 172 casualties during the previous year,[27] but by 1894 that number had risen to 580. The rewards given by the Society in the latter year may be summarized as follows:

RHS: Rewards Voted 1894[28]

Reward	Number voted	Percentage of awards
Stanhope Gold Medal	1	0.2 %
Silver Medal	9	1.4 %
Bronze Medal or Clasp	122	19.6 %
Testimonial on Vellum	306	49.3 %
Testimonial on Parchment	145	23.3 %
Pecuniary Award and Certificate	38	6.2 %
TOTAL	621	

It can be seen that, whilst the Society had shifted its emphasis from the granting of pecuniary rewards to the presentation of medals and testimonials, the proportion of rewards taking the form of medals remained virtually unchanged, with a total of 132 medallic awards (comprising 21.2 percent of all awards voted during the year) being made in 1894, as opposed

---

24 RHS *Annual Report* 1838, 5–6.
25 See RHS *Annual Report* 1838, 18–28.
26 RHS *Annual Report* 1838, 5–6.
27 RHS *Annual Report* 1838, 21.
28 RHS *Annual Report* 1894, 9–10.

to the 36 (19.5 percent) voted in 1837. Bronze medals increasingly came to dominate however, with silver medals normally being issued at a rate of only 10-15 per annum. The way in which the bronze and silver medals were distributed was not identical. Indeed, a detailed comparison of the patterns connected to the awarding of the two types of medal reveals three major differences: very few bronze medals were awarded to members of the aristocracy or landed gentry; a far lower percentage of bronze than of silver medal awards were made to naval or army officers; the proportion of bronze medals awarded to unskilled/manual laborers decreased during the course of the century, whilst the proportion of silver medals awarded to the same group significantly increased (from 1.3 percent in the decade 1840–1849 to 23.8 percent in the years from 1910–1914).[29]

It can accordingly be demonstrated that, throughout the nineteenth century, the social class of rescuers continued materially to affect the nature of any reward that they might expect to receive from the RHS. While working class bravery was regularly rewarded, the Society remained more inclined to give medals to army officers than to private soldiers and very markedly more likely to award a silver medal than a bronze medal to a member of the landed classes.

Practices did however evolve during the course of the second half of the century. The most obvious example of this can be seen in the changing patterns in the forms of recognition granted to civilians for performing brave deeds on land. Here it is possible to demonstrate that an initial inclination to grant pecuniary rewards to working-class rescuers was replaced by an increased use of medals and certificates as the century progressed. Furthermore, whilst initially few awards of silver medals were made, in the period from 1910–1914, almost a quarter of all silver medals awarded were given to manual workers (including 4 miners; 2 cellar-men; a carpenter; a grain-weigher; a gas-worker and a steeplejack). Such developments notwithstanding, a significant status bias continued to be observable in the Society's distribution of rewards. In part, this is doubtless a reflection of the Society's inflexible reporting systems, which for much of the nineteenth century would not even consent to consider a case unless its circumstances could be fully verified by members of the middle classes. In the early years of the century, this requirement was set out in the Society's

---

29 Data derived from RHS *Annual Reports*; Young, *Acts of Gallantry* 1; and Fevyer, *Acts of Gallantry*, 2; Royal Humane Society *Case Books*; Life Saving Awards Society website http://lsars.org.uk/index.htm.

regulations, with Rule XVII specifying in 1838: "That all persons within five miles of London, who claim Premiums offered by this Society, shall produce Testimonials to the Secretary within one month, signed by three respectable Housekeepers acquainted with the accident, and the Medical Assistant, if any attended, or by the Minister of the Parish."[30] By the latter part of the century the requirement for middle-class endorsement had been only slightly reduced, with Rule XVI of the Society as published in 1894 specifying that: "Applications should be substantiated, where possible, by written statements of eye-witnesses, supported by the evidence of two responsible persons acquainted with the circumstances of the case, and the Honorary Medical Assistant, if any attended, or by the Minister of the Parish."[31]

In such circumstances, brave deeds performed in public spaces (such as harbors or rivers) might readily be witnessed by "responsible persons," whilst equally heroic acts performed behind closed factory doors passed unnoticed. Moreover, when the bravery of a gentleman was witnessed by his peers there was perhaps a greater inclination for them to champion his cause with the Society than there would have been had they witnessed the same deed being performed by an anonymous laborer. The granting of medals and certificates represented the culmination of a frequently lengthy paper-driven process that was generally initiated by the reporting of an incident to the Society. On occasion, rescuers continued to submit claims on their own behalf, but the vast majority of the letters that started this process came from government departments, the police, employers, or members of the public.

An examination of the Society's surviving *Case Books* makes it absolutely clear that when letters were received from private individuals their authors were almost invariably members of the professional classes. Indeed, the social standing of many of these reporters was such that the Society's officers regularly entrusted them with making the arrangements to present the medal on its behalf. Furthermore, a high degree of literacy was generally required to frame a case in such a way as to excite the enthusiasm of the Society, while less articulate accounts of brave deeds, no matter how worthy, might easily be overlooked. This effectively reduced the likelihood that nominations made by workers on behalf of their social peers would be successful. Instead, working-class rescuers were forced to

---

30 See, for example, RHS *Annual Report* 1838, 41.
31 See, for example, RHS *Annual Report* 1894, 21.

rely on the sponsorship of their social superiors. The nomination process thus served to ensure that control of the Society's awards remained firmly in the hands of the professional classes. In such circumstances, it is perhaps not surprising that class biases – whether conscious or unconscious – crept into the process.

The success of the RHS encouraged emulation, and the nineteenth century witnessed a proliferation of medal-giving bodies in Britain, as a broad range of philanthropic, civic and commercial bodies established novel awards with which to recognize an ever-widening range of brave deeds. From the outset, the RHS's remit had been limited and its rewards restricted to those who had saved (or attempted to save) others from death by drowning, asphyxiation, or strangulation. Very few RHS awards were given for saving lives from shipwrecks, but the foundation, in 1824, of the Royal National Institution for the Preservation of Life from Shipwreck (later the Royal National Lifeboat Institution) ensured that inshore rescuers would henceforth be recognized appropriately. Indeed, at the inaugural meeting of the Institution, William Wilberforce, the famous anti-slavery campaigner and Yorkshire MP, had proposed "That medallions or pecuniary rewards be given to those who rescue lives in cases of shipwreck."[32] Significantly, the Institution's medals were struck at a smaller size than those issued by the RHS at the time. From the outset, they were intended to be worn suspended from a length of blue ribbon and, as early as June 1825, the Committee had decreed that "a gold or silver loop be attached to every medal."[33] The presentation of a wearable medal bearing the Royal effigy was not without significance. As Prochaska has observed, "in a hierarchical society, the humble subject looks on a royal medal with the same respect as a magnate looks on a peerage."[34]

Those who risked their lives rescuing fellow mariners from vessels in distress on the high seas also began to be recognized by private awards. Lloyd's of London established a lifesaving medal in 1836,[35] whilst the

---

32 Hillary, *An Appeal to the British Nation on the Humanity and Policy of Forming a National Institution for the Preservation of Life from Shipwreck* (London: Whittaker, 1825), 49.
33 B. Cox, *Lifeboat Gallantry* (London: Spink, 1998), 4.
34 F. Prochaska, *Royal Bounty: The Making of a Welfare Monarchy* (New Haven: Yale University Press, 1995), 41.
35 L. Syson, "Designs on Posterity: Drawings for Medals, The British Museum 11 September– 25 October, 1992," in *Designs on Posterity: Drawings for Medals*, ed. Mark Jones (London: British Museum Press, 1992), 225–226. Jim Gawler, *Lloyd's Medals 1836–1989: A History of Medals Awarded by the Corporation of Lloyd's* (Toronto: Hart, 1989), 132–133.

Shipwrecked Fishermen and Mariners' Royal Benevolent Society – a subscription-paying membership society for seafarers – began, in 1851, to issue medals in gold and silver to recognize "heroic or praiseworthy exertions to save life from shipwreck, etc., on the High Seas or coasts of India or the Colonies."[36]

Although awarded to rescuers drawn from all social classes, in many instances the metal (gold, silver, or bronze) from which these medals for maritime bravery were struck was determined by the status of the intended recipient. The unequal treatment of individuals who shared the same risks is particularly evident when examining cases of rescue from shipwreck – there being a general tendency to grant different awards to officers and ratings, even when they had crewed the same rescue boat. A typical example relates to the granting of rewards by Lloyd's of London to those who had manned a boat which went to the aid of 15 shipwrecked mariners in November 1854:

The Honorary Silver Medal to Mr. William Barrett, Master, Royal Navy, Chief Officer in Command of the Coast Guard Station, Balbriggan…

The Honorary Silver Medal to Mr. William Barrett Junr., for his meritorious conduct on the same occasion.

The Honorary Silver Medal to the Revd. Alexander Synge, in acknowledgement of the noble example shewn by him in volunteering and forming one of the boat's crew on the first attempt…

The sum of £20 to the Boat's Crew for their services on the same occasion.[37]

As the Victorian age progressed, charitable middle-class eyes were also increasingly turning towards land-based lifesavers as bourgeois fears and anxieties fed into what Roger Cooter describes as "the Moment of the Accident."[38] Contending that "before the last third of the nineteenth

---

36 A. Wilson & J.H.F. McEwan, *Gallantry* (Oxford: Oxford University Press, 1939), 63. In the first century of its existence, the Society awarded 39 gold and 554 silver medals. See Anon., *The Shipwrecked Fishermen & Mariner Royal Benevolent Society: Brief History of the First Hundred Years* (London: Shipwrecked Fishermen and Mariner's Royal Benevolent Society, 1939) 13–14, and Anon., *Heroism at Sea: A History of Awards for Skill and Gallantry at Sea Presented by the Society since 1851* (Chichester: Shipwrecked Fishermen and Mariner's Royal Benevolent Society, 2009), e-book.

37 Lloyd's of London, *General Minute Book*, March 23, 1853. Gawler, *Lloyd's Medals*, 24.

38 R. Cooter, "The Moment of the Accident: Culture, Militarism and Modernity in Late-Victorian Britain," in *Accidents in History: Injuries, Fatalities and Social Relations*, eds. R. Cooter and B. Luckin (Amsterdam & Atlanta, Editions Rodopi, 1997), 107–157.

century accidental injuries, whether occurring randomly or routinely, were seldom a matter of much public concern,"[39] Cooter argues that, although specific incidents might spark passing concern and comment, accidents in general had, up until this point, continued to be perceived as Acts of God. This view has been echoed by other authors, with Schivelbusch, for example, observing that, in the pre-industrial age, the accident was merely "a grammatical and philosophical concept, more or less synonymous with coincidence."[40] Furthermore, as most accidental deaths and injuries occurred in industrial settings, they remained largely invisible to the middle and upper classes.

Cooter contends that the development of the railways opened up the risk of industrial injury to all social classes and the public nature of rail accidents ensured that they received a disproportionate level of press coverage,[41] contributing, in part, to a public perception of constant looming danger. Indeed, advances in technology could be perceived as increasing, rather than controlling, this danger, with Schivelbusch, for example, observing that "the more efficient the technology, the more catastrophic its destruction when it collapses."[42] Thus, industrial and technological progress helped to engender broader concerns that the city had become a place of danger, analogous to a battlefield. This, in turn, fostered an increased public interest in "first aid" and led a boom in the production of relevant manuals, as well as a demand for the provision of first aid classes.

Cooter's thesis has proved generally sound, although his argument that the "Moment of the Accident" must be confined to the closing third of the nineteenth-century is vulnerable to challenge. There can be little doubt that the advent of the railways brought about a profound transformation in the way in which the public viewed accidents, but it is equally true that the concept of the "technological accident" was firmly embedded in the national consciousness well before the late 1860s.

---

39 Cooter, "The Moment of the Accident," 107.
40 W. Schivelbusch, *The Railway Journey: Trains and Travel in the 19th Century* (Oxford: Blackwell, 1979), 133.
41 Cooter notes that in 1870 over 300 railway accidents received press coverage. During the same period, only 35 mining accidents were covered. See Cooter "The Moment of the Accident," 112.
42 Schivelbusch, *The Railway Journey*, 133.

The fear that a railway engine or other piece of machine might destroy itself "by means of its own power"[43] was well established during the early railway era and the widespread use of engine names suggestive of inhuman or unnatural energy is unlikely to have done much to comfort a nervous public.[44] Railway accidents had no respect for social class and the improvements in communications which the development of a national rail network supported ensured that, when accidents occurred, lurid reports of their horrific consequences could swiftly be distributed throughout the land. The gentleman reading his copy of *The Times* on the train was as vulnerable as the third-class traveler. The nineteenth-century world could seem a very dangerous place; but the support (whether practical or financial) of the diverse organizations dedicated to the preservation of life offered Victorians an opportunity to seize back a degree of control in the struggle to tame the powers of science and nature.

Fire represented a universal peril both to life and property and, in 1836, the Society for the Protection of Life from Fire was founded with significant support from the insurance industry.[45] The main practical aims of the society were to maintain a properly equipped and trained complement of fire-fighters, to assess new inventions relevant to the combating of fire, and to disseminate information relevant to fire safety. But, whilst the prime purpose of the society was initially to provide the wherewithal necessary to save life it also, from its inception, issued a range of awards for gallantry to "such persons as shall distinguish themselves by their endeavours to save life from fire, with special reference to those cases occurring in the Metropolis or its environs."[46] These awards were available not only to the society's own fire-fighters, but also to members of the public, with the secretary noting in his presentation of the Society's annual report at London's Guildhall on January 30, 1854 that, "the awards of the Society are not confined to the conductors or the men in its employ. Among the individuals complimented at the meeting, I noticed several members of the police and several private citizens. The managers of the

---

43 M. Freeman, *Railways and the Victorian Imagination* (New Haven/London: Yale University Press, 1999), 84.
44 Typical of the names given to the Great Western Railway's rolling stock in 1839 were "Vulcan," "Atlas," and "Apollo." See Freeman, *Railways*, 64.
45 See R. Willoughby and J. Wilson, *Saved from the Flames: A History of the Society for the Protection of Life from Fire* (Honiton: Token Publishing, 2012).
46 *New York Times*, August 16, 1854, 4.

Society, like those of the Royal Humane Society, are determined to let no deed of noble daring pass unnoticed."[47]

Perhaps because accidents in mines and factories occurred behind "closed doors" and affected primarily the working classes, middle-class private organizations were somewhat slower to rise to the challenge of rewarding the numerous life-threatening situations that arose in such places. This deficit was not to be addressed until December 15, 1874 when the Chapter General of the Order of St John (at that time a private pseudo-chivalric organization) "instituted Silver and Bronze Medals for saving life on land under conditions which endangered the life of the rescuer."[48] In establishing its own lifesaving award, the Order had recognized that "it appeared that when casualties occur in our mining and colliery districts, and men expose their lives to the greatest risk to rescue their fellow creatures, no recognition from any public body could be obtained, because it was not within the scope of any existing body to reward such merit."[49]

The Order sought to use the lifesaving medals it presented as a means of stressing its inclusivity, with Sir Edmund Lechmere, its Secretary General, posing the question: "And who will say that chivalry is confined to one class? ... Its impulse may beat in every breast whether that breast be the broadcloth of the gentleman or the working dress of the miner."[50] The sentiments expressed by Lechmere may seem to cross class boundaries, but in reality there remained a vast gulf between the membership of the Order and those whom it saw fit to reward with its medals. A miner might hope to gain the Order's lifesaving medal, but he could never expect to be admitted to the Order, as membership was the exclusive preserve of the middle and upper classes. Indeed, the Order of St John can be perceived as an integral part of a highly-structured class system, with the status of its members being confirmed and reinforced by their ability to confer marks of approval on members of the lower orders.

Although the granting of rewards to lifesavers remained a primarily private activity throughout the Victorian age, during the second half of the nineteenth century, the British State, which had initially drawn back from

---

47 *New York Times*, August 16, 1854, 4.
48 E.C. Dawson, "The Life Saving Medal of the Order of St John," *St John Historical Society Proceedings* 5 (1993): 21–22.
49 Anon., *Order of St John of Jerusalem in England: Descriptive History of its Medals for saving Life on Land by Special Acts of Bravery* (London: Order of St John, 1876), n.p.
50 Dawson, "The Life Saving Medal," 22.

taking an active role in the rewarding of martial or non-martial courage, at last succumbed to political and public pressure and instituted a range of medals to reward bravery in battle, at sea and in the mines and factories of Britain and its colonies. These were not however intended merely as gifts for the worthy. Rather, politicians recognized the broader benefits to the state that might be gained through the creation of such rewards, with Lord Newcastle stating that:

> the value attached by soldiers to a little bit of ribbon is such as to render any danger insignificant and any privation light if it can be attained, and I believe that great indeed would be the stimulus and deeply prized the reward of a Cross of Military Merit. ... Such a reward would have more effect in the Army than the grant of Commissions, and the sight of one of these crosses on the breast of a Soldier returning home invalided would bring more recruits than any of the measures we can now adopt.[51]

But even if governmental motivations for the establishment of honors such as the Victoria Cross (1856) and Albert Medal (1866) were at times cynical, by the mid-nineteenth century, British heroes could and did wear badges of honor. These badges – both official and unofficial – were intended to be worn, seen, and to be coveted. For example, in 1908, Baden-Powell reminded Boy Scouts that:

> in war, as you know, the Victoria Cross is awarded to soldiers for performing acts of valour. So, in peace, a decoration is given to anybody who distinguishes himself by bravery in saving life at the risk of his own. ... the Albert Medal and the Edward Medal are the most valued, being given by the King himself, and only in very special cases. So let every Boy Scout prepare himself to win one of these.[52]

Like their military counterparts, civilian medalists from all walks of life could thus perform an inspirational function; particularly if the transient brave deed for which they had earned the medal were to be accepted by the viewer as the ultimate manifestation of a heroic and worthy life.

Those who wore lifesaving medals might accordingly be perceived as paragons of society by an audience who built a heroic narrative around the badge they displayed. Popular literature served to underpin such generalizations, and bodies such as the Religious Tract Society published and

---

51 Nottingham University, Newcastle Collection, NeC 9786, 33. Reproduced in Crook, *Evolution of the Victoria Cross*, 13.

52 R. Baden-Powell, *Scouting for Boys: A Handbook for Instruction in Good Citizenship* (London: C. Arthur Pearson Ltd., 1908), 252.

distributed volumes celebrating not only the deeds of Britain's heroic lifesavers, but also the worthy lives they had led. Such writing was certainly significant for, as Cubitt has observed, a hero is a product not only of heroic deeds but also of the manner in which those deeds are reported. As he put it, "a person becomes a hero, at least in part, by having his or her life and actions and character described in the conventional terms which govern the acclamation and celebration of the heroic within a particular culture."[53] Cubitt further argued that heroic lives are an imaginative social construct, noting that they are

lives, in short, that are not just heroic in isolated detail, but that constitute in some sense a heroic totality. Heroes may be celebrated for particular actions or traits of character, but they are celebrated in a way that implies the essential consistency of action with character, and the dramatic unity of the successive stages of individual existence.[54]

Heroes are thus afforded their special status because their heroism is an inevitable result of their worthy and heroic lives. The classical heroes of Greece and Rome were possessed of an intrinsic ambiguity, combining the attributes of a deity with the vulnerability of a mortal. Within a western Christianized context, a similar dichotomy is to be found in the life and deeds of Jesus, who abandoned the advantages of divinity to sacrifice his life on the cross in order to redeem mankind.

Although members of the upper and middle classes were over-represented among the ranks of the RHS's medalists, few of those who aspired to risk their lives to save others (whether in conscious imitation of Christ or otherwise) fell into the category of what Carlyle would have described as "Great Men." While such humble heroes may not have shaped history, their lives might nevertheless be portrayed as exemplary. Indeed, as Cubitt notes, exemplarity need not be linked to significant historic achievement, being rather "the relationship which pertains when one human existence is taken as a model or the bearer of significant truths for the moulding of others."[55] The portrayal of exemplary lives in their entirety was considered by some, such as Dryden, to be an exceptionally

---

[53] Geoff Cubitt, "Introduction: Heroic Reputations and Exemplary Lives," in *Heroic Reputations and Exemplary Lives*, ed. G. Cubitt & A. Warren (Manchester: Manchester University Press, 2000), 5.
[54] Cubitt, "Heroic Reputations and Exemplary Lives," 6.
[55] Ibid., 9.

effective technique for encouraging a positive didactic moral effect.[56] Cubitt believed exemplars should ideally be individuals with whom their audience might identify, arguing that, "exemplarity involves a perception not just of excellence, but also of relevance – and thus, in a sense, of similarity. Those whom we take as exemplars may be better than we are, but not than we might in principle become – not better in some absolute way that implies a difference of kind, but better relative to some common standard against which we hope to improve."[57]

Exemplarity was at the core of Samuel Smiles's pioneering book, *Self-Help*, which he published in 1859.[58] Promoting the construct of a "manly character" based on "self-restraint, perseverance, strenuous effort, [and] courage in the face of adversity,"[59] it celebrated the labors of self-made men. Drawing examples primarily from the industrious middle-classes, Smiles held up characters such as David Livingstone as exemplars for the aspirational working-classes. The book proved to be extremely popular, remaining in print well into the twentieth century, while its approach to the exploitation of admirable lives as a means of encouraging self-improvement influenced numerous other writers.

Such authors frequently recast the lives of prominent public figures such as Grace Darling. The tale of James Braidwood – a fireman who sacrificed his life to save his colleagues – also proved popular, being featured in several late-Victorian works. The anonymous author of *Everyday Heroes*, an inspirational volume published in 1900 by the Society for the Promotion of Christian Knowledge, was typical of those who sought to weave a fully-formed "heroic life" around the bare bones of his tale. In this telling of Braidwood's story, he not only sacrificed himself to save his men, but: "for many years supported two maiden sisters"; possessed "deep Christian feelings"; "undertook quiet good deeds, quietly wrought out in the poorer districts of London"; "took special interest in the ragged schools of the metropolis"; and was "a model husband and father."[60] The anonymous author sought to ensure that the tale of Braidwood was

---

56 Ibid., 10.
57 Ibid., 11.
58 S. Smiles, *Self Help: With Illustrations of Conduct and Perseverance* (London: self-published, 1859).
59 M. Jones, *The Last Great Quest: Captain Scott's Antarctic Sacrifice* (Oxford: Oxford University Press, 2003), 26.
60 Anon., *Everyday Heroes: Stories of Bravery During the Queen's Reign 1837–1900* (London: Society for the Promotion of Christian Knowledge, 1900), 55–56.

relevant to a primarily working-class target-audience. In so doing, he (or she) was pursuing a well-trodden path.

One of the most prolific of the late-Victorian inspirational writers was Frank Mundell who, in the mid-1890s, penned a series of uplifting volumes – including *Stories of the Humane Society*, *Stories of the Fire Brigade* and *Stories of the Lifeboat* – on behalf of the Sunday School Union. Accessible works such as these both appropriated and celebrated the heroism of ordinary men and women and, through their wide distribution, helped to serve as their memorial. The heroes whose deeds were recorded were in no material way different from their readers, while the style of writing helped to ensure that the audience empathized with the central characters. One of the tales related by Mundell was that of William Brimelow, a Bolton man who saved a fellow workman from suffocation in a gas-filled furnace cupola. As related by Mundell, it was an act of selfless courage which earned him the silver medal of the RHS but cost him his health: "for since that day he performed what has aptly been described as one of the most heroic feats of modern times, he has not known what life really is. Months of weakness succeeded long days of pain, and the occasion which found him a hero left him an invalid."[61] Mundell's book portrayed Brimelow as making a Christ-like sacrifice, but he is nevertheless unquestionably an ordinary man. Indeed, great emphasis was placed upon his modest lifestyle, noting that:

the news of the occurrence soon spread throughout the foundry, and reached the ears of William Brimelow, the son of the proprietor, a man known as a quiet, home-loving fellow, 'who liked to listen rather than to talk.' Few, if any, of his friends suspected he was a man made for some great emergency, but such indeed was the case, as the result proved.[62]

Brimelow was thus portrayed as the embodiment of a range of Victorian virtues: a modest and sober soul who was nevertheless capable of acting with calm and selfless courage when the need arose. His status as the son of the proprietor of the furnace where the accident occurred was referred to in passing, but the account contained no hint that this might have imposed upon him a special duty of care for those employed there. Rather, Mundell chose to emphasize his position as one of the workers, explaining that, "His fellow workmen lamented what they considered his rash action, and thought sadly that two homes would now be desolate instead of

---

61 Frank Mundell, *Stories of the Humane Society* (London: Sunday School Union, c. 1895), 138.
62 Ibid., 134.

one."[63] Brimelow can thus be seen to have been portrayed as a sober and virtuous individual who, whilst not compelled by duty to act, nevertheless felt driven to go to the aid of one of his fellows when the unfortunate man found his life imperiled whilst engaged in everyday activity. Such heroes were part of the normal mass of humanity, but paradoxically somehow elevated above it. As Dr. W.C. Bennett observed in his poem, "Our Heroes of To-day":

Heroes and saints! And do they say
The past had these alone?
Brothers, have we not both to-day,
And both the people's own?
Theirs may be homes in lanes and streets,
But theirs are deeds one hears
With blood that quicker, nobler beats,
And the proud praise of tears.
If e'er your heart ignobly faint
At great deeds in your way
Then think of many a living saint
And hero of to-day.[64]

But if the writing of exemplary lives might be thought of as a specialist art, the master of the genre was perhaps Laura Lane, whose book *Heroes of Everyday Life* provided its readers with 255 pages detailing lives worthy of emulation. She was absolutely clear as to the purpose of her work and the audience at which it was aimed. Lane was acutely concerned about the moral welfare of her audience, bemoaning in the preface to her book that 'We live in a sensational age. Sensational fiction, sensational journalism, sensational speech-making – these are the everyday features of our times."[65]

Lane sought to offer her readers an alternative that could harness and redirect this love of the dramatic, explaining that, "To lovers of the sensational I offer a new, and at the same time healthy, gratification of their taste."[66] Her target audience was likewise clearly identified, with the author explaining that "Such as they are, I venture to dedicate these stories of heroism in every-day life to the working men and boys of Great Britain.

---

63 Ibid., 134.
64 Bennet, "Our Heroes of To-day," *Penny Illustrated Paper*, February 1, 1873, 73.
65 Lane, *Heroes of Everyday Life*, vii.
66 Ibid., vii.

Whatever may be lacking in the completeness of my work, there is certainly no lack of love, no lack of sympathy with the great working class."[67] The tone of Lane's preface strongly suggests that her work was at least partly motivated by a feeling of social anxiety and by an associated evangelical desire to encourage patriotism and stability through the promotion of Christian values in the working classes. As she wrote:

> We live in a transition period. The old order is passing away and giving place to the new. This is inevitable. Change and decay are written in all human institutions. But in all changes that are surely coming (political and social), let us not forget one broad principle – namely that it is "Righteousness" (and righteousness alone) "that exalteth a nation." No material advantages can prove of lasting value unless they are accompanied by the growth and development of the higher nature. "What can it profit a man if he gain the world and lose his own soul?"... And if this little book of mine shall help towards a better understanding of the nobility of nature that lies hid beneath many a toil-stained jacket, my labour will not have been in vain.[68]

Such a preface might be expected to introduce a book which, at the time of its publication, was somewhat anachronistic, for, as Springhall has observed: "Popular juvenile literature, embracing magazines and novels, exemplifies ... a basic shift in the concept of manliness during the second half of the nineteenth century and after, moving away from the strenuous moral earnestness of Dr. Thomas Arnold ... to a greater emphasis on patriotism and athleticism."[69]

But, whilst Lane's preface to *Heroes of Everyday Life* did indeed make emphatic reference to the Christian faith, her writing nevertheless concentrated on the dramatic and created action heroes whose brave deeds were very much in tune with those performed by the fictional heroes of the popular novels penned by G.A. Henty and Arthur Marryat.[70] Thus, although many of the tales related by Lane expressed an explicitly Christian message, that message was not generally allowed to interfere with the flow of the narrative. Crucially, the tales of bravery related by Lane in *Heroes of Everyday Life* were generally those of working class men and women who had risked all for the sake of others. Equally significant was the fact that, in

---

67 Ibid., vii.
68 Ibid., vii–viii.
69 J. Springhall, "Building Character in the British Boy: the Attempt to Extend Christian Manliness to Working-class Adolescents, 1880–1914," in *Manliness and Morality: Middle-Class Masculinity in Britain and America, 1800–1940*, ed. J. A. Mangan, & J. Walvin (Manchester: Manchester University Press, 1987), 61.
70 Arthur Marryat was himself a RHS medalist.

recognition of their valor, most of her heroes had received medals or were otherwise memorialized.

Lane's purpose was to inspire aspirational members of the working classes. To achieve this, she created heroes from those with whom she felt her target audience would empathize. In so doing, not only were the details of their exceptional deeds recorded, but so too was information relating to their backgrounds and everyday lives. Lane sought to look beyond the concrete acts of bravery and to record – or manufacture – a broader heroic context that showed those acts to be the crowning achievements of lives which were not only worthy of but also *capable* of emulation. Thus Walter Cleverly was portrayed as a man whose bravery in leaping into shark-infested waters to rescue a drowning sailor was a continuation of the pluck he had displayed as a child when "thrashing the cowardly bully who was the terror of the weaker and smaller boys."[71]

Lane's account of the early years of the tragic heroine, Alice Ayres, likewise points to a girl who was the child of "poor but honest parents"; who entered domestic service and fulfilled her duties "faithfully and well"; and whose neighbors were reported to have described her as "a quiet-spoken girl with pleasant, gentle ways, quick about her work and very fond of children."[72] Similar worthy, but modest, ambitions were attributed to Hannah Rosbotham, a schoolmistress who earned the Albert Medal:

> The heroine of this sketch evinced from her earliest years a taste and aptitude for the vocation and ministry of a teacher. While yet a mere child – sitting on the benches of the National School of Sutton, Lancashire – she looked forward eagerly to the time when she would be permitted to teach others.[73]

But it was not only the childhoods of her heroines and heroes that were held up for emulation. Lane also went to considerable lengths to stress that the brave acts performed in adulthood represented consistent manifestations of the characters of the men and women whose actions she was describing. Thus, Walter Cleverly's brave act was performed as he was sailing home to visit his mother;[74] while the life-boatman Charles Fish and his siblings were portrayed as exemplarily dutiful offspring, with Lane claiming that "It is pleasant to learn that her sons and daughters proved

---

71 Lane, *Heroes of Everyday Life*, 42.
72 Ibid., 57–58.
73 Ibid., 121.
74 Ibid., 45.

their gratitude to their excellent parent by ministering to her in her declining years."[75] In short, Lane did not merely tell tales of bravery but, rather created fully-rounded heroes, drawing upon the lists of Victorian Britain's lifesaving medalists for her raw material.

The popular celebration of the "everyday hero" is perhaps best exemplified by the near-deification of Grace Darling, but other examples abound. Drawn from all social classes, "everyday heroes" were role models who anyone, through virtuous living, might perhaps hope to emulate. Heroes might even be fashioned from unlikely stock, with the Reverend Henry Woodcock (author of such inspirational tomes as *Wonders of Grace* and *Popery Unmasked*) recording the life-story of John Ellerthorpe, "The Hero of the Humber," who rose above a debauched youth and early adulthood to find a new role as a prodigiously successful saver of lives. Like those of the heroes described by Lane, Ellerthorpe's life-story had important lessons for society. He had led what Cubitt described as an "exemplary life": "one valued and admired not merely (or even necessarily) for its practical achievements, but for the moral or ethical or social values or truths which it is perceived both to embody and, through the force of example, to impress upon the minds of others."[76]

Unlike Lane's writings, Woodcock's story was firmly based in an early nineteenth-century narrative tradition, wherein the protagonist's faith is allowed to occupy center stage. Ellerthorpe's tale, as recounted by Woodcock, was one of redemption through the acceptance of God and the adoption of a life of quiet sobriety. It was a moral and spiritual journey which saw the main protagonist develop from a drunken layabout to a Christian hero; his deeds being rewarded by the granting of medals, honors, and cash rewards. According to his biographer, the linkage between Christian devotion and heroism could not have been closer for Ellerthorpe, who explained that,

ever after my conversion to God, I used to pray, when plunging into the water, 'Lord help me,' and knowing as I did, that prayer melts the heart and moves the arm of Jehovah, I felt confident that he would help me; and so he did ... I always

---

75 Ibid., 130.
76 Cubitt, "Heroic Reputations and Exemplary Lives," 2.

felt it my duty, after rescuing a drowning person, to go to the house of God at night, and return public thanks to the Almighty.[77]

Thus, Ellerthorpe was held up as a Christian role model: a sinner who had found God and, through his faith, had earned worldly rewards and the esteem of his peers. Nevertheless, he was portrayed as both unassuming and modest, with Woodcock specifically noting that, "Though Mr. Ellerthorpe never urged his claims to public recognition, yet we rejoice to state that his deeds were not permitted to pass unnoticed and unrewarded."[78] Indeed, his humble roots and personal reticence were seen as being an integral part of his virtue and were celebrated in verse in the pages of the local newspaper, *The Hull Daily Express*:

Without pretension, who by deeds endears
His name afar beyond its native strand,
A son of toil – yet one of Nature's peers!
Whose worth's acknowledged in his native land![79]

Ellerthorpe died in 1868 as a result of coronary disease, with his physician, Dr. Gibson reporting that, "As his medical attendant, I regret to say, that his frequent plunges into the water, at all seasons of the year, and long exposure in wet clothes, have seriously damaged his health and constitution."[80]

Although Ellerthorpe received many material rewards in his lifetime (including medals from both the Queen and the RHS), it was the nature of his death that provided his biographer with the crowning moment of his career. For Woodcock, Ellerthorpe's demise was a conscious act of martyrdom, and he drew further on the words of Dr. Gibson to stress that "Mr. Ellerthorpe had generously attempted to save the lives of others at the expense of abridging his own life."[81] Thus was the life of "The Hero of the Humber" portrayed as being exemplary. His funeral attracted thousands of mourners and *The Eastern Morning News* resorted to hyperbole

---

77 H. Woodcock, *The Hero of the Humber: or, the History of the Late Mr. John Ellerthorpe* (London: Alford, 1880), Project Gutenberg edition: http://www.gutenberg.org/files/20520/20520-h/20520-h.htm, 30.
78 Woodcock, *The Hero of the Humber*, 57.
79 Reproduced in Woodcock, *The Hero of the Humber*, 63.
80 Dr. Gibson to H. Woodcock, September 26, 1867; reproduced in Woodcock, *The Hero of the Humber*, 74.
81 Dr. Gibson to H. Woodcock, n.d.; reproduced in Woodcock, *The Hero of the Humber*, 74.

in its description of the event, declaring that "it may be questioned whether his career has any individual parallel in the world's history."[82]

The publication of such inspirational works helped to ensure that the work of the RHS and its kindred societies remained firmly in the public eye. Accordingly, the various societies were keen to furnish the authors of such works with every possible assistance. This symbiotic relationship was openly acknowledged. For example, the Society for the Promotion of Christian Knowledge made numerous specific references to the awards of the RHS in its 1900 publication, *Everyday Heroes*.[83] Indeed, Mundell's *Stories of the Royal Humane Society* (published by the Sunday School Union) may be seen as an extended advertisement for the Society and its work: commencing with a brief history of the organization and concluding with an extended personal description of the practical work of the Society's Receiving House in Hyde Park. Significantly, the final paragraph takes the form of a barely concealed appeal for funds couched in the language of patriotism:

> There is no institution more worthy of public support than the Royal Humane Society. Its operations are now world-wide, but unfortunately the voluntary subscriptions, on which it depends, have not kept pace with its extended sphere of usefulness …. Let us hope, for the honour of our country, that the advance of this Society may not be retarded by lack of means.[84]

Authors such as Stanaway and Lane were likewise more than happy to express their gratitude to society secretaries who had "kindly supplied [them] with full and authentic details respecting the deeds described."[85] Mutually beneficial links are further revealed in their published acknowledgements. Laura Lane, for example, thanked representatives of the RHS and the Society for the Protection of Life from Fire by name,[86] whilst Kay Stanaway casts her net more widely to include the RHS, the RNLI, Lloyd's, the Liverpool Shipwreck and Humane Society, the Glasgow Humane Society, the Order of St John and the Carnegie Hero Fund.[87]

The relationship between authors and societies was essentially symbiotic: the societies provided the authors with the stories they needed to

---

82 Reproduced in Woodcock, *The Hero of the Humber*, 75.
83 Anon., *Everyday Heroes*. See, for example, 27–28, 223–224, and 230.
84 Mundell, *Stories of the Humane Society*, 158.
85 Lane, *Heroes of Everyday Life*, vii.
86 Ibid., viii.
87 K. Stanway, *Britannia's Calendar of Heroes* (London: Allen & Unwin, 1914), xiii.

create "exemplary lives" whilst in return, the authors provided the Societies with widely disseminated publicity and the prospect of garnering much needed funds and support. As a patriotic award-making body, the RHS must also have been well aware of the value of such collaboration in the development of the public perception of its awards as aspirational objects. Indeed, the Society was keenly conscious of the esteem in which its rewards were held, and many of their early awards actually had their edges inscribed with the words "Go thou and do likewise." The medal and its wearer thus performed the same function as the Watts memorial, namely to act as a source of inspiration. As J.A. Froude urged: "there is a man – such a man as you ought to be … see what he was, and how he made himself what he was, and try to be yourself like him."[88]

---

88 J. A. Froude, *Short Studies on Great Subjects* (London: Longman's Green & Co., 1888), 583–584.

Everyday Heroism for the Victorian Industrial Classes: *The British Workman* and *The British Workwoman*, 1855–1880

Christiane Hadamitzky and Barbara Korte

Heroism in an Everyday Medium

In his famous lectures on heroes published in 1841, Thomas Carlyle may have regretted that the days of hero worship were over, but Victorian society still widely accepted the heroic as a template for perpetuating and negotiating its dominant ideals and values. The heroic was a pervasive presence in the media of everyday life: public monuments, paintings and performances, as well as the books and periodicals a rapidly expanding print market offered the "common" reader.[1] These periodicals targeted various segments of the public and so reached readers of different generations, genders, and classes. In the period this chapter is concerned with, the mid-1850s to the late 1870s, the major part of the Victorian readership was comprised of middle-class readers. However, working-class readers were on the rise, and their reading materials, including periodicals,[2] were a concern for the dominant classes, who aimed to provide them with content they deemed "suitable."

The two publications on which the following pages focus belong to the periodicals that were produced *for* and not *by* working-class people and so reflect the value system of a middle class that was concerned about public order and had an interest in channeling the ethos of the working classes into certain directions. Industrial communities in the second half of the nineteenth century were regularly unsettled by strikes, and workmen were politically organized with increasing efficiency. The Second Reform Act of

---

1 See Richard Altick, *The English Common Reader* (Chicago: University of Chicago Press, 1957), J. Don Vann and Rosemary Van Arsdel, *Victorian Periodicals and Victorian Society* (Toronto: Toronto University Press, 1994), and Andrew King and John Plunkett, *Victorian Print Media: A Reader* (Oxford: Oxford University Press, 2005).
2 See Joel H. Wiener, "The Press and the Working Class, 1815–1840," *Victorian Periodicals Newsletter* 11 (1971): 1–4, and Jonathan Rose, *The Intellectual Life of the British Working Classes* (New Haven: Yale University Press, 2001).

1867 extended the vote to working-class electors in the boroughs. The discourse of heroism gained special poignancy in this context, because heroic figures and concepts of the heroic transport social values and ideals. It is no coincidence that the historian James A. Froude also had the working classes in mind when he wrote his reviews about books with a heroic theme for major middle-class papers of the early 1850s.[3] An "everyday" heroism was of particular importance in relation to the working classes because it could be closely related to the real-world experiences of "common" men and women.

The British Workman (1855–1892) and *The British Workwoman* (1863–1896) were monthly educational or "improving" papers available for a mere penny. They were popular and influential.[4] We will argue that they reflect a levelling of class boundaries in the appreciation of heroism, and thus the progressive democratization of the heroic during the 19th century[5] and especially the construction of a working-class heroic civilian. At the same time, however, their scope of heroic actors and agencies is significantly narrower than in most periodicals for middle-class

---

[3] See, for instance, his review of Emerson's *Representative Men* in *The Eclectic Review* May (1852): 568–582: "Yet, far off we seem to see a time when the lives, the actions of the really great, great good masters, great good landlords, great good working men, will be laid out once more before their several orders, laid out in the name of God, as once the saints' lives were; and the same sounds shall be heard in factory and in counting-house as once sounded through abbey, chapel, and cathedral aisle – 'Look at these men; bless God for them, and follow them'" (579). See also his review article on editions of early modern travel writing, "England's Forgotten Worthies," *Westminster Review* July (1852): 32–67. Here he explicitly regrets that the common sailors had not been heroized in their own period: "The heroes themselves were the men of the people – the Joneses, the Smiths, the Davises, the Drakes; and no courtly pen, with the one exception of Raleigh, lent its polish or its varnish to set them off" (35).

[4] See "British Workman" and "British Workwoman," in Laurel Brake and Marysa Demoor, *Dictionary of Nineteenth Century Journalism* (Gent: Academia Press, 2009), 80; "British Workman" and "British Workwoman," "Waterloo Directory of English Newspapers and Periodicals: 1800–1900,", http://www.victorianperiodicals.com; and Simon Cooke, "The British Workman,", http://www.victorianweb.org/periodicals/bw/cooke.html; Frank Murray, "Often Taken Where a Tract is Refused: T.B. Smithies, *The British Workman*, and the Popularisation of the Religious and Temperance Message," in Laurel Brake and Marysa Demoor, *The Lure of Illustration in the Nineteenth Century: Picture and Press* (Basingstoke: Palgrave Macmillan, 2009).

[5] On this levelling, see also Melvin Charles Smith, *Awarded for Valour: A History of the Victoria Cross and the Evolution of British Heroism* (Basingstoke: Palgrave Macmillan, 2008), and John Price, *Everyday Heroism: Victorian Constructions of the Heroic Civilian* (London: Bloomsbury Academic, 2014).

readerships. *The British Workman* and *Workwoman* share with middle-class publications a special interest in, and an appreciation of, moral heroism and exemplary, imitable heroic figures.[6] But, while Victorian middle-class magazines recruited most of their heroes from the middle and upper classes, *The British Workman* and *Workwoman* were especially concerned with acts of heroism performed by people of "humble" origin. Some of these people were "everyday heroes" according to John Price's definition: ordinary people who performed brave deeds in commonplace surroundings.[7] But in addition to (and often intermingled with) this understanding, the *Workman* and *Workwoman* also promoted heroism *in* everyday life: praising a heroic spirit that enabled men *and* women to live up to high moral standards on a daily basis and in all circumstances, albeit with certain gendered biases concerning the kinds of heroic behavior promoted, as well as the textual and pictorial rhetoric with which they were depicted.

The British Workman and *The British Workwoman*

The British Workman and *The British Workwoman* had different owners and publishers,[8] but they were linked in public perception. The fourth issue of the *Workwoman* quoted an appreciative comment from the *Weekly Record* that pronounced: "We are sure there is room for the 'British Workwoman' wherever the 'British Workman' is taken in. They should go side by side, and aid each other as man and wife, brother and sister."[9] Both had an obvious family resemblance, sharing a strong didactic tone, a firmly Christian orientation, and a paternalistic attitude towards the working classes.

The *Workman* had set the tone by declaring itself to be "commenced with an earnest desire to promote the Health, Wealth, and Happiness of the Working Classes," and thus "solicit[ed] the support of both employers and employed, believing that the interests of both are firmly linked together, and that whatever injures one, affects the other."[10] Propagating a

---

6 See Geoffrey Cubitt and Allen Warren, *Heroic Reputations and Exemplary Lives* (Manchester: Manchester University Press, 2001).
7 Price, *Everyday Heroism*, 29.
8 S.W. Partridge for the *Workman*, and Hall, Smart & Allen and Job Caudwell for the *Workwoman*.
9 *The British Workwoman* February (1864): 32.
10 "[Editorial]," *The British Workman* February (1855): 1.

harmonious relationship between the classes when that relationship was strained, its full title declared an element of class friendship twice: *The British Workman and Friend of the Sons of Toil: Dedicated to the Industrial Classes, By Their Sincere Friend, the Editor.* This editor and owner (until 1883) was the Methodist reformer and temperance campaigner Thomas Bywater Smithies, who managed to keep the price of the periodical consistently low, despite its high quality.[11] Like many other working-class periodicals, the *Workman* was published as a large broadsheet, which meant that it could not be easily carried around and could only be consumed in a domestic environment.[12] It was very attractively illustrated with woodcuts, for which Smithies engaged leading artists of his day. The full-page title illustrations were an eye-catcher, and so were many pictures inside the periodical. Murray characterizes the *Workman* as "a pioneering paper for adults premised on a technically and morally elevated style of illustration, and complementary letterpress."[13] Cooke likewise emphasizes the important contribution of the images to the *Workman*'s message, claiming that they "condense the *Workman*'s teachings into monumental designs" and have "an unambiguous directness, and effect, ultimately, like those appearing in an emblem book."[14] He adds that they "represent a particular notion of Victorian paternalism in which the key messages are expressed in words and images and in the interaction between them."[15] It is significant for the *Workman*'s key messages – and also its depiction of everyday heroism – that these illustrations emphasized the public *and* the domestic sphere as references for male working-class life. As Murray notes, the magazine was marked by an "overwhelming dominance of 'genre' subjects depicting scenes from everyday life either in public space (the workplace), or in the private arena (the home)."[16] According to the *Workman*, men's lives were meant to be grounded in the domestic because, in this civilized (and feminized) space, the element of violence commonly associated with both

---

11 On Smithies, see Peter Roger Mountjoy, "Thomas Bywater Smithies, Editor of *The British Workman*," *Victorian Periodicals Review* 18, no. 2 (1985): 46–56.
12 See Simon Cooke, "Periodicals of the mid-Victorian period: the physical properties of illustrated magazines," http://www.victorianweb.org/periodicals/cooke.html.
13 See Francis Allan Murray, "Thomas Bywater Smithies and *The British Workman*: Temperance Education and Mass-Circulation Graphic Imagery for the Working Classes, 1855–1883" (PhD thesis, University of Salford, 2007), 7.
14 Cooke, "The British Workman."
15 Ibid.
16 Murray, "Thomas Bywater Smithies," 135.

the male gender and lower strata of society could be contained. This was also communicated through the *Workman*'s textual contributions, which came in a wide range of forms and topics: "poetry, anecdotes, short stories, and serial stories. There were factual items, pieces of statistical information, notices on new publications and items of interest and advice for men and women."[17] On the large pages of the magazine, heroic stories were placed next to many different pieces, all of which, however, promoted values such as cleanliness, health, social care, kindness to humans and animals, temperance, charity, piety, industry, perseverance, and selflessness.[18]

The Heroic Profile[19] of *The British Workman*

The British Workman printed only a comparatively small number of articles that explicitly dealt with heroic figures and acts. Some of these were dedicated to great and famous men like Abraham Lincoln (July 1865), Sir Henry Havelock (June 1858), Garibaldi (January 1861), Columbus, "the hero of many a boy" (May 1868, 162), and King Alfred the Great (March 1869 and August 1869). Unsurprisingly, the *Workman* also heroized the Smilesean self-made man who had elevated himself above his class through hard work: like the engineer, George Stephenson (January 1859), whose portrait the *Workman* reprinted from Samuel Smiles's biography. However, most figures designated as heroic in the periodical are workmen who distinguished themselves through acts of everyday heroism.

Indeed, several pieces in the periodical explicitly address class differences in order to maintain that working men are just as capable of noble heroism as their betters. In no. 121, for instance, the *Workman* published a ballad entitled "Cornish Heroism, A True Tale of the Land's

---

17 Ibid., 127.
18 The periodical's attention to human-animal relations included a "canine hero" in "The Newfoundland Dog's Revenge," *The British Workman* November (1856): 90. The dog's name is Napoleon. He rescues a captain who has fallen overboard and is attacked by a shark.
19 For the notion of a periodical's heroic profile, see Barbara Korte, "Viele Helden für viele Leser: Das Heroische in viktorianischen Publikumszeitschriften," in *Bewunderer, Verehrer, Zuschauer. Die Helden und ihr Publikum* (Helden – Heroisierungen – Heroismen), ed. Ronald G. Asch and Michael Butter (Würzburg: Ergon, 2016), 93–115.

End."[20] Its author is identified as "John Harris, the Cornish Miner" (who was a regular contributor to the publication). In the ballad's narrative, a middle-class traveler is enclosed by the rising sea and rescued by a young farmer. When the traveler wants to reward this act of courage with a golden watch, the rescuer's father rejects the present with a lesson to the middle-class man that heroism cannot be materially rewarded:

Go, learn that nobleness of soul
Is found in every grade
'Tis not confined to princely courts
Or won by warrior's blade;
Full oft it walks in rustic garb,
Where weeds of labour cling:
Take back your gold, take back your gold!

A similar example is the poem "Noblemen" by C.H. Stuart in April 1855:

The noblest men I know on earth,
Are men whose hands are brown with toil;
Who, backed by no ancestral birth,
Hew down the woods, and till the soil;
And thereby win a prouder fame,
Than crowns a king's or warrior's name.[21]

The *Workman*'s illustrations confirmed such verbal affirmations of working-class heroism and nobility. The title illustration of the February 1860 issue (Fig. 1) is characteristic of the kind of hero the magazine preferred: "a heroic version of the working man."[22] As the caption emphasizes, it depicts the "life-like portrait" of a "Real Hero," the seaman Joseph Rodgers, who "swam ashore with a rope, by means of which thirty-nine lives were saved from the wreck of the 'Royal Charter.'"[23]

---

20 "Cornish Heroism, A True Tale of the Land's End," *The British Workman* January (1865): 2.
21 C. H. Stuart, "Noblemen," *The British Workman* April (1855): 11.
22 Cooke, "The British Workman."
23 "Joseph Rodgers, the Hero of the 'Royal Charter,'" *The British Workman* February (1860): 245.

Figure 1: "A Real Hero," The British Workman (February 1860), with kind permission of the Working Class Movement Library, Salford, United Kingdom.

The man looks calm and confident, but not proud; he is clad in clean everyday clothes and holds the everyday work tool of his heroic deed in his hands. Those who saved other people's lives form the main hero group in *The British Workman*. This group includes the one-time hero (such as Rodgers), as well as members of life-saving professions: policemen,[24] firemen,[25] and life-boatmen, for whom the *Workman* had a special

---

24 See, for example, an article about "Sergeant Brett," who was shot while doing his duty in Manchester (*The British Workman*, March 1868: 156).
25 The September 1861 issue was dedicated to the brave deed of James Braidwood, chief of the London fire department, who had died while performing his duty in the great fire at London Bridge in June that year. Braidwood's portrait and deed were seen on the cover, followed by an obituary with the title "Braidwood, the Brave," which includes the following lines: "We reverence the true hero, we love the good, simple-hearted man – the friend and peacemaker – the humble Christian. We hardly dare lament him. His career was so exalted – his death, notwithstanding our first shock – so painless and impressive. To follow him in his great work of mingled daring and mercy may be far beyond our feeble powers. To follow him, as we follow Christ, is our privilege and

partiality.²⁶ Significantly, these are all professions that serve the community, and while articles about their heroic members appreciated courage and the willingness to take risks, they also often emphasized kind-heartedness. The title of the November 1864 issue, for example, shows a "Kind-Hearted Policeman" who has helped a hungry child. The accompanying poem on the next page points out that this was not an act of conventional, agentive heroism ("'Twas no heroic deed; in fact / 'Twas but a trifling, kindly act"), but then proceeds to suggest that this "kindly act" should not be diminished and is heroic in its own right: "Yet 'twas no trifle to relieve / A childish heart unused to grieve; / No trifle that could end in good, / Or earn a mother's gratitude."²⁷

Another group of articles is dedicated to heroism at the workplace and, here again, special esteem is reserved for those who selflessly came to the rescue of their fellow workers.

---

duty." (322) The obituary was followed on the same page by C.L.R.'s poem "On the Death of Braidwood," whose third stanza identifies him as "a hero true." The January 1874 issue likewise had an image of "The Brave Fireman" on its cover and included an article on "Our Brave Firemen," which emphasized the human element in a fireman's action: "Greatly has the commander been aided by the floating engines, powerful land steamers, and manuals of the brigade; yet with all the advantages of perfectly arranged gear, in many of our large fires would be every effort but for the steady and enduring perseverance of the men" (194).

26 See, for example, "Life-Boat Services," March (1857): "We rejoice in being able to record the heroic deeds of various life-boat crews, whereby not a few of our fellow men were saved from a watery grave" (105–106). The January 1870 issue presented John Parsons (3–4), who acted for the Royal Humane Society at the London Serpentine, and the November 1870 issue had "Coxwain Cox and His Comrades on Their Mission of Mercy" on its cover, accompanied by an article about "The Brave Old Coxwain" (42), who not only received several medals for his deeds, but was also an exemplary Christian and teetotaler. A poem printed in the September 1866 issue entitled "The Life-Boat" (83) voiced appreciation for the brave men on the boat, and the cover of the December 1876 issue showed "Our Brave Lifeboat Men." An article commented on this illustration: "We may add that the illustration of 'Our Brave Lifeboat Men' represents two able and gallant men, who have on many an occasion rendered excellent service on the east coast of England in saving life from shipwreck" (94). Even an arctic explorer, a type of hero popular at least since Sir John Franklin's ill-fated expedition, was presented not as a man of great courage and endurance but as a man who saved a comrade's life: "We believe that very few instances of greater self-devotion, persevering courage, true friendship, and painful toil for the safety of another, have been known in the world's history," in "The Heroic Deed of Sergeant Woon, of the Royal Marines," December (1875): 47.

27 "The Kind-Hearted Policeman," *The British Workman* November (1864): 474.

Figure 2: "The Hartley Colliery Accident," The British Workman (April 1862), with kind permission of the Working Class Movement Library, Salford, United Kingdom.

The cover of the April 1862 issue shows a dramatic scene drawn by the famous illustrator John Gilbert (Fig. 2). It depicts miners during an accident in a colliery that had taken place in January that year. The following page features a poem about this accident by John Harris which highlights the bravery of Thomas Watson, who tried to help his injured colleagues – or at least pray with them in their hopeless situation. The poem explicitly compares him to a soldier and claims that his humanitarian, "true" heroism was greater than the belligerent heroism of a warrior:

He risked his life for others,
Who trembled near the goal;
If he could save their bodies,
Or cheer the parting soul.
O hero! Noble hero!
Not shedding human blood,

But walking in the footsteps
Of thy Redeemer, God.

The song of after ages
Thy story shall rehearse;
And harps not yet enkindled,
Embalm thy deed in verse.
And glory, fairer, brighter,
Than ever warrior won,
Shall stream upon thy pathway,
And gild thy setting sun.[28]

The need to distinguish between "true" (or "real") and false heroes is a concern that comes to the fore in a number of *Workman* articles. Misdirected hero-worship is always condemned, as can be seen in the piece "Who Is the True Hero." Here the author is outraged by a group of workmen who confuse the reputation of a popular prize-fighter with the truly deserved fame of national heroes such as Nelson and Wellington. To him, the men have been "led astray," and have misdirected their admiration to the representative of a useless and brutal sport, rather than to models of moral excellence. The author gives vent to his irritation in a long discussion of the nature of true courage – the only kind of courage which every man should admire and strive to imitate. He carefully distinguishes it from cowardice, but also from mere physical daring or pluck (which lacks the civilized qualities of moral heroism):

Courage is a quality which all men are disposed to admire. Cowardice as certainly calls forth contempt. ... The value of courage, however, ought to be determined by the *nature* of its *object*, and the *circumstances* under which it is exercised. A pugilist, who engages in the prize-fight may display great "pluck," and astonishing disregard of physical danger and suffering, he may excite wonder by his powers of endurance, and dogged determination to conquer, and those who are sufficiently inhuman to find pleasure in seeing two men try who can most successfully bruise and maim each other, may cry "bravo! bravo!" and hold them up as heroes; [sic] But in what does their courage exceed that of the *wild beast*? ...

In fact, the excellence of courage is always proportioned to the excellence of the cause in which it is exercised. There are *moral Heroes*, men who for the sake of great moral principles and interests have braved reproach, ignominy, imprisonment,

---

28 "The Hartley Colliery Accident," *The British Workman* April (1866): 350. See also another poem by John Harris, "The Two Miners; or, Christian Heroism," *The British Workman* May (1866): 66.

tortures, and death; and this not merely in reference to themselves, but to others also. In this class we must include the large number of worthies who in every age have suffered for conscience'-sake, and whose heroic bravery has been acquired, not by gymnastic training, but from the influence of Christian principles upon the heart. Nor has it been confined to one sex only, it has been nobly displayed by the delicate maiden, and by the aged matron, nay, even by the child of tender years.[29]

As represented in this long and sermonizing passage, moral heroism is superior because it impregnates "the heart": it is not spent in the single deed but emerges in a person's entire behavior, and thus sustains everyday life. In addition, as the last sentence of the passages emphasizes, moral heroism is ungendered and unrestricted with regard to age (and, one might add, to class): it is an ideal to which everybody can strive in all situations of life.

The British Workman's Christian bias and esteem for moral heroism not only prohibited the heroization of a violent sport. They also help to explain the magazine's very reserved attitude towards military heroism – perhaps the most prototypical form of the heroic.[30] Indeed, military feats are rarely mentioned on its pages (in contrast, for instance, to contemporary magazines for boys such as *The Boy's Own Magazine*), and where they are, it is usually in a highly critical light. While the necessity of belligerent heroism may be granted, it is presented as inferior to heroism in civilian life.[31] A poem entitled "The Heroes of Industry," published in 1859, makes this statement at the very beginning:

Let others write of those who fought
On many a bloody field –
Of those, whose daring deeds were wrought
With sword, and spear, and shield;
But I will read of heroes bold,
The bravest of the brave,
Who fought for neither fame nor gold –
Who fill an unmarked grave.[32]

---

29 'Uncle David,' "Who Is the True Hero," *The British Workman* July (1860): 266.
30 See Graham Dawson, *Soldier Heroes: British Adventure, Empire and the Imagining of Masculinities* (London: Routledge, 1994).
31 See "Real Heroes," May (1862): 356, which gives an excerpt from a speech by the Bishop of Durham, who had visited the site of the Hartley Colliery accident and was impressed by the men who had tried to save their fellow miners: "I call these men the real heroes of the people"– in contrast to soldiers who kill other people.
32 G. P. R., "The Heroes of Industry," *The British Workman* September (1859): 226.

The article "Our Brave Firemen" (1874) even insists that "we should possess a volume of courageous narrative by the side of which military triumphs would pale."[33] In March 1873, the *Workman* printed a poem by John Harris about "Samuel Westlake, the Brave Engine Driver," who had saved many passengers in October 1872 when he "coolly kept his place" and prevented a crash with another train. To the working-class poet, Westlake seems to translate old chivalric valor into modern and more democratic times:

Gone is the age of knighthood,
The palfrey and the squire;
And he who would revive it
But overstrains his lyre.
Yet there are real heroes,
Their fellow-men to cheer,
Without the shining corslet,
Without the pointed spear.

Where moral darkness reigneth,
Where young feet turn astray,
Where age and want are weeping,
With kind hands there are they.
And in the path of danger
They boldly stand to save,
Through raging fire and water,
Their comrades from the grave.

Where Cornwall's rocks are rising,
Where Scotland's mountains stand,
By many a rolling river,
In many a distant land,
The true-born hero dwelleth,
Who seeks his country's weal,
Not in the soldier's glitter,
Not in the warrior's steel.

....

How thrills the heart to hear it!
In vales where cowslips grow

---

[33] "Our Brave Firemen," *The British Workman* January (1874): 194. A popular book collection with stories about military heroism was Lawrence Drake, *The Heroes of England: Stories of the Lives of the Most Celebrated British Soldiers and Sailors* (London: Joseph Cundall, 1843).

The Tale shall be repeated
As autumns come and go;
For oft of SAMUEL WESTLAKE
Beside the hearth we'll boast,
Who is a greater hero
Than if he slew a host.[34]

Apart from humanitarian concerns, there was another reason why a publication for working-class men shied away from an appreciation of martial heroism (even while soldiers were becoming increasingly important in the spread and defense of the British Empire[35]): A worker who was disposed to admire soldiers (or prize-fighters) might also have been disposed to raise his fist against his masters — a pervasive fear of middle-class employers in the decades after Chartism. Heroism in male workers had a precarious element since it might have been activated in social protest, and it therefore had to be carefully channeled, as the *Workman* attempted to do through word and image. It seems fitting in this light that *The British Workman* only rarely mentioned — and never heroized — the great fighters for workers' and, more generally, social rights of the preceding decades.[36] The issue for January 1862 presents Tom Paine, the author of

---

34 John Harris, "Samuel Westlake, the Brave Engine Driver," March (1873): 155. The July (1877) issue printed another poem by John Harris about the accident at "Throedyrhiw Colliery" (122). The rescuers are here referred to as "these noble hero-workers," and the poem ends with the lines: "Thank God for British heroes, / Who never wore a sword!"

35 See, for instance, John M. MacKenzie (ed.), *Popular Imperialism and the Military 1850–1950* (Manchester: Manchester University Press, 1992); Jeffrey Richards, "Popular Imperialism and the Image of the Army in Juvenile Literature," in *Popular Imperialism and the Military 1850–1950*, ed. John M. MacKenzie (Manchester: Manchester University Press, 1992), 80–108; and Michael Lieven, "Heroism, Heroics and the Making of Heroes: The Anglo-Zulu War of 1879," *Albion* 30, no. 3 (1998): 419–438, who states that "the military hero was an exemplar, teaching the young the qualities they must develop and reassuring adults of those qualities on which they had been taught to rely" (419).

36 The Chartist weekly newspaper *The Northern Star* (1837–1957), founded and owned by the Chartist leader Feargus O'Connor, has a very different heroic profile. It portrays many heroes of the Chartist movement and contemporary democratic movements all over Europe, as well as historical heroes of freedom and democratization, such as William Tell or Robin Hood. Working men are also heroized, for instance in an address "To the Frame-Work Knitters of the Mansfield District" in the January 1847 issue: "You who glory in singing of the heroic deeds of your ancient sires, how they fought, bled, and conquered, in the cause of humanity, justice, and liberty, copy their glorious example, be energetic, act nobly, and posterity will regard you as their benefactors and deliverers" (6).

The Rights of Man, who had died in 1809, as a meek, old, and quite unheroic man, both on its cover (captioned as "The Last Moments of Tom Paine") and in an associated article[37] that claims that Paine returned to Christianity before his death.

The Heroic Profile of *The British Workwoman*

The British Workwoman shares many features and values with *The British Workman*, since the latter was never exclusively directed at a male audience but also included some pieces aimed at female readers (for instance on the household and food). However, it is marked by a conspicuous use of heroic templates and a heroic vocabulary in relation to working women and their lives.

The British Workwoman's Christian orientation is reflected in its epigraph in the masthead (from 1863 to 1871): "'A Woman that feareth the Lord, she shall be praised. – Give her of the fruit of her hands, and let her own works praise her.' Prov. Xxxi."[38] This citation not only places the publication in a Christian context and sets an intention to praise working women, but also hints at the fact that the praise of female work is to be performed quietly, in private, through "her own works." The periodical, whose full title was *The British Workwoman Out and at Home*, was a monthly publication which first appeared in November 1863. The connection between *The British Workwoman* and *The British Workman* could be found not only in the name, but also in the size, price, and style of the publications, even though they had different publishers. The *Workwoman* was also priced at one penny, was printed in folio size, and had a large front-page illustration. Despite these formal similarities, a different vocabulary and visual language were needed, since the publication exclusively targeted women, whose societal status was – generally, but especially in relation to work – much more disputed than men's.

In its opening issue, the periodical states that "we have no organ exclusively devoted to the interests of the British Workwoman, and it will

---

37 "Paine's Last Moments," *The British Workman* January (1862): 338.
38 See, for example, the November 1863 issue and all following ones until 1871.

be our earnest effort to supply this want."[39] As the "centre of all social influence," women are to be instructed by the periodical on how to improve "the religious, moral, and social progress of our country"[40] along the lines of the Earl of Shaftesbury's recommendations.[41] Women's precarious position between the private and public spheres is already mirrored in the periodical's dilemma of how to define what a "workwoman" actually is: The article "Who are Workwomen?" answers this question first with a catalogue of well-known examples, headed by Queen Victoria[42] and followed by Florence Nightingale and prominent philanthropists such as Angela Burdett Coutts, Caroline Chisholm, and Maria Rye. Only after listing these women does the article mention the "hundreds of others doing a good moral work, whose names are not so well known to us."[43] The main field of work for women is defined as "moral" work within the household or in Sunday school. This "good and Christ-like work" in a private or educational setting constitutes the main definition of female work in the publication, while a note on manual labor in the public sphere done by those "compelled to work in order to live" reads like a mere afterthought.[44] The tension between the publication's title, which clearly suggests more than household work, and its definitions of female work remains present throughout its entire publication run. This is remarkable because advertisements for the publication clearly signal that many of its readers were laboring women. Most issues end with a note encouraging employers to buy the publication for their female employees: "All Masters, Mistresses, Fathers, Husbands, Brothers, and the Employers

---

39 "The British Workwoman. Out and At Home," *The British Workwoman* November (1863): 2.
40 Ibid.
41 Shaftesbury is quoted in many articles of the journal and is the only male hero figure in the whole run of the periodical. He is praised for his ideas on education and social improvement. With quotes such as "I believe that any improvement which could be brought to bear on the mothers, would effect a greater amount of good than anything that has yet been done" (Ibid.) he stresses the influence women exerted in the private sphere on society as a whole.
42 The first yearly volume of the publication was dedicated to "her most gracious majesty" (*The British Workwoman* May 1865) as well, and throughout the run of the magazine Queen Victoria is constructed as a model for a workwoman. Not her regal qualities are stressed in most of the cases, but her private efforts as a wife and mother, which she manages to maintain alongside her public duties.
43 "Who Are Workwomen?," *The British Workwoman* November (1863): 2.
44 Ibid.

of Workwomen and Girls, are invited to place before their Servants, Mothers, Wives, Sisters, and Employees, copies of the 'British Workwoman,' under a full assurance to themselves that great good may result."

Like in *The British Workman*, the texts in the *Workwoman* are written in accessible prose and promote a similar set of values, although with shifts in emphasis. Values such as perseverance, industry, temperance, altruism, and kindness are stressed, but the most important virtue is selflessness. Quite strikingly, and in contrast to the *Workman*, articles which label actions as "heroic" appear frequently. Since female work was located primarily in the domestic sphere, even the vocabulary of martial heroism is employed without hesitation or restriction. The *Workwoman* contains a vast number of texts that heroize women,[45] and most of them describe their heroism in a language of war and battle. For example, an article in the publication's second issue, "Good Women," states that women are "morally heroic in the great battle of life."[46] Within this battle, women perform a charitable and altruistic role (just like the examples of "workwomen" such as Nightingale, Chisholm, or Rye mentioned in the periodical's first editorial). It is their task to "lighten heavy toil, to guide the erring, to instruct the ignorant, to console the suffering, and to cast something of heaven's own light on a world overgrown within thorns and thistles."[47] Significantly, all of the women of the "noble army" are performing these actions within "the sacred circle of home."[48] Female heroism is thus not only given weight through the use of war metaphors, but is also depicted as God-given work through its placement in the "sacred circle" of the household – a circle in which it is also safely contained.

This idea of life as a battle to be fought bravely is a frequent metaphor in the publication and even used as a theme in the editorial of April 1864. "What have England's women to do with battles?" is its opening question. After establishing that during violent national wars, women's fate of waiting, watching, and hoping makes them "suffer as much as the husbands and brothers," the editorial turns to a different battlefield:

But there is another battle, from which not the feeblest woman is exempt. A battle for every individual, in which we must all stand up and take our part, whether we

---

45 The only exception is the aforementioned Earl of Shaftesbury.
46 "Good Women," *The British Workwoman*, December (1863): 12.
47 Ibid.
48 Ibid.

will or not. We may be young, or old, weak, or ignorant, feeble, or active; no matter, the sword is thrust into our hands, we choose our side, and are compelled to take our part in the proceedings. ... There are, however, many noble-minded women taking their part in life's battle on the right side. These are fighting evermore for goodness, for truth, for gentleness, for integrity. ... God's soldiers of the cross are they, who follow in the steps of the Saviour, loving and serving him. ... Side by side, with all the heroic sisterhood, you may fight for goodness and truth by your own firesides. Better husbands, better fathers, better brothers, better sons shall go forth peace-laden into the outer world, because of your efforts. The fell destroyers which blast so many joys may come up to your well-barred doors and windows, but your hands shall push them back. Gentle words and loving counsels, and pleasant advice shall make music wherever the light sound of your footstep is heard. A barrier of love shall be built around the unstable ones of your household, so that they must needs be kept from harm, vice, dishonesty, fraud, intemperance, impurity: and all that is wicked shall shrink abashed from your presence, *if only you will be true to yourselves*, if you will watch and pray, if you will be careful and industrious and noble. O women of England![49]

The imagery of war is prominent in this article. Its strong connection to the Christian faith[50] evokes not only a violent battlefield, but also medieval crusades. At second glance, however, this battlefield is located in contemporary society's everyday life, with the "right side" found in the domestic sphere, into which the public, outside world as the "wrong side" tries to intrude. The elevated style stresses the importance of female work within the domestic sphere. The women are presented as crusaders, though their weapons are peaceful: love, faith, and industry in their domestic actions enable them to prepare the male members of their family for the public sphere and help them to resist "fraud, intemperance, impurity." They themselves, however, do not seem to be able to cross the threshold, but protect the domestic circle from within with their "barrier of love." Similar imagery can be found in the editorial of June 1871: "But unless we keep constant guard at the threshold, there are foes innumerable ever ready to

---

49 "What Have England's Women to Do with Battles?," *The British Workwoman* April (1864): 43.
50 This and other texts clearly evoke a Christian form of martial rhetoric and are reminiscent of many popular Christian hymns. The "kind" of battle action evoked in the texts is reminiscent of the "mental fight" proclaimed, for instance, in the famous "Jerusalem" or the "good fight" in John Monsell's 1863 hymn "Fight the Good Fight with All Thy Might." The appeal to "fight" is thus strengthened by the fact that it is not only depicted as a familiar, individual duty, but as a Christian one as well, which makes it an even more significant fight for the grand collective of the Christian faith.

invade our domestic strongholds. Drunkenness, wastefulness, pride, lying, indolence, and a great many other evil influences are apt to creep in and destroy the peace and happiness of a family."[51]

Articles such as this construct the image of a battling housewife who heroically protects the domestic sphere against dangers and vices that threaten it from outside. This notion, which is repeated time and again, stands in the greatest possible contrast to the actual "weapons" and "manoeuvres" it describes. Although the imagery of the battlefield would be associated with physical violence, noise and chaos, women's acts are described as "silent acts of heroism."[52] And the periodical's most pronounced characteristic of the female hero is her "heroic love."[53]

What is striking is the homogeneity of female heroism depicted in the publication – especially when juxtaposed with the kind of heroes presented in *The British Workman*. While the *Workman* shows heroes in different situations outside the home, the *Workwoman* places its female heroes firmly in the household and relates their heroic behavior to the influence they exert on the other members of their family.[54] Female heroism is thus made accessible to all readers who are motivated by the same values as the women represented in the periodical: "The heroine may be simply a daughter (a 'girl of her period') who has laid aside sweet dreams of her own that she may help her brothers. Or she may be a mother, who thinks of nothing day or night but how she may be more helpful."[55] Thus, the acts of female heroism could rather be described as non-acts. Female heroes are silent, humble, selfless, and restrained, and their heroic deed is often the omission of active involvement in order to allow room for the actions

---

51 "Home and Its Influences," *The British Workwoman* June (1871): 348.
52 "Woman's Courage," *The British Workwoman* March (1869): 132.
53 "Incidents in the Time of the Plague," *The British Workwoman* June (1870): 251. See also the articles "What are we doing? What can we do?" September (1867): 372; "A Noble Woman," July (1872): 79; "Heroism of the Present Day," May (1873): 144; or "A Woman's Heroism" August (1879): 83.
54 This is exemplified by articles such as "John and Mary Scott; or, Ill Effects of a Mother Leaving Home," February (1864), which presents the negative effect of a working mother on her family, and its companion piece in the same issue, "Lucy Norcott; or, the Wife at Home," which contains an appeal to the female reader to "Stay at Home!" (26). In a similar vein, women's rights are also restricted to the private sphere. The poem "Women's Rights" contains stanzas such as "A Right to watch when others sleep, / To soothe the bed of pain, / To cause the weary troubled heart / To wake to hope again," December (1878): 19.
55 "Heroism of the Present Day," *The British Workwoman* May (1873): 144.

of others. The paradox of this heroic passiveness and invisibility appears to be compensated by the martial vocabulary with which it is described and praised – use of this vocabulary being possible because the behavior and attitudes to which it referred were peaceful and had no potential for uproar.

Female heroics are defined very narrowly in the publication, and the rhetoric of war and heroism may have given the female readers a feeling of purpose and duty. The contributors to the magazine did not only make the role of housewife more appealing and rewarding. They also created a sense that this role was endangered by contemporary political and societal developments such as women's labor and the rising women's movement. Indeed, they implied that it needed to be defended with force, although the weapons described were those of love, understanding, selflessness, and piety. The fact that many women of the working classes not only worked in the domestic sphere, but actually contributed to their families' income with paid labor in mills and mines, makes the *Workwoman*'s rhetoric of female heroism even more remarkable. In its articles, *The British Workwoman* either criticizes or overlooks its intended readers' actual role as laboring women. This meant that the only niche left for active, female everyday heroism was in the area of life-saving, where women could prove their courage and strength under extraordinary circumstances. It was women such as these to which the *Workwoman* occasionally paid tribute in articles from the 1870s, with several articles recounting the well-known incident of Grace Darling. However, these stories are not described in a martial language, but through a more peaceful rhetoric.[56] In "ordinary" everyday life, however, "heroism" is conceived as passive and private – and in this respect the magazine evokes middle-class ideals of female domesticity.

In this light, it is significant that on the pictorial level, which conveys its messages more concretely than text, *The British Workwoman* never suggests the martial. Where the magazine's verbal rhetoric seems paradoxical, its

---

56 One poem, "Woman's Heroism," is written from Grace Darling's perspective and shows her as a dutiful, loyal and pious daughter: "God will give me strength, I know, / Since my mother cannot go; / He whose word could still the wave / Sends his angels now to save," August (1879): 83. Other articles compare Darling's heroic act to the heroism of a woman in the household and emphasize that the former's behavior was situation-bound and singular and constitutes an inferior form of heroism: "[the] common-place good woman ... is not Grace Darling. No, because she does not live in a lighthouse, and looks only upon the stormy sea where lives are being lost" in "Heroism of the Present Day," May (1873): 144.

visual rhetoric is decidedly not: The front pages usually show peaceful scenes of women surrounded by their children and/or husbands. The scenery, for example on the title page of issue 50 (December 1867, Fig. 3), is a harmonious, domestic one.

Figure 3: "Mother's Home Training," The British Workman *(December 1867), with kind permission of the Working Class Movement Library, Salford, United Kingdom.*

The mother in this illustration is surrounded by her five children, all of whom are involved in the act of reading, making it clear that they have apparently already received some form of education. Their mother has fulfilled her role, and the image shows her in the very moment of exerting her "social influence" on her children. The toys around the children show that the mother not only takes care of their education but also has their pleasure in mind. The same scene could be depicted for a middle-class household (and it often was in contemporary women's magazines). But the minimalist furniture and decoration of the room, the lack of the Victorian "clutter" so characteristic of middle-class interiors, signal that the setting is distinctly *not* middle-class.[57] Furthermore, the impression of a "dangerous" urban public, as constructed in the articles on female heroics, is omitted. Most illustrations set within the household feature a window or opened door which affords a view to a peaceful landscape. Those illustrations which depict the outside world predominantly show a rural environment but still communicate domestic values. For example, the cover of the May 1867 issue (Fig. 4) displays a pastoral setting in which two girls are standing against a background of trees, meadows, and sheep. The only building to be seen is a church in the background, which shows that civilization and Christianity are close, while the fence and bench behind the children make it clear that the represented rurality is man-made.

Figure 4: "The Little Mother," The British Workman (May 1867), with kind permission of the Working Class Movement Library, Salford, United Kingdom.

---

57 See, for example, Kathryn Ferry, *The Victorian Home* (Botley: Shire Publications, 2010).

The illustration emphasizes domestic values: The girls have apparently been picking flowers. One of them has torn her sleeve and the older girl does not even wait until they get home, but fixes the garment on the spot. The caption "The Little Mother" marks this as a desired behavior of young girls, who are expected to become "proper" mothers one day.

The only pictorial representations of violent female acts in *The British Workwoman* are religious allegories, such as one which shows "Faith" as embodied by a woman (April 1865, Fig. 5). The personification of faith ("the substance of the things hoped for," as one can read in the ornamented frame) not only embraces the cross as a way of arming herself and crushes the embodiment of evil with her foot, but she can also be seen as a role model for "common" women.

Figure 5: "Faith," The British Workwoman (April 1865), with kind permission of the Working Class Movement Library, Salford, United Kingdom.

Her outstretched hand, which marks her as a leader, is on a direct line with the opened Bible on the left-hand side. The Bible is thereby shown as the foundation of modern faith and an inspiration for every "battling" woman. As an established discourse which uses martial rhetoric but at the same time does not call for active realization, religious representations such as this one can be seen as a clear reference point for the depiction of the heroic woman in *The British Workwoman*.

Conclusion

The British Workman and *The British Workwoman* created images of everyday heroism that focused primarily on the moral implications of heroic behavior and attitudes. "Everyday" heroism in *The British Workman* and *The British Workwoman* can consist of brave, risk-taking acts, but also in a disposition that manifests itself in the living of daily life. In both instances, heroism is synonymous with moral exemplarity and has an ennobling quality. Heroic workmen and workwomen are presented as the cream of their class and morally equal to the best examples of people with a higher social standing. In this respect, the *Workman* and *Workwoman* contributed to the processes and institutions through which the heroic was democratized in the course of the nineteenth century, and so stand side by side with the medals and monuments for "common" heroes that proliferated in Britain during the second half of the 1800s. At the same time, the *Workman* and *Workwoman* were not produced by working-class people but for them, and so served as a middle-class fabrication of an ideal working class. The values embodied by heroized figures in the two periodicals were adopted from the dominant Victorian middle-class value system. Thus, while widening the social scope of the heroic and heroizing the working classes, the *Workman* and *Workwoman* also molded working-class heroics in a certain ideological way. Specifically, in times of unsettled class relations, and especially unstable industrial relations, they responded to middle-class anxieties about threats to the social order and were produced to appease these anxieties by constructing a spirit of class friendship and the image of a peaceful and socially compatible working class, whose role models were peace-loving, pious, and socially responsible men and women.

Both publications carefully navigate the image of heroic behavior: True and false heroism are openly distinguished, and heroic qualities are always of a nature that could and should be admired and imitated by every man and woman. Heroic figures in the *Workman* and *Workwoman* are never transgressive or even subversive, while pro-social behavior is clearly meant to be encouraged. This seems to come almost "naturally" in the case of women, whose heroism, as defined in *The British Workwoman*, is manifested in passive values and qualities of care and social responsibility. Indeed, their heroic behavior has communal and relational tendencies that are culturally closely connoted with femininity. That women are also capable of agentive, risk-taking heroism, as when they save other people's lives, is acknowledged and appreciated, but also marked as an exceptional departure from the norms of female behavior. The seemingly "natural" habitat for the seemingly more "natural" passive heroism of women in everyday life was the home, which the *Workwoman* emphasizes through its illustrations in particular. Interestingly, domesticity is also always portrayed as a background for the heroism of the working man in *The British Workman*, where textual and pictorial representations of heroism are embedded in numerous articles that promote caring, communal, and pious qualities for men as well. *The British Workman* prefers non-belligerent heroism to martial and military heroism, with the working men on its pages proving their masculinity by acts of civil heroism rather than on the battlefield. Their deeds of everyday heroism require courage, strength, and stamina, but they also demonstrate communal and relational qualities since everyday heroism is performed for the benefit of others. Male everyday heroism in the *Workman* is thus significantly permeated with qualities typically associated with the heroic behavior of women and in domestic settings. The representational strategies of the *Workman* thus contained the threat of heroic agency in a potentially radicalized working class. This agency was, in quite a literal sense, domesticated.

What seems even more remarkable are the representational strategies for heroism in *The British Workwoman*. With its preference for a passive and decidedly domestic female heroism – which saw active female heroism as an absolute exception – this periodical translated ideals of middle-class femininity into the working classes. As indicated above, this translation entailed a significant tension of the ideal and the real since readers of the *Workwoman* were aware of the fact that many workwomen had a workplace outside the home. That a language of belligerent heroism was used to describe female daily heroism in the home (while it was carefully avoided in the parallel publication for men) is a paradox that might at least partly be explained as a compensation for the desired passivity.

Both periodicals employed templates of the heroic, and especially a heroism linked to everyday life, in a highly politicized manner: Their careful navigation of desirable heroic behavior in the working classes was intended to help stabilize the social order and reinforce the dominance of middle-class values at all levels of Victorian society.

Everyday Heroism in Britain, 1850–1939

John Price

During a ferocious storm on March 23, 1866, a cargo ship named *Spirit of the Ocean* was swept off course and wrecked upon the notorious Start Point rocks on the southwest coast of England.[1] A local farmer, Samuel Popplestone, witnessed the incident and, grabbing a coil of rope, he ran to the cliffs and climbed down to the shore. Clambering out onto the rocks, Popplestone was swept off several times but, nevertheless, eventually manage to lift four men out of the water and drag them up the cliff to safety. On April 23, 1885, a terrible fire engulfed a shop and house in Union Street in south London.[2] Alice Ayres, a young woman who lived in the house, managed to throw a feather mattress out of the window and, while smoke and flames billowed around her, she calmly dropped three young children, one after the other, onto the mattress below. Alice then tried to jump but, apparently overcome by smoke and exhaustion, she fell limply, missed the mattress, and hit the pavement. Conveyed to Guy's hospital with severe spinal injuries, Alice's condition deteriorated and, two days later, she died. During a night shift at the Baxter Chemical Works in St. Helens, Lancashire on September 23, 1908, a workman fell into a well where he was quickly overcome by poisonous fumes.[3] Another worker, Thomas Wright, despite being warned of the danger, climbed into the well to try and help his co-worker. Wright, though, was also overcome by the fumes, and it was some time before rescuers could obtain suitable rescue equipment to lift the two men out. Remarkably, the first man was

---

1 "Mr. Popplestone, the First Recipient of the Albert Medal," *Illustrated London News*, June 2, 1866; Lambton J. H. Young, *Acts of Bravery* (London: printed in Edinburgh, 1872), 306.
2 "The Fatal Fire in the Borough," *The Times*, April 30,1885; "The Fatal Fire in Southwark," *Lloyd's Weekly Newspaper*, May 3, 1885; John Price, *Postman's Park; G. F. Watts' Memorial to Heroic Self-Sacrifice* (Compton: Watts Gallery, 2008), 57–64.
3 Carnegie Hero Fund Trust, Dunfermline, *Annual Report* (1908), The British Library, London.

resuscitated but, unable to be revived, Wright died, leaving a widow and seven children.

Although separated by forty-two years, these three incidents all share one prominent thing in common: they are all examples of what was known in Britain during the nineteenth and twentieth centuries as "everyday" heroism. The term "everyday" heroism was used to describe acts of life-risking bravery, undertaken by otherwise ordinary civilian individuals, largely in the course of their daily lives and within relatively commonplace surroundings.[4] What is more, not only were these three incidents all examples of everyday heroism, each of them also acted as the catalyst for the establishment of prominently public schemes to recognize, commemorate, and reward such acts. Samuel Popplestone became the first recipient of the Albert Medal, the first Crown-sanctioned decoration for civilian gallantry; the death of Alice Ayres inspired the Victorian artist George Frederic Watts to construct a unique monument to everyday heroism in Postman's Park, London; and Thomas Wright's family were the first people in Britain to be supported by a pension from the Carnegie Hero Fund Trust, which was established by the retired steel magnate, Andrew Carnegie. Crucially, these organizations were not anomalous or isolated examples; rather, they were part of a broader landscape of discourses and activities in Britain focusing on everyday heroism. The State and numerous charitable organizations created medals and awards to honor it; authors wrote books and poems about it; artists created paintings illustrating it; communities erected monuments to commemorate it; intellectuals discussed and debated the merits of it; groups sought to control or appropriate it; and, most importantly, people from all walks of life embraced and championed it. It is surprising that, for an idea that was so pervasive, everyday heroism has not received more attention from scholars until fairly recently.

This is a point raised by Simon Wendt in his introduction to this volume, where he also provides a salient and useful comparative framework for studying everyday heroism that will be employed in this chapter. Firstly, there is a need to identify and examine the contexts within which people, and/or their behavior, were considered and defined as being "heroic," and the extent to which "heroism" was constructed by specific

---

4 The idea of "everyday" heroism in Britain in the Victorian and Edwardian period is analyzed in detail in John Price, *Everyday Heroism: Victorian Constructions of the Heroic Civilian* (London: Bloomsbury, 2014).

groups for particular audiences. The evidence suggests that in Britain in the nineteenth and early twentieth century, there were three prominent contexts within which everyday heroism was considered and defined. There was an "establishment" context, in which everyday heroism was specifically constructed by the State, predominantly through the awarding of Crown-sanctioned medals, and aimed at the general public – in particular, the increasingly enfranchised working classes. There was also an "organizational" context, driven chiefly by private and charitable bodies, which championed particular types of heroism and sought the widest audience possible since they were reliant on subscribers and patrons. Thirdly, there was a "radical" context, principally composed from networks of progressively-minded individuals who were keen to appeal to the aspirational working classes as well as policymakers and power holders.

Based on their context, the functions and purposes that such constructions (be they social, cultural, political, racial, or gendered) may have served, and whether they were designed to stabilize and unify, or destabilize and contest, should also be scrutinized. Within the establishment context, awards such as the Albert Medal and the Edward Medal were introduced in order to increase public awareness of state recognition of civilian gallantry so as to encourage and foster public allegiance and loyalty to Crown and country. Thus, while it was very much about bolstering and unifying the state and nation, this also had an impact on the types of people considered worthy of reward. In the organizational context, charities and private bodies such as the Royal Humane Society and the Society for the Protection of Life from Fire were primarily concerned with promoting and disseminating their work so as educate and inform the public about certain hazards and methods for preventing them. But, generally speaking, they were also subscription-funded organizations that tended to avoid controversial or contested constructions of heroism, as they needed to publicize their work so as to encourage and retain patrons. Progressive liberal networks were also keen to use everyday heroism for educational and instructional purposes, though they had their own more radical contextual agenda. For some, the purpose was to highlight the morality and decency of the working classes and to stimulate and foster social and cultural improvement beyond the realms of simple citizenship. For others, it was to promote pacifist and humanist ideas that were somewhat at odds with the militaristic and imperial rhetoric of the state. For the radicals, acts of everyday heroism were employed because they believed them to be more relevant and better understood by working-class audiences, thus giving them a greater didactic potential. As a result, progressive, liberal, philanthropic, and pacifist motivations contributed significantly to shaping, consolidating, and encouraging an alternative discourse on everyday heroism that, to a great extent, contested with the one presented by the state.

In addition to context and purpose, the extent to which these definitions, constructions, functions, and purposes were products of their time, and the propensity for the meaning of "heroism" to change over time, also needs to be taken into consideration. Heroism is not a single, static, or rigidly understood notion, but rather a flexible and malleable constellation of ideas which can be shaped or constructed along different lines by different groups or people. This is why the study of heroism is particularly useful and important for scholars, as it offers a window onto, for example, the social, cultural, and political atmosphere in which it existed. Essentially, if you want to identify the characteristics of a group or a society at a given point in time, much can be learnt by studying those which it held up as heroic. During the timeframe selected for this chapter, 1850–1939, it can be argued that, in Britain, the idea of heroism became progressively more inclusive and egalitarian; in fact, more "everyday" in nature. The process of change was relatively slow and distinctly incremental, but it is clear that the widening of the sphere of heroism was reflective of broader changes and reforms in Victorian and Edwardian society. Prior to 1850, there was little or no recognition or reward for the heroism of the working-class man or woman. Yet, by the early twentieth-century, everyday heroism was almost entirely integrated into wider discourses, and there is some evidence to suggest that it was even strong enough to act as a bolster during the interwar period when military and imperial heroism had become problematic ideas.

The Establishment Context

Within the establishment context, the Albert Medal, introduced in 1866 as the first Crown-sanctioned award for everyday heroism, represents an ideal case-study through which to identify the establishment context and to examine the functions and purposes that it served.[5] The Albert Medal was explicitly introduced by the government on the basis of a belief that publically recognizing civilians who undertook acts of heroism in their everyday life would stimulate the emulation of patriotic attitudes and civic behavior within British society. Generally speaking, military heroism, which occurred within the context of "serving the country," was easy to promote and interpret as heroism "on behalf of the nation" and thereby underline a serviceman's allegiance to the Crown.[6] Providing state recognition and endorsement of everyday heroism widened the idea beyond the battlefield, meaning that, potentially, any of the monarch's subjects could receive a state reward for heroism, become a "national" hero, and represent allegiance to the Crown and service for the country. Furthermore, instituting a Crown decoration for civilian heroism promoted the idea that every citizen in the country was capable of performing a heroic act and, consequently, the admirable qualities of a heroic individual could be perceived as belonging to the national character. Thus, in an establishment context, the intended function and purpose of promoting and rewarding everyday heroism was to encourage allegiance to Crown and country, and promote the idea that the nation was underpinned by high and honorable ideals.

However, bestowing Crown medals for everyday heroism had to be approached carefully. If individuals were to receive highly publicized state endorsement of their behavior, it was vital, in the establishment context, that the correct kinds of people and personal qualities were promoted as being worthy of emulation. There was clearly a lot of anxiety and suspicion about extending state recognition of heroism beyond the military and into the everyday, where there was a danger of rewarding the wrong sorts of people despite their having undertaken acts of heroism. When the medal was first proposed in 1864, Queen Victoria raised two specific concerns about Crown recognition of everyday heroism. The first was that "it might frequently happen that these daring acts might be performed by men of irregular life and immoral habits," and the second that "the present proposal would give decorations to men for gallant acts performed as citizens, in their ordinary life, and would be vouched for by people of their own

---

5 Donald V. Henderson, *Heroic Endeavour: A Complete Register of the Albert, Edward and Empire Gallantry Medals and How They Were Won* (London: J. B. Hayward, 1988); Price, *Everyday Heroism*, 31–63.

6 For example, see Melvin C. Smith, *Awarded for Valour: A History of the Victorian Cross and the Evolution of British Heroism* (Basingstoke: Palgrave Macmillan, 2008).

class, probably their friends and neighbours."[7] Ultimately, it was these anxieties and suspicions that informed the way in which the establishment constructed its idea of everyday heroism.

There was no formal public application procedure for nominating an individual for the Albert Medal, nor was there very much in the way of rules or guidelines to assist government officials when deciding whether to agree or refuse an award.[8] Without any real guidance, they were left to adopt their own sets of standards, qualifications, and judgements as to what constituted an act worthy of recognition; something which they believed would be relatively straightforward to do. They would consider the facts of the matter and apply their collective knowledge and reasoning to reach an informed consensus. However, by and large, their judgements were based upon their personal assumptions and opinions about the nature of heroic behavior, as well as being heavily influenced by a desire to restrict the medal to people who, they believed, exemplified the core values of the nation. In doing so, they shaped a construction of everyday heroism that focused more on the perceived qualities and character of the individual person and was thus less concerned with the specific facts of the case.

With the Victoria Cross and other gallantry medals, what most often exists in the archives are the registers for those who were awarded the medal. The Albert Medal is particularly interesting because documents relating to refusals have also survived. Refusing a nomination was effectively saying that the individual did not qualify for the award and, therefore, reasons for refusal can inversely be interpreted as qualifications. Surveying the most predominant and consistent reasons for refusal reveals that, to be considered worthy of an Albert Medal, individuals had to substantially, consciously, and voluntarily endanger their own lives while trying to save another. In addition, they could have no professional duty or responsibility to do so, they could receive no outside assistance and, while undertaking the act, they needed to exhibit a significant degree of self-control, sound judgement, and presence of mind. What becomes clear is that the majority of refusals were based upon judgements relating to the

---

7 Board of Trade memorandum, "Rewards. Granting of awards; and interpretation of the terms 'Distress at Sea' and 'Peril of the Sea'" (1886), MT9/288 (former dept. reference M.17381/86), The National Archives: Public Record Office, Kew, Surrey (hereafter TNA: PRO, Kew).

8 Home Office case notes file, "ALBERT MEDAL: Edward James Battersby" (1906–1907), HO45/10349/146953, TNA: PRO, Kew.

personal character of the individual and their perceived suitability as an exemplary role-model, rather than their bravery.[9] Behavior such as facing danger, being in control, standing firm, acting independently, relying on your own abilities, and making informed decisions were regarded as being indicators of sound and exemplary personal character – these being the types of heroes that that the establishment wanted to recognize. In the establishment context, the manner in which the heroic act was undertaken, and the personal characteristics displayed by the individual during that act, were crucial to determining whether or not the rescuer was suitable to be considered "heroic."

The establishment context was underpinned by a relatively narrow construction of everyday heroism, reliant upon exacting standards, and largely limited to a particular type of individual, exhibiting specific characteristics, under certain circumstances. It was overwhelmingly influenced by ideas such as character, altruism, pure motive, integrity, and the triumphant or civilizing nature of British national identity. This is why the Albert Medal was, implicitly, restricted to acts which were perceived to represent the very pinnacle of pure and exemplary national character. Everyday heroism within the establishment context was also constructed by white, British, middle-class men in government departments and very few women or children were recognized. Thus, it did little to challenge or modify the existing model established by military and imperial heroism. Instead, it sought, rather unsuccessfully, to simply encompass everyday heroism within it. Consequently, to the public, the establishment context appeared to be somewhat out of touch with the average working-class man in the street, not to mention the average women or child, while lacking the radical edge of reform that was increasingly driving popular politics and discourse in the latter half of the nineteenth century.

The Organizational Context

The establishment context was far from being the only realm within which everyday heroism was constructed and employed during the nineteenth and early twentieth centuries. Another prominent arena was the organiza-

---

9 Home Office case notes file, "ALBERT MEDAL: Henry William Curtis – refused" (1911), HO45/10650/211488, TNA: PRO, Kew.

tional context. One of the key players in this context, the Royal Humane Society, is discussed in detail by Craig Barclay elsewhere in this volume, but there were other organizations within the same context undertaking similar work and shaping ideas and concepts of heroism.

Following the success of a temporary fund to relieve the victims of a hurricane in January 1839, a permanent charity was established in April of that year. This was provisionally named the Liverpool Humane Society but, in January 1840, it became the Liverpool Shipwreck and Humane Society (LSHS). The stated purpose of the LSHS was, "saving human life, particularly in cases of shipwreck in the neighbourhood of Liverpool" and, in order to achieve this, pecuniary or honorary awards were given to "persons instrumental in rescuing human life from danger."[10] In addition to pecuniary awards, the LSHS generated publicity through various medals for saving life. Three were for acts of bravery at sea: the Marine Medal (1884), designed by William Wyon, Chief engraver at the Royal Mint; the Camp and Villaverde Medal (1872), named after Captain Bernardino Camp and his mate Villaverde who rescued people from a Royal Mail ship in the Gulf of Mexico in 1847; and the Bramley-Moore Medal (1872), funded by the chairman of the Liverpool Dock Committee, John Bramley-Moore, and particularly awarded for incidents within the port of Liverpool. The Society also gave two awards for saving life on land: the Medal for Saving Life from Fire (1882), funded by Roger Lyon Jones, one-time councilor for Liverpool, who in 1875 left a donation of £2000 to the Society; and the LSHS General Medal (1894), introduced to allow an honorary award for any case that did not currently fall into an existing category. Interestingly, over eighty percent of the General Medals awarded by the LSHS between 1894 and 2005 were awarded for the act of stopping runaway horses on the streets of Liverpool.

The history of another organization, the Order of St. John of Jerusalem can, in the words of one historian, "be traced back so far that it is difficult to name an exact date for its beginning," and there is no shortage of literature for those interested in its earliest history.[11] In Britain, the Order

---

10 Sydney Jeffery, *Liverpool Shipwreck and Humane Society* (Liverpool: Daily Post, 1939), 16.
11 Edward D. Renwick, *A Short History of the Order of St. John of Jerusalem* (London: St. John's Gate, 1958), 7; for example, William K. R. Bedford, *The Order of the Hospital of St. John of Jerusalem* (London: F. E. Robinson, 1902); Henry E. Collett & E. C. B Merriman, *A Short History of the Knights of the Order of St. John of Jerusalem* (London: W. H. Smith Ltd., 1920); Eva M. Tenison, *Chivalry and the Wounded: The Hospitallers of St. John of Jerusalem 1014–1914* (London: L. Upcott Gill, 1914).

began organizing an ambulance service for mining and pottery areas as early as 1872. Then, in 1877, the St. John Ambulance Association was formed, followed ten years later by the creation of the St. John Ambulance Brigade. In 1869, "recognition by the Order of those who had distinguished themselves by acts of personal bravery and humanity on occasions of accident and danger" was proposed, and it was decided to award parchment testimonials and medals in bronze and silver.[12] Awards were limited to acts carried out on land and excluding rescues from fire so as not to encroach upon the work of other societies, namely the Royal Humane Society and the Society for the Protection of Life from Fire. Unlike the state, the Order formalized its application process and a printed form was produced for applicants to complete. This required the name, address, age, and occupation of both the applicant and the person rescued, as well as the date, time, place, and particulars of the incident. The application had to be accompanied by statements from one or more eyewitnesses, in their own handwriting, which had to be countersigned by the nearest clergyman, magistrate, or the witness's employer. Interestingly, both the applicant and the eyewitnesses were asked to provide details of "the *precise* nature of the *exertions* used and of the danger known or *risk* incurred by the applicant," demonstrating that risk to life, rather than just saving life, was an important consideration when evaluating the claim.[13]

The organization that was to become the Royal National Lifeboat Institution (RNLI) in 1854 began as the National Institution for the Preservation of Life from Shipwreck in 1824.[14] Later that same year, it received the patronage of King George IV and the Royal prefix was added to the name. The primary purpose of the Institution was to provide the means of rescuing people from shipwrecks. This was initially conducted through twelve lifeboats manned by volunteers and relying on voluntary contributions for funding. In addition to providing the means of rescue, the Institution also sought to encourage rescue through the provision of rewards, with one of its founding resolutions being, "that medallions or pecuniary rewards be given to those who rescue lives in cases of ship-

---

12 Order of St. John of Jerusalem, *Descriptive History of Medals and Grants for Saving Life on Land by Special Acts of Bravery* (London: Order of St. John, 1876), 3.
13 Order of St. John of Jerusalem, *Descriptive History*, 6.
14 For more information on the RNLI, see Alec Beilby, *Heroes All! The Story of the RNLI* (Somerset: Patrick Stephens Ltd., 1992).

wreck."[15] Furthermore, according to RNLI minute books, awards were given in recognition of "great risk to life" or actions undertaken "without consideration of the risk involved," which places the recognition above the realm of purely lifesaving and into that of heroism: life risked and not simply life saved.[16] The Institutions medals, engraved by William Wyon, were initially awarded in gold and silver, with the introduction of a bronze format in 1917.

In addition to medals, the RNLI awarded pecuniary awards and there was a marked and interesting distinction between the two. Generally speaking, the officers were awarded medals, while the crewmen were given monetary awards. For a rescue in which an officer received a gold medal, the Institution's highest award, a crewman could receive a monetary reward in the region of three to five sovereigns, the equivalent of many weeks' wages for a fisherman. Notwithstanding this, pecuniary awards were not universally accepted by those upon which they were bestowed. In 1825, the Institution's Committee awarded the sum of three sovereigns each to three men described as being "persons in a humble sphere of life," who had assisted three "gentleman of property" in saving life during the wreck of the *Fanny*, off St. Helier, Jersey.[17] One of these humble awardees, Philip Nicole, declined the sovereigns on the basis that, "pecuniary reward was foreign to his feelings," and was eventually awarded a silver medal instead.[18] It is interesting how, throughout the nineteenth century, societies and charities offering pensions to support men or families who had been disadvantaged through an act of heroism was regarded as perfectly acceptable, whereas if money was perceived as a "reward," it attracted a degree of criticism and resistance; attitudes also encountered by Andrew Carnegie in the early twentieth century (see below).

The Society for the Protection of Life from Fire (SPLF) was formed in 1836. The 1837 annual report stated the association's purpose as "the preservation of Life from Fire, by organising a body of men who shall be provided with … public fire escapes … and also by exciting Fireman, Policemen and others to a prompt attention to the scene of danger – by holding out rewards, as the merit of the case may deserve." Its main work at that time was the provision and maintenance of fire escapes at around

---

15 Quoted in, Barry Cox, *Lifeboat Gallantry* (London: Spink & Son, 1998), 3.
16 Cox, *Lifeboat Gallantry*, 1.
17 Edward Wake-Walker, *Gold Medal Rescues* (Newton Abbot: David & Charles, 1992.), 18.
18 Ibid.

seventy central London locations. As this extract from an 1865 periodical explained:

The Society maintains, in different parts of the Metropolis, 73 fire-escape stations, usually at distances of about half a mile from each other. At each station there is a fire-escape, attended throughout the night by a conductor well instructed in its use, and provided with all necessary implements. From 1843 to March 31, 1861, the Society's fire-escapes have attended no less than 5211 fires, and rescued 670 lives.[19]

The Metropolitan Fire Brigade Act (1865) made the Metropolitan Board of Works responsible for running the fire brigade and, soon after, all the equipment and staff of the SPLF was absorbed into the new organization. In the long term, this stimulated changes in the remit of the SPLF and, by 1908, its stated purpose had become "the Protection of Life from Fire, by the grant of rewards for saving life from fire, to persons who shall have distinguished themselves or received injury while engaged in the rescue of life from fire."[20]

This definition of its work, with the emphasis on risk to life rather than just attempting to save life, situates the SPLF as recognizing heroism, rather than simply promoting or endorsing lifesaving. This was also inferred in one of its five "specific objects," which was "to bestow rewards, at the discretion of the Society, on such persons as shall at any time distinguish themselves by their endeavors to save human life in case of fire."[21] SPLF awards included certificates, watches, monetary awards, and, in particularly meritorious cases, a medal. An indication of the quantity, scope, and reach of the Society's awards can be ascertained by looking in depth at particular periods. For example, between 1908 and 1914, the Society recognized 547 individuals with awards, including eighty-one bronze medals, forty-six silver medals, eighteen silver watches, and 293 certificates.[22] Awards were also given for the design or construction of fire escape equipment and bringing equipment to the scene of a fire, but it was awards for directly saving life, and at personal risk, which were most admired. In 1837, it was noted that, "presenting the medals to the persons to whom they were awarded, produced a gratifying and interesting

---

19 G. F. Cruchley, *London in 1865: A Handbook for Strangers* (London: G. F. Cruchley, 1865).
20 Society for the Protection of Life from Fire, London, *Annual Report of the Society*, (1908), CLC-014, (former reference MS 34978- 84), London Metropolitan Archives, London (hereafter, LMA, London).
21 Ibid.
22 Price, *Everyday Heroism*, 135.

sensation on the minds of the assembly, which was very numerous; and those who received them ... returned thanks, appearing to value them as an inestimable treasure."²³

These organizations were primarily concerned with the saving of life or the prevention of circumstances in which life was put at risk. They all shared a common goal, which was to endorse and encourage a particular set of ideas or practices, directly linked to the ethos and objectives of the organization, and they all utilized incidents of everyday heroism to promote and further their work. In doing so, they increased the public profile of everyday heroism and demonstrated that it could be a powerful and potent mechanism for attracting press attention, bringing publicity to a particular cause, and affecting real change in terms of behavior or best practice. The organizational context also did much to widen the definitions and construction of everyday heroism beyond the narrow establishment channels; views about who was and was not suitable for recognition were less fixed, with women and children featuring more often in their rolls of honor.

However, although the organization context was wider than the establishment one, the construction of heroism within it was still restricted in certain ways and shared key elements with the establishment model. Due to the nature of the organizations, certain types of incidents tended to be privileged, which, in turn, contributed to the shaping of what was considered to be everyday heroism, so that rescues from shipwrecks, drownings, and fires accounted for the vast majority of awards in this context. It must also be noted that the organizational context existed, by and large, alongside the establishment one and, moreover, acted as an adjunct and reinforcement to it rather than presenting much alternative or challenge. At one time or another, all of the major organizations, received Royal patronage, which, as with the Albert Medal, served, to some degree, to link the awards of the organization with the state and nation. Furthermore, within the organizational context, medals and decorations were still the predominant mode of recognition and the focus was very much on living heroes and heroines rather than those who perished in the act – much as it was in the establishment context. Although it widened the field of everyday heroism and helped to make it more reflective of the society in which it existed, the organizational model not only received endorsement

---

23 Society for the Protection of Life from Fire, London, *First Annual Report of the Society*, (1837), CLC-014, (former reference MS 34978- 84), LMA, London.

from the establishment, but also shaped its activities along similar lines and represented continuity rather than introducing anything particularly new or radical.

The Radical Context

The Victorian artist, George Frederic Watts was, without doubt, a highly influential figure in the conception, development, and dissemination of the idea of everyday heroism in Britain. Considered by many to have been the greatest painter of the Victorian age, Watts enjoyed an unparalleled reputation as a portraitist, sculptor, landscape painter, and symbolist; talents and skills which earned him the title "England's Michelangelo."[24] Around the 1850s, as incidents of everyday heroism became more widely reported, Watts became absorbed by the subject and began formulating ambitious plans for various public sculptures to commemorate it. While his initial plans did not come to fruition, the artist's passion and commitment were undaunted and, in 1900, he created the Watts Memorial to Heroic Self Sacrifice in Postman's Park, London, which still stands as the most significant monument to everyday heroism in Britain.[25]

Notwithstanding this, Watts' influence extended far beyond his own work with the full impact on his ideas about everyday heroism stemming from the wider social network of broadly liberal-minded reformers and radicals who coalesced around him and his ideas. Within this context, acts of everyday heroism (and in particular working-class examples) were highlighted and promoted in the belief that they were generally undertaken by honorable people of good moral fiber, leading conscientious, dutiful lives, and with fruitful contributions to make to society. Thus, everyday heroism could provide models of exemplary character which could then be utilized as mechanisms to inculcate and instill "respectable" behavior and education among the working-classes as a whole.

---

24 Mark Bills & Barbara Bryant, *G. F. Watts: Victorian Visionary* (London: Yale University Press, 2008); Veronica Franklyn-Gould, *G. F. Watts: The Last Great Victorian* (London: Yale University Press, 2004).
25 John Price, *Heroes of Postman's Park: Heroic Self-Sacrifice in Victorian London* (Stroud: The History Press, 2015); Price, *Postman's Park*.

It might be argued that the motives and intentions within the radical context appear to have little difference to those in both the establishment and organizational contexts: the recognition and promotion of everyday heroism as a vehicle to modify the ideas and actions of the masses. However, as discussed above, the establishment approach was to try to encompass everyday heroism within an existing military model which equated heroic acts with loyalty to the crown and country, while the organizational context, although wider in terms of qualification, did little to challenge or move beyond those establishment mechanisms. Conversely, within the radical context, reformers, philanthropists, artists, writers, and other public figures acted in novel and varied ways to recognize and commemorate everyday heroism outside of the usual state mechanisms. There were various goals, all of which were essentially beyond the remit of the establishment and organizational contexts: improving the lives and outlook of the working classes; providing exemplary working-class role-models for "respectable" working-class behavior; inspiring the working classes to take more control of their lives; and, for some, fostering a sense of class consciousness and conflict.

Furthermore, it was a radical context because, instead of merely encompassing or accommodating civilian heroes, those within it were championing them and celebrating them; showing that there was more to the working classes than the sensationalized claims of social explorers or the judgmental conclusions of government officials. Within the radical context, ultimate self-sacrifice was part of the construction of everyday heroism and, unlike the establishment model, deceased heroes were very much recognized and commemorated. The radical context also challenged the manner in which everyday heroism was recognized and, rather than conforming to establishment mechanisms of honors and decorations, it opened up new avenues in areas such as art, sculpture, literature, poetry, and politics. Ultimately, the radical context of the nineteenth century continued into the twentieth and paved the way for the Carnegie Hero Fund Trust which, in many ways, superseded all three contexts by challenging establishment conceptions, monetarizing organizational structures, and initially taking everyday heroism to new heights of radicalism.

Watts' landmark contribution to the character and construction of everyday heroism in the nineteenth and early twentieth centuries was through his Memorial to Heroic Self-Sacrifice in Postman's Park, London. The memorial consists of fifty-four ceramic tablets, fixed to a wall about

15 meters long and covered by an open-sided wooden cloister that stands about 4 meters high. Each tablet, manufactured using small glazed tiles, briefly documents a person, or people, who lost their own life while attempting to save another. The narrative on the tablet provides the name of the individual, and the date and details of the incident in which they perished, an example being, "William Donald of Bayswater, aged 19, Railway Clerk, was drowned in the Lea trying to save a lad from a dangerous entanglement of weed, July 16 1876." Sixty-two people are commemorated on the memorial: eight children, nine women, and forty-five men. The ages range from 8-year-old Henry Bristow to Daniel Pemberton, who was 61 when he died. The earliest recorded incident is that of Sarah Smith, a pantomime artist who perished in 1863, and all but one of the people who feature died between 1863 and 1827. Six Metropolitan Police officers and two members of the Fire Brigade are commemorated but, essentially, the memorial is dedicated to otherwise ordinary and unremarkable people.

One of the interesting things about the radical context is the way in which various projects interweaved with one another, involved many of the same people, and drew their inspiration from a shared network of ideas and incidents. One example of this is a scheme of decoration conceived for the Red Cross Hall in Southwark which was inspired by Watts' ideas about everyday heroism.[26] The Hall and adjacent cottages were the brainchild of the housing reformer Octavia Hill, and when it came to devising the interior decoration for them, an associate of Hill's, Mrs. Emilie Barrington, who was also a close friend of G. F. Watts', came up with a fitting scheme. Barrington commissioned the decorative artist and art theorist Walter Crane, who also moved in the same circles as Watts, to design a series of nine three-meter by two-meter murals, each depicting a real-life scene of everyday heroism. The titles for the murals were as follows: "An Explosion in a Mine," "Rescue from Drowning by a Youth," "Rescue from fire," "A Sister of Mercy holding back a dog from attacking her school-children," "the rescue of a boat's crew from the rocks," "the man who took the bull by the horns," "Rescue from a well," "Jamieson," and "Alice Ayres."[27]

---

26 John Price, "Octavia Hill's Red Cross Hall and its Murals to Heroic Self-sacrifice" in Elizabeth Baigent & Ben Cowell, *"Nobler imaginings and mightier struggles": Octavia Hill and the remaking of British society* (London: Institute of Historical Research, 2016).
27 Emelie Barrington, "The Red Cross Hall," *English Illustrated Magazine*, vol. x, June 1893, 610–618.

Ultimately, only the final three designs in this list were translated into full-size versions and erected in the hall; the most notable being the one commemorating Alice Ayres who had died just a few streets away from the location. The death of Alice Ayres is an interesting case because it was the one explicitly cited by Watts when proposing his plan, it was the first of the murals to be completed, and it also featured in several other projects within the radical context.

In a notable letter to *The Times* in 1887, Watts referred to civilian heroism as "heroism in every-day life." Less than a year later, the novelist Laura M. Lane, inspired by Watts, published a book entitled *Heroes of Every-day Life* containing twenty dramatically embellished narratives of everyday heroism.[28] While there was no personal connection between Lane and Watts, it is clear that the radical discourse on everyday heroism being fostered in liberal circles was the catalyst for the publication. In the preface, Lane provided a lengthy quotation from Watts' 1887 letter and asserted that, "these words mark an epoch. They are the legend of the Victorian era."[29] The book also featured the case of Alice Ayres who, as already discussed, was something of an iconic figure within the radical context. Furthermore, Lane herself was a somewhat non-establishment figure: she had run charitable schools; worked on behalf of feminists and trade unionists; collected evidence about sweated female labor; and, later in life, worked for the Women's Liberal League of New South Wales and the Australian League of Honour for Women and Girls.[30] Lane was clear regarding her purposes and objectives for documenting tales of everyday heroism, stating that, "no material advantages can prove of lasting benefit unless they are accompanied by the growth and development of the higher nature," by which she meant that the working classes required more than financial assistance to lift them out of their lives of deprivation.[31] What they required, according to Lane, was moral and social guidance, as well as political and financial assistance – things she believed could be achieved by using cases of everyday heroism as exemplary role models of correct behavior.

---

28 Laura Lane, *Heroes of Every-day Life* (London: Cassell & Co., 1888).
29 Ibid., p. v.
30 Margaret Bettison, "Luffman, Lauretta Caroline Maria (1846–1929)," *Australian Dictionary of National Biography* 10 (1986): 167.
31 Lane, *Heroes*, vii–viii.

Another author who contributed to the radical context was Canon Hardwicke Rawnsley. In 1896, he published a collection of thirty-eight poems about acts of everyday heroism titled, *Ballads of Brave Deeds*.[32] Rawnsley was also a member of the wider liberal-radical network, and he and Watts were close friends and associates. As Eleanor Rawnsley wrote in her biography of her husband: "Hardwicke greatly valued the friendship of G.F Watts and his wife, for they were in sympathy with him in many of his aims and ideals."[33] Two of the cases featured in the book were well known within radical circles; those being, once again, Alice Ayres and also an incident at an East Ham sewage works in which four workmen died. For Rawnsley, everyday heroes were chivalric and captured Christian virtues of self-sacrifice and the giving of life for one's brother.[34] This differed very much from the establishment model of heroism, exemplified by the Albert Medal, which did not, on the whole, subscribe to chivalric ideals and placed service to the nation above service to God in terms of self-sacrifice. Rawnsley's approach also diverged from much of the organizational context, as he focused on the self-sacrificial nature of heroic acts and the creation of exemplary martyrs rather than living figures.

Lane and Rawnsley were not the only writers to focus on everyday heroism. Indeed, literature was a key component in the radical context, with titles such as *Everyday Heroes: Stories of Bravery during the Queen's Reign* (1889), *Beneath the Banner* (1894), and *Deeds of Daring: Stories of Heroism in Every Day Life* (1900), focusing almost exclusively on it.[35] The radical credentials of literature on everyday heroism can clearly be seen when considering acts undertaken by women and children. In the establishment context, everyday heroism was seen as very much the domain of adult men. In the lifespan of the Albert Medal, only nineteen awards were made to women, just six of which were made prior to 1916, and not a single woman ever received the first-class decoration, while children did not fare

---

32 Hardwicke D. Rawnsley, *Ballads of Brave Deeds* (London: J. M. Dent & Co., 1896).
33 Eleanor F. Rawnsley, *Canon Rawnsley: An Account of his Life* (Glasgow: Maclehose, Jackson & Co., 1923), 127.
34 Hardwicke D. Rawnsley, "The Lamp of Chivalry," *Sermons preached in St. Kentigern's Church, Crosthwaite, Keswick 1898* (Keswick: Bakewell, 1900), 1–12.
35 Lane, *Heroes*; Christian Knowledge Society, *Everyday Heroes: Stories of Bravery During the Queen's Reign 1837–1888* (London: Christian Knowledge Society, 1889); Frederick J. Cross, *Beneath the Banner* (London: Cassell & Co., 1894); Rawnsley, *Ballads*; Charles D. Michael, *Deeds of Daring: Stories of Heroism in Every Day Life* (London: S. W. Partridge & Co., 1900).

much better. This was not the case in literary circles where, for boys, there were titles such as, *Heroism of Boyhood* (1865), *Fifty-Two Stories of Heroism in Life and Action for Boys* (1899), and *Deeds of Daring: Stories of Heroism in Every Day Life* (1900) – all of which contained dramatic tales of heroic boys.[36] Perhaps more radically, girls were also well served, with books such as *Brave little Women: Tales of the Heroism of Girls* (1888), *Heroines of Daily Life* (1886), *Noble Deeds of the World's Heroines* (1903), and *Heroines: True Tales of Brave Women – A Book for British Girls* (1904) aimed at fostering the spirit of heroism in young women through true stories of heroic acts undertaken by female civilians.[37] Overall, the broad range of accessible literature on everyday heroism, with its wider focus encompassing women and children, provided another element in the radical and contentious discourse being promoted by Watts and those influenced by him.

Finally, there is one other organization, founded prior to the First World War, which should be considered within the radical context. The Carnegie Hero Fund Trust, established in 1908, was the brainchild of the philanthropist Andrew Carnegie and, since it was specifically created to assist "heroes" (as opposed to those who had simply saved or attempted to save life), it reveals much about how ideas of everyday heroism had developed by that time. The Hero Fund Trust was the first extension of the U.S. Hero Fund Commission, discussed in the introduction to this volume. After the establishment of the U.K. Fund, nine further Hero Funds were established across Europe, with Carnegie endowing 10.5 million dollars to the foundation of funds recognizing everyday heroism.[38] Essentially, the purpose of the Hero Fund was to provide pensions or one-off payments to individuals who had been injured or financially disadvantaged as a result of undertaking an act of heroism or, in the case of

---

36 William Martin, *Heroism of Boyhood* (London: Darton and Hodge, 1865); Alfred H. Miles, *Fifty-Two Stories of Heroism in Life and Action for Boys* (London: Hutchinson and Co., 1899); Michael, *Deeds of Daring*.

37 Marie Trevelyan, *Brave little Women: Tales of the Heroism of Girls* (London: J. Hogg, 1888); Frank Mundell, *Heroines of Daily Life* (London: Sunday School Union, 1896); Charles Moore, *Noble Deeds of the World's Heroines* (London: Religious Tract Society, 1903); Charles D. Michael, *Heroines: True Tales of Brave Women* (London: S. W. Partridge & Co., 1904).

38 The European hero funds and the initial endowments were as follow: France (1909) $1 million; Germany (1910) $1.5 million; Norway (1911) $125,000; Switzerland (1911) $130,000; Netherlands (1911) $200,000; Sweden (1911) $230,000; Denmark (1911) $125,000; Belgium (1911) £230,000; Italy (1911) $750,000. The U.S. Hero Fund Commission (1904) received an initial endowment of $5 million.

those who lost their lives through such an act, to provide for the family or other dependents. The Hero Fund provides a useful case study for examining changing notions of everyday heroism because it was both a new initiative but also one that needed to take account of, and to some degree accord with, the ideas around heroism which had developed in the preceding half century. By 1908, public recognition and commemoration of everyday heroism in Britain was relatively commonplace and the idea had become a reasonably well-known and well-understood. Those behind the Hero Fund undoubtedly worked to position it harmoniously alongside existing mechanisms of recognition, including those of the establishment.

The Hero Fund Trustees adopted key elements from the establishment approach, particularly judgements about the amount of risk to life involved and also whether or not the person involved had a professional duty to save life. As already discussed, within the establishment context, heroism was seem as being the preserve of morally decent people, and the performance of a heroic act was indicative of a respectable and upstanding character. The Hero Fund was one of Carnegie's charitable trusts specifically designed by him to redistribute his immense wealth to those in society who he deemed to be worthy of his benevolence. Carnegie did not believe in indiscriminate charity or in assisting those who, in his mind, were the architects of their own poverty through laziness, drunkenness, or gambling. He was, instead, very much in the business of helping those who, in his opinion, appeared willing but unable to help themselves; essentially, those he considered to be the deserving poor. Thus, for Carnegie, according with and following the establishment, construction of everyday heroism was, in effect, a practical "quality control" mechanism through which to identify disadvantaged but upstanding citizens who deserved his support. Ultimately, the Carnegie Trustees had to look beyond this narrow stream of recognition, because the stringency and exclusivity of the establishment construction did not provide anything like the numbers needed to stimulate publicity or to dispense the huge sum of money that Carnegie had given them. Consequently, the hero fund quickly shifted and adopted a much more egalitarian and all-encompassing attitude towards candidates and their actions which, consequently, put them out of step with the establishment context.

The Carnegie Hero Fund can be considered part of the radical context for a number of reasons. Firstly, its all-encompassing attitude led it to recognize heroic acts of every conceivable nature and, as a result, it established far wider boundaries than the establishment for what was considered to be everyday heroism. Preventing someone from being killed by tackling a runaway horse was highly unlikely to merit an Albert Medal and would have been outside of the remit of both the Royal Humane Society and the Society for the Protection of Life from Fire. Yet it was something very much recognized by the Hero Fund and, consequently, actions such as tackling out of control animals, incidents with road or railway vehicles, particular types of medical treatment, and common industrial accidents became regarded as heroic when they might not have otherwise. The Hero Fund also, to some extent, subtly redefined the parameters for acceptable methods of rewarding everyday heroism, suggesting that, under certain circumstances and with effective judgement, financial reward could be seen as appropriate recognition. It is not that the Hero Fund was the only organization ever to give pecuniary awards, because many of the private subscription organizations did. But, there were two things that made it comparatively radical: the fact that pecuniary awards were the mainstay of the Hero Fund, and the organization's position that the monetary award was for "heroism" rather than lifesaving. There was, though, one aspect of the Hero Fund which, above all others, set it at odds with the establishment model.

One of the Hero Fund's founding stipulations was "confining the operations of this Fund to those who have shown true heroism in the peaceful walks of life." This focus on civilian, rather than martial, heroism was related to Carnegie's strong belief in pacifism and his quest to facilitate world peace.[39] Between 1904 and 1914, Carnegie donated over $25 million to the cause of achieving world peace through initiatives including founding the Church Peace Union; constructing three "Peace Palaces," including the International Court of Justice at The Hague; and, finally in 1910, founding the Carnegie Endowment for International Peace with its professed aim "to hasten the abolition of international war."[40] Carnegie was an ardent believer in the idea of heroism, viewing it as something which could not be ignored or overlooked and something which, particularly in the case of young men, would find expression through one means or another, having stated that, "there is an instinct in man that seeks

---

39 S. N. D. North, *A Manual of the Public Benefactions of Andrew Carnegie* (Washington: The Carnegie Endowment for International Peace, 1919), 118.
40 Figure of $25million derived from, Simon Goodenough, *The Greatest Good Fortune: Andrew Carnegie's Gift for Today* (Edinburgh: Macdonald, 1985).

to wrestle with some foe. The heroic impulse demands expression."[41] When explaining the purpose of the Hero Fund to his close friend Frederick Lynch, Carnegie argued, "We have got to show young men that there are just as great battles to be fought in peace-time as in war-time and just as much heroism demanded, just as much opportunity for the hero."[42] The goal, then, was to direct the heroic impulse into everyday rather than military heroism and that was a key purpose of the Hero Funds.

Moreover, it was, from Carnegie's perspective, an entirely applicable and necessary time to be accelerating his campaigns for peace. The destabilizing of many nineteenth-century military and political alliances had generated something of a resurgence of imperialism in Europe, and the formation of new agreements and powerbases, coupled with an accelerating arms race, was visibly building towards conflict in the region. Carnegie's intention was to show young men that heroism in peaceful pursuits could be every bit as rewarding and well regarded as the military variety. He also hoped to remove one of the arguments for the necessity for young men to go to war, which held that it provided the best opportunity for the performance of heroism. Undoubtedly, both Carnegie and the Crown wanted to utilize civilian heroism to capture the hearts and minds of British citizens. However, the two positions were distinctly at odds, with the State attempting to link heroism to national allegiance, while Carnegie wanted it to reflect a deeper philosophy of allegiance to humanity. Consequently, although to some degree it drew from both the establishment and organizational contexts, the Hero Fund was ultimately much more in tune with the liberal-radical philanthropy extolled and acted upon by Watts and others like him.

Change Over Time

The final element in the analytical framework that needs to be addressed is the propensity for the meaning of the term "heroism" to alter or modify over time. As already mentioned, in Britain, during the period 1850–1914, the idea of heroism became progressively more inclusive, more egalitarian,

---

41 Quoted in, Frederick Lynch, *Personal Recollections of Andrew Carnegie* (New York: F. H. Revell Co., 1920), 145.
42 Ibid.

and more "everyday" in nature. It was a relatively slow and incremental process, reflective of broader changes and reforms in Victorian and Edwardian society, and, although applicable to men, women, and children, attitudes towards female heroism offer a particularly vivid example. The construction of female heroism undoubtedly grew and altered in parallel with changes and developments in the status and position of women in Victorian and Edwardian society. Furthermore, in the same way that those political and societal changes took place gradually, with society negotiating and adjusting to the shifts over time, while different elements coexisted alongside one another during periods of transition, so too with the construction of heroism. Heroines at the turn of the nineteenth century were certainly constructed differently than those of the mid-Victorian period, but the differences were often subtle and some elements of previous constructions persevered alongside them. This not only illustrates the complexities of the construction of female heroism, but serves to underline the malleable and adaptable nature of everyday heroism more generally.

Up until the turn of the nineteenth century, the construction of female heroism in Britain largely mirrored dominant ideas of domestic ideology and "separate spheres." Acts of bravery were considered all the more remarkable if they were undertaken by a woman, largely on account of perceptions of weakness and fragility. Furthermore, demonstrations of heroism and strength were regarded as anomalous and believed to stem from innately "womanly" attributes such as compassion or motherhood. Any bravery or courage on the part of the woman was seen as being fleeting and circumstantial, with men usually being required to step in at some point and render assistance in some capacity. A strikingly comprehensive example of this construction can be seen in the reporting of a fire which took place above a tailor's shop in Surrey, in September 1888.

A fifteen-year-old maidservant called Minnie Murrell, who was employed by Mr. and Mrs. Inglis to look after their three children, was woken by the fire and proceeded to raise the alarm and set about rescuing the children. Opening the window, Minnie called to the crowd below catch the children and then dropped each one safely from the window. At this point, Mr. Inglis appeared, forcing his way through the flames to assist Minnie, and just as well that he did. For as the report continues:

Having been hitherto as cool as a salamander and as gallant as a fireman, Minnie promptly regained the privileges of her sex, and was on the point of making a fool of herself by shrieking and jumping out of the window. She had at this crisis a sort of hysterical or fluttering fit, and would have leaped headforemost to probable death, had not her master caught hold of her in time and lowered her carefully to the enthusiastic arms below.[43]

Although Minnie's mothering instincts and duty to care for the children provided her with the strength and courage to undertake her remarkable heroic act, she then "regained the privileges of her sex" and it was necessary for a man to step in and rescue her on account of her irrational, yet distinctively female, behavior. This quotation clearly and succinctly illustrates the predominant construction of female heroism. While this, or slight variances upon it, was the most common construction of female civilian heroism in Britain in the mid-to-late nineteenth century, by the turn of the century, things had very much altered.

On March 30, 1899, the SS *Stella* left Southampton bound for St. Peter Port in Guernsey with 190 passengers and crew on board. Later that day, in thick fog, the ship struck the notorious Casquets rocks and the granite reef ripped an enormous gash into the hull of the vessel. Water poured in and the Captain gave the order for the lifeboats to be launched, following which there was, according to survivors, an orderly evacuation with women and children first in the queue. Just eight minutes later, the ship sank and although four of the five lifeboats were successfully launched, eighty six passengers and nineteen crew lost their lives. In the following days, a story emerged about the heroism of Mary Anne Rogers, the senior of the two Stewardesses on board, who had, it was reported, given up her own lifebelt to a female passenger and refused to take a place in a lifeboat, choosing instead to go down with the ship.[44]

Elsewhere on the *Stella*, in accordance with nineteenth-century ideas about gendered modes of behavior during shipwrecks, one woman passenger was "pressed into a boat by her husband, who refused her entreaty to be allowed to stay with him," and there were numerous accounts of husbands "putting" their wives into lifeboats against their

---

43 "The Rescue of Three Children from a Fire at Dorking," *The Illustrated Police News*, 2 February 1889.
44 *The Jersey Weekly Press and Independent*, April 15, 1899, 1.

protestations.[45] Attitudes to Mary Rogers, however, were very different. No man attempted to force her into a lifeboat and, when she refused male entreaties to join them on account of it being overcrowded, no man offered up his seat for her.[46] Acknowledging Mary's professionalism and dedication to duty, a *Derby Mercury* editorial contended that, "she appeared, from all accounts, to regard herself as part and parcel of the ship," as evidenced by her response to a passenger's plea for her to save herself, to which Mary reportedly replied, "no, my place is here." By choosing to undertake her professional duty, rather than exercising the priority for escape accorded on the basis of her gender, it would appear that Mary viewed herself as a stewardess first and a woman second. Furthermore, and perhaps more interestingly in relation to the construction of female everyday heroism, those aboard the *Stella* were also willing to consider Mary as a professional and heroic crew member rather than a weak, fragile, and dependent woman.

The changing nature of the construction of everyday heroism that allowed Mary to be treated thus was very much situated in the wider context of the significant social and political changes of the late nineteenth century. Improvements in educational provision dramatically widened the occupational field for women, while more progressive attitudes towards female sexuality allowed women greater control over family planning and prompted re-evaluations regarding motherhood. Even minor changes, such as increasing participation in sports or the enthusiastic female embracing of the bicycle, had a distinct impact on shaping an alternative image of women. As Barbara Caine has concluded, "one can see the whole discussion of the 'new woman' of the 1890s as the reformulation of the early and mid-Victorian 'woman question' in accordance with the broad economic, social, political and intellectual changes in society at large."[47] Change, however, was a negotiated process, and full acceptance would take time and a period of transition during which both old and new ideas operated alongside one another while competing for supremacy. This dialectic was also clearly at work in relation to notions of everyday heroism: a limited acceptance of new ideas permitted Mary Rogers to be treated as a professional and independent heroic woman, while the long

---

45 *The Jersey Weekly Press and Independent*, April 8, 1899, 7; *Jersey Times*, April 5, 1899, 4; *The Evening Post* (Jersey), May 9, 1899, 2.
46 *The Jersey Weekly Press and Independent*, April 15, 1899, 1.
47 Barbara Caine, *Victorian Feminists* (Oxford: Oxford University Press, 1992), 250.

established belief in "separate spheres" ideology continued to determine the patriarchal behavior towards female passengers.

The overall timespan for this chapter has been 1850–1939 so it is not really possible to examine the changing nature of the construction of everyday heroism throughout that period without discussing the potential impact of the First World War and the position of everyday heroism in Britain in the interwar period. Since this latter period represents relatively unchartered waters, inquiries and conclusions are, at the present time, rather tentative and speculative. There is, however, some evidence to suggest that everyday heroism came through the war relatively unscathed and may actually have benefited and even gained further legitimacy as a result of its military and imperial counterparts becoming problematic and somewhat debased ideas.

Within scholarship on heroism, there seems to be somewhat of a consensus that the First World War fundamentally and intractably sullied the idea of heroism in Britain and that, consequently, heroism in the interwar period was viewed negatively and as something of a corrupted and degraded concept. Paul Fussell, for example, argued that the majority of men who fought in the war had obtained their ideas of heroism from works of "Victorian pseudo-medieval romance" such as William Morris' *The Well at the World's End*, published in 1896 and that this idea perished in the modern mechanized warfare that followed.[48] However, as this chapter has shown, there were a myriad of other "wells," not associated with that discourse, from which men in the late Victorian and early Edwardian period could have drawn their inspirations for heroism. Melvin Smith, in his book *Awarded for Valour: A History of the Victoria Cross and the Evolution of British Heroism* (2008), has dramatically declared that "the Victorian army died in the mud of Flanders and with it died the Victorian ideals of Heroism."[49] This may well have been true for the military construction of the idea, but heroism, as demonstrated in this volume, extends far beyond that narrow furrow and, therefore, the landscape of analysis must be widened. In his book, *Heroes' Twilight: A Study of the Literature of the Great War*, Bernard Bergonzi discussed interwar literature and argued that many works, such as Richard Aldington's *Death of a Hero* (1929) and Ernest Hemmingway's *Farewell to Arms* (1929), represented "a savage debunking of

---

48 Paul Fussell, *The Great War and Modern Memory* (Oxford: Oxford University Press, 1975), 135–136.
49 Smith, *Awarded for Valour*, 111; see also 131, 163–165, 185.

the whole concept of heroism," and were designed to show how heroism had been wasted and betrayed and that the war had marked a "collapse of the heroic ideal."[50] According to Bergonzi, "after the mechanised large-scale slaughter of the Somme … the traditional mythology of heroism and the hero … had ceased to be viable."[51]

Keeping with Bergonzi's idea of "debunking," another work which has been said to have contributed to the interwar disillusionment with heroism was Lytton Strachey's pedestal-shaking *Eminent Victorians*, which, as Edward Bereson has recently concluded, "served as an epitaph to a Victorian era eclipsed … by the shadow of war."[52] These sentiments are echoed by scholars, including Nigel Hamilton, who has argued that "the grotesque waste of human life in the First World War … spurred Lytton Strachey into mockery of public figures," and Julie Anne Taddeo, who has declared that "the war undermined the tradition of heroism, and the faith in progress gave way to 'Stracheyesque' cynicism and despair."[53] However, in a recent publication on the subject of General Gordon, Max Jones set out to "challenge this orthodoxy" about the collapse of the heroic ideal following the First World War. Jones has convincingly demonstrated that Gordon's reputation "proved far more resistant to Lytton Strachey's barbs that most historians have assumed," and, in fact, "Strachey helped to extend his [Gordon's] appeal, inspiring … more sympathetic portraits of a flawed hero with a complex interior life."[54] Likewise, it can be argued that, far from destroying or debunking the idea of heroism, the First World War can be seen to have had variable influences on different types of heroism and, while it may perhaps have damaged some military and imperial constructions of the idea, that it actually increased and strengthened ideas of everyday heroism.

---

50 Bernard Bergonzi, *Heroes' Twilight: A Study of the Literature of the Great War* (London: Constable, 1965), 173–174.
51 Ibid., 17.
52 Edward Berenson, *Heroes of Empire: Five Charismatic Men and the Conquest of Africa* (Berkeley: University of California Press, 2011), 266.
53 Nigel Hamilton, *Biography: A Brief History* (Cambridge, MA: Harvard University Press, 2007), 186; Julie Anne Taddeo, *Lytton Strachey and the Search for Modern Sexual Identity: The Last Eminent Victorian* (New York: Haworth Press, 2002), 115.
54 Max Jones, "'National Hero and Very Queer Fish': Empire, Sexuality and the British Remembrance of General Gordon, 1918–1972," *Twentieth Century British History* 26, no. 2 (2015): 201.

Within the establishment context in the interwar period, the Albert Medal continued to be awarded as an endorsement of exemplary national and civic gallantry, although the average number of awards per year did fall from five to two. However, in 1907, another establishment decoration, the Edward Medal, had been introduced in order to recognize gallantry undertaken by industrial workers in factory accidents and disasters.[55] Since awards of this medal increased during the interwar period, it may well indicate the establishment attempting to distance itself from the overtly patriotic and nationalistic ideals promoted through the Albert Medal and, instead, aligning itself more with the idea of recovery and investment in the building of a new world. By the mid-twenties, there was a sense that Britain was not delivering the "land fit for heroes" promised by Lloyd George. Thus, the increased state recognition of working-class heroism through the Edward Medal may have been designed to try and counteract that negativity. Whichever the case, it is clear that establishment recognition of everyday heroism continued after the war and a more "industrial labor" construction of the idea appears to have been favored over the more problematic nationalistic one.

Examining the organizational context, it appears that all of the major institutions active in the nineteenth century continued their work in the interwar period. It can be argued that these organizations stood to gain additional social and cultural currency because the heroism that they recognized, predominantly non-military and taking place outside the theatre of war, could be regarded and championed as relatively pure and untainted. If societies do indeed require heroes, heroism, and examples of exemplary behavior in order to function, then it stands to reason that, if the martial examples have become debased in some way, people will inevitably turn to other alternatives.

Finally, with regard to the radical context, there is not only continuity but also growth and expansion. After the installation of tablets on the Watts Memorial in Postman's Park initially ceased in 1908, work recommenced in 1927, with suggestions for new cases resulting in 4 tablets being unveiled in 1930.[56] Despite the death of Andrew Carnegie in 1919, the Hero Fund continued its work. Again, given that one of Carnegie's

---

55 For a full history of the Edward Medal, see Donald, V. Henderson, *Heroic Endeavour: A Complete Register of the Albert, Edward and Empire Gallantry Medals and How They Were Won* (London: J. B. Hayward, 1988).

56 Price, *Postman's Park*, 31–35.

central aims for the fund was to put an end to war by promoting heroism in peaceful pursuits, it is plausible to suggest that the brutal carnage of the First World War and the anti-militaristic sentiments of the early interwar period provided much fuel for his project rather than damaging it. Furthermore, 1923 saw the creation of a new award for everyday heroism: The Daily Herald Order of Industrial Heroism.[57] The *Daily Herald* was funded by the Trades Union Congress (TUC) and the Labour Party, and was essentially designed to be a newspaper for British workers. The award was established in 1923 because, according to the *Daily Herald*, there had "not yet been established a method of recognising the bravery of the toilers, though scarcely a day passes without some example of valour or self-sacrifice in the industrial field."[58] The principal award was a bronze medal, designed by Eric Gill, which became popularly known as the "Workers' VC" (referencing the Victoria Cross) and was often awarded posthumously. The Order was awarded on 440 occasions between 1923 and 1964, and was discontinued after the sale of the TUC's stock in the *Daily Herald*.

What makes the Order of Industrial Heroism particularly interesting is the idea that the *Herald* deemed it necessary because there was no suitable award for recognizing the bravery of British industrial workers, despite the fact that the establishment's Edward Medal was intended to do just that. It has been demonstrated that there a lack of public engagement with the Albert Medal and that alternative schemes garnered far more popular support.[59] It would appear that there was a similar disparity between the Edward Medal and the working men of Britain and, in that way, the Order of Industrial Heroism continued the radical and alternative challenge to the establishment modes of recognition, much in the same way that G. F. Watts and his associates, and Andrew Carnegie had done in relation to the Albert Medal.

---

57 W. II. Fevyer, et. al., *The Order of Industrial Heroism* (London: Orders and Medals Research Society, 2000).
58 *Daily Herald*, June 9, 1923, 7.
59 Price, *Everyday Heroism*, chapter 1.

Conclusion

This brief overview of the idea of everyday heroism in Britain in the period 1850–1939 has demonstrated that it was a prominent, visible, and contested concept that could be variably constructed by different bodies, for different purposes, at different times. Because each distinct construction was very much a product of the social, cultural, and political landscape of the time, concepts of everyday heroism were not static, but rather they evolved in relation to the ideas around them. Everyday heroism could be constructed in a myriad of ways, but there were three prominent contexts within which it most often originated or was constructed: an establishment context, an organizational context, and a radical context. While each of these undoubtedly interacted with the others, many key aspects of everyday heroism such as risk to life, lack of duty, and perceived moral fiber were represented across all three. However, the different contexts also presented challenges to one another. Particularly in the case of the establishment and radical contexts, there were, without doubt, contestations and differences of opinion about how everyday heroism should be constructed and the types of people and activities that could be regarded as constituting heroism or heroic behavior.

What is also clear from this study is that constructions of heroism in Britain in the period 1850–1914 most certainly altered over time. Within the overarching idea of heroism, the "everyday" variety grew in prominence alongside military and imperial constructions to the extent that, by the outbreak of the First World War, it was an idea which was well known, well understood and, most importantly, very well respected. A reasonable argument might be made, and conceded, that the First World War must have had some impact upon ideas and perceptions of heroism in Britain, and indeed Europe, both during the conflict and in the years that followed it. However, it is absolutely incorrect to suggest, as some scholars have, that the war caused a complete collapse of the heroic ideal. Although there is much research to be done, it is already abundantly clear that, in Britain, the idea of everyday heroism survived the First World War relatively unscathed and it continued to be a well-regarded, well-respected and much admired concept throughout the interwar period. Not only did everyday heroism continue to be constructed in the same three contexts, but those contexts widened to encompass and react to the social and cultural changes in Britain following the war. One particular example of that was an increasing shift towards recognizing the courage and resilience of the working-class men and women who were underpinning the post-war rebuilding of the nation, thereby focusing upon the living heroes who were bringing positive change and modernity, rather than the millions of deceased heroes who, for many, represented a past that they wanted to forget. If, as argued throughout this volume, societies do indeed *need* heroic figures in order to function, then for Britain, everyday heroism must, to some extent, have gained strength and ground in the interwar period, when, in comparison to military heroism, it remained relatively unsullied by the mud and the blood of the battlefields.

As this chapter has shown, the idea of everyday heroism in Britain has a long and colorful history and it is one which is populated not solely by the great men of history, but also by the masses of men, women, and children who might otherwise have gone unnoticed; making it all the more interesting and valuable to scholars. Everyday heroism, as defined in this chapter, was predominantly undertaken by otherwise ordinary working-class people; the kinds of people who would have remained "hidden from history" were it not for the newsworthy circumstances of their actions. Historically, they are the kinds of people who are notoriously difficult to locate because they tend not to feature in many records. Moreover, when they do feature, it is often in negative contexts: when they break the law, when they enter an institution like a workhouse or an asylum, or in surveys of their poverty and deprivation. The circumstances of everyday heroism, especially in fatal cases, may not always have been "positive," but they do, in many ways, provide a more neutral or objective perspective from which to gain insights into everyday life in Victorian and Edwardian Britain. The records detailing acts of everyday heroism briefly illuminate the lives of "ordinary" people and, however briefly and tragically, bring them into focus, so that we can finally get a better look at them. From such a single "snapshot" moment of action, some sense of that life can be reconstructed – and not just the individual life but the lives around it, the communities in which that life was lived, and the times that person experienced. When all is said and done, everyday heroes were, essentially, "people like us," and that is why, although they are long since gone, their stories, their experiences, and the ways in which their societies recognized them, can continue to inform and educate, as well as to captivate and inspire.

Volunteers and Professionals: Everyday Heroism and the Fire Service in Nineteenth-Century America

Wolfgang Hochbruck

In an age of deconstruction, the fact that ideas and ideologies of heroism have become questionable, along with a lot of other formerly revered institutions, should not come as a surprise. There are few exceptions. Among the least questioned forms of heroism is that of rescue personnel. Notably, firefighters are renowned for allegedly risking their lives on a daily basis. Whereas the reputation of the U.S. military suffered considerable damage as an effect of the war in Vietnam,[1] firefighters are still widely considered America's finest. Yet this is not necessarily a given, or natural development – in fact, it might be the result of a strategic effort, because there is a strange bend in the history of firefighting in the U.S. in the mid-nineteenth century.

For about fifteen years, between 1850 and 1865, urban volunteer departments were vilified in newspapers and political speeches as rowdy and unreliable. Within roughly the same timeframe, all major U.S. cities disbanded their often numerous and colorful volunteer fire companies, and turned to paid fire departments. In Boston, this had started even earlier, but as a more gradual process, whereas some of the cities that had made the change from volunteers to professionals between 1853 (Cincinnati) and 1866 (San Francisco) left hardly any time for the transition period.

With the professionalization of fire services, first in the bigger cities, then increasingly also in smaller communities, the role of firefighters started shifting both technically and in terms of the economic relationship between the parties concerned – city officials, the public at large, and the rescue forces. The members of fire departments changed from being

---

[1] Wolfgang Hochbruck, "Dennis Smith's *Report from Engine Co. 82*, Or, How to Win in Vietnam," Unpublished Paper, given at the EAAS Biannual Conference, Den Haag, April 4, 2014.

supposedly altruistic volunteers to being paid service personnel. Technically speaking, being paid for being heroic defies the original idea of heroism, but as I will try to show, the transition from volunteer forces to paid personnel was managed in a rather astute way. The most important factor was the transfer of the original idea of fameworthiness[2] that the eighteenth century associated with the republican form of volunteerism, to the paid replacement of the fire volunteer.

Considering that the move from volunteers to paid personnel translated into a considerable increase in the costs of firefighting to some cities – Cincinnati, for instance, had to pay $90,000 to its paid department, triple the sum the city treasury had needed for its volunteers[3] – the change to professionalization does not seem very sensible nor likely. Generally speaking, city treasurers tend to curb expenses rather than to enlarge them, so saving money cannot serve as an explanation. Nor have the explanations furnished by the school of urban studies scholars like Sean Wilentz and Bruce Laurie[4] been of much help: either over- or understating assumed class and labor-aspects, they arrived at statements like: "Fire protection was originally provided by middle-class volunteer fire companies, but by the 1830s they had become lower-class fraternal and athletic clubs, centers of ethnic, occupational and neighborhood gangs more interested in racing or in fighting than in quenching fires."[5] These problems were supposedly resolved almost instantly by converting the volunteer companies into paid departments.

There are several points in this line of argumentation which neither the older generation of scholars, among them George D. Bushnell, Stephen F. Ginsberg, Glen E. Holt, and Anthony B. Lampe, nor the most recent scholarship by Amy S. Greenberg and Bruce Hensler, on whom I largely

---

[2] David K. Hart, P. Artell Smith, "Fame, Fame-Worthiness, and the Public Service," *Administration & Society* 20 (1988): 131–151.

[3] Amy S. Greenberg, *Cause for Alarm: The Volunteer Fire Department in the Nineteenth-Century City* (Princeton: Princeton University Press, 1998), 125.

[4] Sean Wilentz, *Chants Democratic: New York City and the Rise of the American Working Class* (New York: Oxford University Press, 1984); Bruce Laurie, "Fire Companies and Gangs in Southwark: The 1840s," in *The Peoples of Philadelphia: A History of Ethnic Groups and Lower Class Life, 1790–1940*, ed. Allen F. Davis and Mark H. Haller (Philadelphia: Temple University Press, 1973), 71–88.

[5] Stephen A. Riess, "The City," in *Encyclopedia of American Social History*, Vol. 2, quoted in Greenberg, *Cause for Alarm*, 8.

rely, have been able to explain.⁶ One is that most villages and smaller cities in the U.S. are to this day serviced by volunteer fire departments. If there really was a structural problem with the quality and reliability of volunteer firefighting, their continued existence demands an explanation. A second problem lies in the fact that a service performed by specially abled members of a community for the benefit of all should, in a republican democracy, at least theoretically be held in higher esteem than the same service rendered by a paid force. This, however, was apparently no longer the case with American firefighting in the mid-nineteenth century.

There is, then, a necessity to account for the paradoxical observation that the transition from what might be called the everyday heroism of volunteers to the equally everyday professionalism of a paid force left the public hetero-stereotype of the firefighter largely intact. Beginning in the late nineteenth century and continuing through the twentieth, the heroic image of *professionalized* firefighters even increased in its heroic components in the United States. At the same time, the reputation of volunteers has continued to diminish to the point where, to this day, the gradual replacement of volunteer departments by professional services continues in all regions of the United States, without much resistance. In addition, in some regions there is an increase in the privatization of fire services, meaning that only paid-up members or communities are being served. Otherwise, firefighters will stand by, or protect adjoining structures, while the involved structure burns down.⁷

---

6 George D. Bushnell, "Chicago's Rowdy Firefighters," *Chicago History* 2, no. 4 (1973): 232–241; Arlen R. Dykstra, "Rowdyism and Rivalism in the St. Louis Fire Department, 1850–1857," *Missouri Historical Review* 69, no. 1 (1974–1975): 49–64; Glen E. Holt, "Volunteer Fire-Fighting in St. Louis, 1818–1859," *Gateway Heritage* 4, no. 3 (1983–1984): 2–13; Stephen F. Ginsberg, "Above the Law: Volunteer Firemen in New York City," *New York History* 50, no. 2 (1969): 165–186; Anthony B. Lampe, "St. Louis Volunteer Fire Department, 1820–1850: A Study in the Volunteer Age," *Missouri Historical Review* 62, no, 3 (1967–1968): 235–259; Bruce Hensler, *Crucible of Fire: Nineteenth-Century Urban Fires and the Making of the Modern Fire Service* (Washington: Potomac, 2011).

7 The "pay for spray" policy in Obion County, Tennessee demands that people living in unincorporated areas outside of the town of South Fulton pay an annual service charge to receive the same fire protection as South Fulton residents. In several highly publicized cases since 2010, firefighters were forced to stand by and watch as structures burned. Dave Statter, "South Fulton, Tennessee's Fire Department Makes News After Watching Another House Burn," http://www.statter911.com/2011/12/06/south-fulton-tennessees-fire-department-makes-news-after-watching-another-house-burn-obion-county-pay-for-spray-subscription-policy-causes-brings-more-heat-for-firefighters/.

Volunteer History

The origins of fire departments in the U.S. lie in the efforts of ordinary citizens in the eighteenth and nineteenth centuries, and were characterized by a republican spirit of communality and a desire for fameworthiness: The volunteer firefighters performed their services for the community, allegedly asking nothing more than the praise of their fellow citizens as a token of appreciation. This, at least, is a part of the *grand récit* of firefighting as a community service. The narrative commences with the Union Fire Company, a club founded in 1736 by Benjamin Franklin and some twenty other citizens of Philadelphia. The difference between Franklin's and other fire companies existing before that date was that the Union Fire Co. eventually resolved not only to come to the aid of their paid-up members in case of a fire, but to help everyone within their district. Originally, members of the company were required only to help each other.[8] Within the next fifty years, more and more fire companies organized themselves, notably in urban areas, and on the premise that they would fight all fires in their area of operation.

This movement, from a specific in-group to a more encompassing social frame of reference, was typical of a wave of enlightenment-inspired humanitarianism that informed urban, white, middle-class capitalist societies in the second half of the eighteenth century.[9] As a movement, it fell on fertile ground as long as Jeffersonian democracy sought to teach and inspire responsibility towards the community. The rise and distribution of volunteer fire departments in the late eighteenth and early nineteenth centuries was as much a rising to a republican challenge as it was a response to technological innovation. The late mediaeval and early modern urban bucket brigades receded behind the new hand-pumper fire engines which could not only throw water a greater distance but, with the use of riveted leather hose, also made fighting a fire at close quarters possible. However, this new machinery needed an additional degree of skill and a considerable amount of physical strength to operate it. The volunteer companies attracted primarily younger men. In addition to providing an opportunity for a physical lifestyle that was gradually disappearing from the

---

8 Paulet, Cori, prod., *Benjamin Franklin*, PBS 2002 http://www.pbs.org/benfranklin/l3_citizen_firefighter.html.

9 Thomas L. Haskell, "Capitalism and the Origins of the Humanitarian Sensibility, Part I," *American Historical Review* 90, no. 2 (1985): 339–361.

everyday life of office clerks and shopkeepers, they offered a sort of value-added adulation for extra heroism from one's peers and neighbors.

The fire volunteers of this period, then, are a form of assertive male republican self-empowerment. Their organizational modus was close to *syndicalism*: individuals investing time, physical as well as psychological effort, and risking their health for the benefit of their community. In that process they transgress class membership as well as professional divisions. Volunteers came from all venues of society. Many urban companies had high percentages of white and "high white" collar members well into the 1850s. Contrary to the myth, the working-class structure of the culture of firefighting is a phenomenon from the period following the dissolution of the urban volunteer departments.[10]

There were two structural aspects to urban volunteer firefighting, however, that became part of a particular problematic, beginning around 1830 with the Jacksonian turn in American democracy. Being a company member came with considerable benefits. The volunteers received the respect and praise of their peers and of the community in general. Dependent on the self-help and mutuality system, non-firefighters were originally quite ready to support the volunteers. Private donors and admirers bought and financed equipment, and outfitted and supplied the firehouses. The volunteers themselves also contributed a lot of funds and effort – thus the impression of social clubs was not unjustified. Life in the volunteer company in this respect "offered some of the trappings of the middle class – fine houses, libraries, even an occasional piano – along with the physicality and excitement of working-class culture. It offered a home that was a 'warming place' for the firemen."[11] This combination of the cultural atmosphere of the aspiring middle class, and of working-class heroics, was both inspirational and attractive.

It needs to be considered that there was no experience with this kind of system at the time. The fameworthiness basis of the volunteer system might have continued to work in a society based on the kind of rational frugality envisioned by a Franklin and a Jefferson (not that they always lived it themselves). However, in the era after the War of 1812, the American political economy, with its proliferation of graft and get-rich-quick schemes, did not necessarily support this idealism. Besides, there were serious organizational flaws. In the majority of cities, the volunteer

---

10 Greenberg, *Cause for Alarm*, 67.
11 Ibid., 68.

fire companies were independently organized, and only loosely, if at all, coordinated. Often, city fire chiefs had to be content with controlling the condition of the apparatuses.[12] Without a city-governed system of distribution and allocation, engine companies in the same city quarters vied for what was believed to be the most honorable position at a fire: first in line. The necessary cooperation between pumper-engines, hose, and hook and ladder units did, of course, work, more or less.

The appearance of many of the volunteer fire companies and their equipment should have given reason for concern already by the 1830s. Not only did the firefighters exhibit a proto-carnivalesque pride in parading in gaudy uniforms with their "masheen," but their pride in the apparatus was often expressed in elaborate paint-jobs and adornments. While some of them were artistically quite remarkable, they were also entirely impractical in terms of a culture of firefighting that needs to rely on functionality. The gradual shift from functional pieces of machinery to exhibition pieces signals one of the factors that contributed to the alienation of the "fire laddies" from exactly the middle class they were trying to emulate. In some cities, they did not stop at emulation: some firehouses in San Francisco, for instance, apparently excelled in libraries, valuable paintings, and other "fancy fixens"[13] – to the point where "normal" middle-class Americans apparently started to think of this kind of splendor as rather extravagant. Certainly the size and temple-like adornment of some firehouses, like the Gothic castle the Vigilant Fire Company No. 9 of San Francisco were planning for themselves in 1855,[14] must have created resentment.

There were other problems. Many of the younger, unmarried firefighters gave their residence as the firehouse, and even though technically they continued to be volunteers, it was not as if their services remained entirely free – not in their own eyes, nor in those of city councils, or of an increasing percentage of the population. Respect and honor gradually gave way to increasingly tributary systems of support as firefighters had become used to the support and supply from donors and admirers. Furthermore, by the 1840s, with cities often growing exponentially, and new fire

---

12 Hensler, *Crucible of Fire*, 51.
13 Quoted in Greenberg, *Cause for Alarm*, 55.
14 Ibid., 35. However, the *Guardians of the City* webpage, http://guardiansofthecity.org/sffd/companies/volunteer/vigilant_engine_co_no9.html, indicates that, while the building may have been planned, in 1860 the Vigilant fire company was still in a two-story brick building that belonged to the city.

companies being founded to meet the demand, most cities had to resort to subsidizing their fire departments – often with considerable sums of money.[15] This, however, did not prevent these departments from asking for more. Chief Engineers were salaried civic employees anyway. So if fire companies were still perceived as heroic, by 1840 they were also receiving their dues in tributes of honor, donations, and money spent at balls, banquets, and other fundraisers on behalf of the fire companies.

As long as the public at large felt that there was a balance between the services rendered by the volunteers, and the amount of tribute they required for their maintenance, this system could remain operational. Towards mid-century, however, the volunteer companies and their class-transcending difference from the rest of society, their lifestyle away from the family environment, and their potential political influence were beginning to be looked askance at by influential forces in society.

Volunteers in the Political Market Economy

It is highly telling that, around this time, the effectiveness of the system was coming under scrutiny. The market economy started to have effects on the labor-force; most notably in the urban centers. By 1850, professionality and business-like attitudes had taken the place of minute-man readiness. Men in responsible positions spent longer hours on the job and saved their free time for quality time with their families. To volunteer for something that was not remunerated gradually came to be seen as unprofessional, which was syllogistic with amateurish, while the amateurish in turn was seen as not geared towards efficiency.[16] Paid-for services became the order of the day. Everyday heroism was redefined as faithfully doing one's duty at the job one got paid for – a notion possibly advocated first in Britain, but readily picked up in the U.S.[17] In this context, an important factor arose in the notion that shop- and factory-owners, finding themselves in increasingly competitive situations in the market economy, could not

---

15 Greenberg, *Cause for Alarm*, 35.
16 Ibid., 75–78.
17 I am grateful to Christiane Hadamitzky for alerting me to this fact, and to a copy of D. Chalmers, "What is Heroism?" *Chalmers's Journal*, May 9, 1857, 297–298.

afford to let workers – especially highly skilled ones – run off at any time of the day to follow a fire-alarm.

Consequently, the mid-century citizens increasingly looked at volunteers no longer as a familiar force recruited from their own ranks, but as something different from themselves – even suspiciously different in so far as volunteers apparently had too much time at their hands to idly hang around their firehouses. This might not have been a problem had they limited themselves to loitering primarily *inside* their firehouses. However, complaints increased about the noise and rowdyism in front of and around fire company quarters.[18]

This, however, is a factor that has been represented from an odd angle in many of the local histories of fire departments. Concentrated on the fire companies, and based primarily on newspaper reporting, departmental documents, and city council records, rowdyism and even criminal activities in these histories appear seemingly unmotivated and matter-of-factly.[19] This requires further investigation and a widening of the perspective to encompass the broader societal picture.

As a result of the Jacksonian turn in American politics, the mid-nineteenth century saw increasing problems in terms of class relations. Equality was increasingly understood not in the de Crevecoeurian sense as the ubiquity of educated yeoman farmers, but that there was no difference between intelligence and ignorance. Enlightened republican rationalism gave way to get-rich-quick schemes and egotism on all levels of society. One of the consequences was an increasingly physical, and even violent, everyday culture which involved not only the lower but also parts of the middle classes. By the 1840s, the violence aspect appears to have gotten out of hand as political altercations became more serious, and the republican sense of cooperation deteriorated in the face of increasing moral and religious intransigence, collective self-righteousness, and oppositional conspiracy theories.[20] Theatre audiences rioted, Christmas revelers attacked what they perceived as immoral institutions and, notably, election

---

18 George D. Bushnell, "Chicago's Rowdy Firefighters," *Chicago History* 2 (1973): 232–241.
19 An exception to the similarity in range and scope between Bushnell, Holt, Lampe, and others, is Geoffrey Giglierano's article on the genesis of the Cincinnati paid fire department in the 1850s and 60s: "'A Creature of Law': Cincinnati's Paid Fire Department," *Cincinnati Historical Society Bulletin* 40, no. 2 (1979): 78–99.
20 Michael Butter, *Plots, Designs, and Schemes: American Conspiracy Theories from the Puritans to the Present* (Berlin: de Gruyter, 2014), chapter 4.

campaign meetings deteriorated into inner-city pitched battles that lasted for days and cost numerous lives in the 1850s.

However, even within a political and social environment that was, in more ways than one, headed towards Civil War, clashes between rivalling fire companies still had a different quality, and posed a substantial danger: Politicians' supporters and theatre audiences were not part of the city's volunteer rescue forces, whose purpose was to provide safety and restore order rather than to endanger and subvert them.

This is where the physical aspect of firefighting disarticulated from middle-class culturedness. Being a member of a volunteer company was, as noted above, "a physical way of life" which "offered the action, adventure, and autonomy denied in the workaday realm. ... Volunteer fire companies offered a chance for real heroics, rough masculine camaraderie and colorful display."[21] At least in the first decades of the century, the life of a volunteer "offered the fulfilment of a vision of masculinity that celebrated strength, courage, speed, and appearance" – all of which were necessary in a technical environment that celebrated and necessitated physical strength above everything else. After all, pulling a pumper by hand to the scene of the fire, as well as pumping by hand, required physical strength and stamina on a scale almost unimaginable from today's point of view. Whether this was, however, "a vision of masculinity which was not tied to class, in a period when class increasingly divided and defined cultures in America"[22] is a more difficult statement to evaluate, in so far as the divisions appear not to have been tied as much to class as to the idea of division and competition, rather than consensus and cooperation.

From the notes and records that Greenberg, Hensler, Dykstra, Bushnell, and others have sifted through, it becomes apparent that the competitive spirit between volunteer units, especially in New York, Baltimore, and St. Louis, was getting more and more out of hand in the 1840s. Even where apparatuses were positioned in line to transport water over longer distances to a fire, competitions set in to either "wash" the pumper ahead of one's own, or to "suck dry" the one from which the water came, rather than to provide a steady supply. Engine companies raced each other to fires, which included risking damage. Even worse, hiding "plugs" (i.e. early water hydrants) and even cutting another engine's hose were extremes to which the competitiveness was taken. It is also

---

21 Elliot Gorn, quoted in Greenberg, *Cause for Alarm*, 66.
22 Ibid., 79.

evident that this rowdyism could only attain such proportions, and turn into a system-threatening problem, because fighting between companies was initially not taken seriously, possibly even condoned for a while, downplayed in newspaper reports, and often not followed by legal action even when members were killed. This reluctance to act in the face of a serious and increasingly disabling problem is even less comprehensible in view of the fact that this kind of behavior clearly ran counter to the original idea and ideals of the volunteer fire service.[23] Strangely enough, in Cincinnati for instance, one of the sources of the increasing descent into disorder has been identified as the absence of a chief fire engineer who would control all companies and take charge on site. This function had originally been part of the system, and its reintroduction came simultaneously with the introduction of paid firefighters – to which the reestablishment of order has been credited.[24]

From circa 1848, the course of the fire services diverged from developments in the political climate: as firefighting as a practice became less and less efficient, there was a gradually swelling chorus of voices that started turning against the volunteers and later becomes an identifiable, concerted effort to undermine their public image, while propagating their replacement by paid firefighters.

It must have come as a surprise to many volunteers, notably in cities where the collective disorder had not spread to the same disturbing extent as, for instance, in St. Louis.[25] Amy Greenberg comes to the conclusion that there was a shift in American political culture which increasingly "identified interest in terms of class and ethnicity, and ... which elevated the businessman over the manly fireman as the ideal citizen."[26] Another acting force in the field was the "modern city" where "men would find their value in their paid work and turn to their biological families as the basis of their community."[27] Both of these statements, while logical, are also loaded with moments of ascribed agency that makes the fall of the volunteer and the rise of the paid system look like natural developments, which they were not.

---

23 Hart and Smith, "Fame, Fame-Worthiness, and the Public Service," 134.
24 Giglierano, "A Creature of Law," 93; Hensler, *Crucible of Fire*, 50.
25 Robert Vote, "When Men Were Men and Firemen: San Francisco's Volunteer Fire Department," *American History Illustrated* 17, no.3 (1982): 32–37.
26 Greenberg, *Cause for Alarm*, 40.
27 Ibid., 164.

One of the main forces behind the shift in tone, and the anti-volunteer propaganda, were the underwriters for fire insurance companies, as Greenberg and Hensler point out.[28] Seen as natural tributaries by many fire departments, the insurance companies desired to lower their expenditures at least in this direction, so they lobbied both behind the scenes as well as openly for the installation of paid fire departments – which would cost the municipalities a lot more, but which the underwriters hoped would also increase effectivity. With promises of cutbacks on insurance rates, the underwriters managed to pull the majority of business owners and stakeholders over to their side, and thus also influenced city councils. According to Mark Tebeau and Amy Greenberg,[29] this did more to end the urban volunteer system than anything else, since the insurance companies, and their allies among the business class, wielded a financial power and influence on city councils that the firefighters could not stand up against.

As far as efficiency and effectivity were concerned, much has been made of the advent of the steam engine, and of horses to draw them, on the 1850s firefighting scene. The often-repeated argument that volunteers could not take care of horses and steam-engines 24/7, however, is one of the myths that do not hold up to closer scrutiny. As records and histories show, a number of first generation steam-pumpers were acquired by or for volunteer companies.[30] With a substantial number of the younger members of fire companies usually sleeping at the fire-house anyway, the presence of a maintenance-crew was not the problem. The initial effectivity of the steam engine over the hand-pumper was not all that evident in the 1850s either – the first generation of steamers were huge, unwieldy, and rather unreliable contraptions.

The radical shift that affected the volunteer system most damagingly was the re-definition of the central myth and metaphor which had propped up the volunteer system for almost a century: that of fighting fire effectively. The practice of pulling their engines and hose wagons to fires quite literally ran up against the increasing size of cities, the size of house

---

28 Hensler, Crucible of Fire, 183; Greenberg, *Cause for Alarm*, 57.
29 Mark Tebeau, *Eating Smoke: Fire in Urban America, 1800–1950* (Baltimore: Johns Hopkins University Press, 2003); Greenberg, *Cause for Alarm*, 148–149.
30 Anon. David Crockett Steam Fire Company No. 1 [Gretna, LA] http://www.davidcrockettfire.com/our-history.html.

and factory constructions, and the increasing risk of high-damage fires. This showed, for instance, in the disastrous 1845 fire in Pittsburgh.[31]

The American industrial system of the 1840s and 50s becomes increasingly a system of steam engines and of machines. Advertising billboards and journal illustrations celebrated industrialization. The very idea of the heroic, and, consequently, the public and even more so the publicized display of heroism, shifted from the show of physical, muscular prowess – as shown in dragging the "masheen" to the fire, and manning the pumps – to a display of technology. An operational steam pumper could be handled by a fraction of the manpower needed to drag a fire-engine to the site of the fire and then keep up a steady stream of water. This reduction in numbers was clearly in the interest of company owners, who did not receive recompense from the city if their workers ran off at the sound of the alarm.[32]

Consequently, as stated above, some volunteer companies acquired steam pumpers and learned to work them. However, within the world of the volunteer companies, the job of a teamster was not one that was considered desirable, nor was the job of a fireman – not as in fighting fires but as in stoking one, maintaining the heat of the water in the steam pumper. But that was exactly what was required now, and images of steam engines started to dominate news reports about fires being fought successfully. Even in the theatre, the novelty of steam pumpers put them quite literally center stage – a poster advertising Dion Boucicault's *The Poor of New York* shows a steam engine in the front, and firefighters operating a hand-pumper in the back.

Deprived of a central pillar of their masculine heroism, some firefighters resigned in indignation. In some cities, whole companies disbanded. The transition went badly in some places, better in others. One company in St. Louis set fire to their own firehouse, while another one – named, of all possibilities, after Benjamin Franklin – was taken over into the paid service. They sold their apparatus to the city of St. Louis, founded a library out of the funds thus obtained, and continued to use their engines as professionals.[33]

The heroic image of the firefighter as such in the public mind was less affected by this shift than might have been expected. To be paid for being

---

31 Hensler, *Crucible of Fire*, 49–52.
32 Ibid., 94.
33 Dykstra, "Rowdyism and Rivalism," 63.

heroic – strongly in disagreement with the original idea of the fame-worthy volunteer – turned into the new normal.

It needs to be kept in mind that there had been shifts before. The original firefighter of the eighteenth century was a protector of private and public properties. Every member of Benjamin Franklin's Union Fire Company "agreed to furnish, at his own expense, six leather buckets and two stout linen bags, the latter to receive and hold property which was in danger, to save it from risk of theft."[34] Already by the early 1800s, however, the imagery of firefighting had shifted from protecting property to decidedly more traditionally heroic efforts at saving lives; especially those of women and children. Romanticized and often tear-jerking poems, songs, paintings, and melodramatic plays, like Samuel D. Johnson's *The Fireman*,[35] celebrated heroically physical firefighters. Consequently, and no doubt much to their chagrin, insurance company underwriters had to hire their own helpers to salvage property. These men were dressed to look like firemen, even though they were not attached to fire companies.

It is arguably the positive range of the firefighter image that transgresses the shift from salvage crew to heroic volunteers to heroic professionals. The continuity can be seen in a set of lithograph prints issued by Nathanael Currier in the 1858 "American Fireman" series.[36] At first, the men in these prints look like they might be either volunteers or members of paid departments – the dress is the same, the then new protective leather helmets were obtained by professionals and volunteers alike in the 1850s. However, there are a number of instances that indicate that the makers of these prints were very much aware of being right in the middle of the transition period.

---

34 John Thomas Scharf, Thompson Westcott *History of Philadelphia, 1609–1884*, Philadelphia 1884, quoted from http://en.wikipedia.org/wiki/Union_Fire_Company.
35 Samuel D. Johnson, *The Fireman* (New York: Samuel French, 1856).
36 Both Nathaniel Currier and his later brother-in-law and partner James Merritt Ives served with volunteer firemen in New York during the 1850s.

Figure 1: The American Fireman: Facing the Enemy, Louis Maurer, lithograph, Currier & Ives, New York, 1858.

Figure 2: The American Fireman: Rushing to the Conflict, Louis Maurer, lithograph, Currier & Ives, New York, 1858.

Figure 3: The American Fireman: Always Ready, Louis Maurer, lithograph, Currier & Ives, New York, 1858.

Figure 4: The American Fireman: Prompt to the Rescue, Louis Maurer, lithograph, Currier & Ives, New York, 1858.

The only hint of the traditional volunteer culture in these pictures is visible in one of the prints showing a hose-cart being drawn out of the firehouse by hand; but then not all paid fire-departments had horses for all their apparatuses from the start. All four prints (Figs. 1-4) create symbolic impressions of competence and deliberation, and at least one shows a heroic savior. None shows a salvage bag. The "modern" image of the heroic proved not to be tied effectively to the fame worthiness of the republican, community-oriented actor, but to turn the rational protector of civic property into a pre-modern mediaeval knight. The images of heroism are romantic qualities – they show the stalwart, the strong, and reliable – shared by volunteers and professionals alike. There is also a strongly religious overtone to the images. As Amy Greenberg points out quite convincingly, the nozzle-man emulates a Saint George fighting the dragon. Likewise, the officer with the trumpet can be seen as a Christ-like leader, and the man pulling the apparatus as a Samson, while the rescuer of a young woman can be seen as an angel, or Saint Christopher.

It might be assumed that this set of images was possibly designed to accompany the transition from the volunteer to the paid system – at least it served both clienteles for positive identification, based on identical sentiments and key attributes.

Other images, dating to the late 1840s and early 1850s, are structured more ambivalently. There was an earlier lithograph series, published in 1854 and based on images by the German painter Louis Maurer (not Maurier, as Greenberg writes). This series sequentializes a fire-alarm. The locations are all identifiably New York, a city in which, at the time, the amount and degree of fire-company rowdyism was only topped by police graft and corruption. The first one of this series of consecutive prints, *The Night Alarm*, shows the men of volunteer Excelsior Company No. 2 (including both Currier and Ives, who were members) pulling their apparatus out by hand with the help of long ropes from their station on 21 Henry Street (Fig. 5). The second in this very popular set shows old-style volunteer companies pulling their apparatuses to a fire. Apparently racing each other, such behavior was one of the methods by which volunteer companies asserted their manhood, but which also served as a source of criticism.[37] The fire in the third print is being fought with determination, but it is a huge conflagration – the two attack lines trained on the flames by the companies visible in the foreground appear hopelessly inadequate.[38] Consequently, the fourth image shows a ruin, with the fire department

---

37 https://springfieldmuseums.org/collections/item/the-life-of-a-fireman-the-race-jump-her-boys-jump-her-nathaniel-currier/.
38 https://springfieldmuseums.org/collections/item/the-life-of-a-fireman-the-fire-now-then-with-a-will-shake-her-up-boys-nathaniel-currier/.

taking up their hose even before the fire is completely subdued (Fig. 6). This is in keeping with a number of reports from the period that commended the firefighters for their "almost superhuman effort" but at the same time admitted that they had not been particularly successful.[39] It is important to note that for everyone who wanted to revel in the glory of the old days, this set of prints constructed mainly positive evidence. Criticism, as far as it can be identified, is only present in the lack of effectivity.

Figure 5: *The Life of a Fireman: the Night Alarm – "Start her lively boys"*, Louis Maurer, lithograph, Currier & Ives, New York, lithograph, Currier & Ives, New York, 1854.

---

39 See Greenberg, *Cause for Alarm*; Hensler, *Crucible of Fire*.

Figure 6: The Life of a Fireman: The Ruins – Take up – Man your Rope, Louis Maurer, lithograph, Currier & Ives, New York, 1854.

Exactly this lack of effectivity, however, is foregrounded in the most popular, and simultaneously the most misinterpreted, "fire laddie" of them all: the stage figure of a New York volunteer, "Mose, the Bowery B'hoy." His stage career started in 1848 in a two-act melodrama entitled *Glance at New York*. Of the nine known Mose-plays, it appears that Benjamin A. Baker's text is the only one to have survived. However, the most strident characteristics of Mose, as far as they are known from folklore and mythology, are all there.[40] He "runs wid der masheen," saves babies, and puts out fires. In the process, he knocks over bystanders, and he never leaves a site without a "muss" – either fighting another fire company over the use of a hydrant, another fireman from his own company over the nozzle, or just about anybody else for the sake of a fight.[41] In this, Mose represents the best and the worst contemporary citizens were hearing

---

[40] Richard Mercer Dorson, "Mose the Far-Famed and World-Renowned," *American Literature* 15, no. 3 (1943): 288–300.
[41] George A. Baker, *Glance at New York* (New York: Samuel French, 1848).

about volunteer firefighters. Simultaneously Mose has to be seen in the context of other early to mid-nineteenth century American folk heroes.[42]

The rough frontiersman Davey Crockett, the lumberjack Paul Bunyan and the "king of the river" Mike Fink were all extremely physical, boisterous figures, heroic in their performances, and courageous to the point of recklessness; claiming they could "out-run, out-hop, out-jump, throw-down, drag out, and lick any man in the country."[43]

But this is exactly where the scales regarding cultural refinement in the 1840s tipped against these figures, and against the fire volunteers. Already in the first of Cooper's Leatherstocking Tales, *The Pioneers* of 1823, Natty Bumppo, the free hunter of the woods, runs afoul of the law, and is punished. Likewise, the fighting and brawling of the folk heroes became legendary, and, as a consequence, they were relegated to children's books and other forms of entertainment. To the urban middle classes, they represented a form of unrefined and uncouth savagery that these people increasingly left behind in terms of manners and behavior. Their overabundant and outrageous display and performance of physicality and violence was increasingly seen as comical at best. In connection with the fire service, the insistence on brawling physicality also became an indication of ineffectiveness: In a widely reproduced image of Frank Chanfrau as Mose there is a ruptured hose on the ground that prevents water from reaching the hand-pumper "tub." In the background behind Mose, idlers even sit on a fire plug while the situation appears to be still developing.[44]

The reception of the Mose-plays is quite telling. A fair number of volunteers in urban environment appear to have misunderstood Mose as a role-model – Amy Greenberg has noted that incidents of brawling and fighting at, and on the way to, fires seem to have increased in number in the late 1840s. This might, however, have been due to the marked increase in critical reporting about questionable volunteer performances, rather than due to a real increase. The lower-class audiences in whose theatres the Mose-plays were staged certainly liked the rough and physical "Mose," and even middle-class audiences might have enjoyed the performance – but would they have wanted the Moses of the Bowery as their protectors in a dangerous situation?

---

42 https://de.pinterest.com/pin/111464159497615655/.
43 Paul O'Neill, *The Old West: The Rivermen* (New York: Time-Life Books, 1975), 71.
44 https://de.pinterest.com/pin/111464159497615655 /.

Mose signals the limitations of the volunteer system – the volunteers almost run over the country bumpkin visiting the big city, and their competitive physicality is described as comical. At a time when an increasingly rational allocation of resources was the economic order of the day, this comicality is a signpost of inadequacy: the old volunteers are likeable, but dated. That they are representative of an outdated model is also visible in the hat and uniform worn by Frank Chanfrau in the lithograph. He is not wearing the ergonomically reasonable patent leather fire-helmet, but a stovepipe chapeau.

The "plug," and a positively ancient, early nineteenth-century style overcoat are also worn by the volunteer firemen appear in three of four Harrison & Weightman cartoons (Figs. 7–10) from the same decade as the Courrier and Ives prints. These literally old-fashioned volunteers are, man by man, the opposites of their Currier & Ives counterparts. They overturn apple-baskets and hit bystanders with ladders as they pass a hose (which has a hole in it). In one of the four pictures, the fireman has not brought enough length of hose to reach the fire, so one bystander is accosted for assistance, and another young bystander gets sprayed with water by an inattentive fireman. The underlying message is that the boy will no longer be enamored with the fire laddies– nor will the gentlemen who get hit by the ladder and are recruited, unwillingly, into the fire service. In any case, the latter gentleman does not look as if he would relish being handed the nozzle – something considered an honor in the early volunteer days, and one over which Mose the bowery b'hoy often fought other fire-laddies. Here the separation of urban citizen and urban volunteer is at its most visible.

Figure 7: The Firemen, No. 1, Running to a Fire, A Collision, Harrison & Weightman, lithograph, Philadelphia, 1858.

Figure 8: The Fireman, No. 2, Near a Fire, An Awkward Attachment, Harrison & Weightman, lithograph, Philadelphia, 1858.

Figure 9: The Fireman, No. 3, Near a Fire, Harrison &Weightman, lithograph, Philadelphia, 1858.

Figure 10: The Fireman, No. 4, At a Fire, What Boys May Expect when They Get in Firemen's Way, Harrison & Weightman, lithograph, Philadelphia, 1858.

The time-gap is decisive here. The old volunteer format is shown as outdated in costume as well as behavior. Once the decision for paid departments was made, cultural product lines celebrating firefighters and the new technology at their disposal became the order of the day. Quite tellingly, two images were added to the continuously popular Currier and Ives series in 1861 and 1866, and they show the next generation – a modern horse-drawn steam pumper on the run to a fire, and a mixed steam and hand-pumper department fighting a fire with "steam and muscle" (Figs. 11 and 12). Furthermore, within less than twenty years, even those volunteers who had crossed the line and were retained as members of the paid force became objects of adoration, as if there had never been a rowdy volunteer culture.[45] Thus, the memories of the positive aspects of volunteerism were combined with the new everyday heroic of technology and professionalism.

Figure 11: The Life of a Fireman: The New Era, Steam and Muscle, Charles Parsons, lithograph, Currier & Ives, New York, 1861.

---

45 See, for instance, the figure of Joe Jones, an old retained volunteer, in Joseph Arthur's popular firefighting melodrama *The Still Alarm*, 1885.

Figure 12: The Life of a Fireman: The Metropolitan System, John Cameron, lithograph, Currier & Ives, New York, 1866.

This reassignment of ideas and images of heroism had a considerable impact in the process of transition from volunteer to professional fire departments. Attributes originally connected to the volunteer firefighters were transferred to the professionals. However, what sounds like a simple equation can, upon closer inspection, be seen to shows signs of a more intricate pattern that is typical for the modern and the consumerist phase of capitalism.

Professional structures of command were installed to ensure efficiency. For example, racing each other, though never completely eradicated, gave way to an enforced coordination of efforts, at least once the firemen arrived on site. Stratification modeled on military structures, with battalion chiefs and company officers of military rank, replaced the syndicalism of the volunteer system. It came complete with a system of orders and strict obedience which the lessons of the Civil War taught were problematic for many freedom-loving Americans, but which seemed, at least at the time, unavoidable.

In the light of this context, the firefighters' rowdyism, most frequently mentioned as the reason for the transition from volunteer to paid, starts to look almost like a pretext for a change that insurance companies, and the social compound of company and business owners and shareholders propagated and pursued once they had come to the conclusion that their financial benefit lay with the professionalization of the fire services. All scholars that have written on the history of firefighting in this period concur that the urban volunteer fire companies were regularly lavished with praise during the first half of the nineteenth century. Then, around 1850, the situation changes. Praise continues in some publications but, as Amy Greenberg has shown, at the same time newspaper editors in St. Louis, Birmingham, and San Francisco begin complaining about volunteer firefighters being rowdy, disorderly, and – worst of all – inefficient. The model American of the second half of the nineteenth (and all of the twentieth century) was the efficient businessman.

With urban areas ever growing, and the pressure of liberal market competition demanding both the presence of employees as well as the safety of production processes, the decreasing efficiency of the volunteer system, as well as the absence of employees from the workplace, did not match systemic demands made by the increasingly all-pervasive capitalist structures. The logic of administrative orders under capitalism meant that the much higher cost of professional departments could be socialized, i.e. redistributed to the citizenry at large. Also, the disappearance of middle and upper-class volunteers meant that a re-classification of firefighters as predominantly working class was possible, thus ensuring that the costs for the paid professionals did not rise too high. A second factor to keep payments low was the continuation of the heroic image of firefighters. The appearance and impression of everyday heroism were transferable from the volunteers to the professionals because the shift to paid departments coincided with the advent of new technological systems which reduced numbers, but asked for special technical skills that were identified with the working class. A new heroics of technology, combined with the traditional physicality of rescue heroics, ensured that firefighters in the U.S. to this day can be paid relatively low wages, but enjoy a very high reputation. As a side effect, this new heroics of rescue-plus-technology made sure in the long run that the remaining volunteer companies in small towns and rural areas also attracted a mostly blue-collar membership.[46] Other than their urban successors – notably in New York, Chicago, and Boston – the volunteers henceforth suffered at the hands of intellectuals (dramatists, filmmakers, and cartoonists) who turned them into usually amiable but thick-headed, slightly comical figures along the lines of Mark Twain's Scotty Briggs.[47]

The days when future presidents (as had been the case with George Washington, Millard Filmore, and John Buchanan) were members of a volunteer fire company during early phases of their political careers were over. But at least there wasn't another "Boss" Tweed of Tammany Hall fame either, whose political ascendancy had also started in a volunteer fire department. Depoliticized, and reduced to a strangely para-romantic professional admixture of physical plus technological prowess, and life-saver qualities, the everyday heroism of American firefighters would continue to provide a mythological rallying point for all Americans, regardless of political affiliation. The transgressive phenomenon of all levels of the social body being attracted to the everyday heroism of serving as a volunteer firefighter, however, receded largely to rural communities with a strong sense of cohesion.

---

[46] Charles R. Simpson "A Fraternity of Danger. Volunteer Fire Companies and the Contradictions of Modernization." *American Journal of Economics and Sociology* 55, no. 1 (1996): 17–34; Kenneth B. Perkins, "Volunteer Fire Departments: Community Integration, Autonomy and Survival," *Human Organisation* 46, no. 4 (1987): 342–348.

[47] Mark Twain, "Buck Fanshaw's Funeral," Ch. XLVII *Roughing It*, (Hartford: American Publishing Company: 1872), 329–338.

Narratives of Feminine Heroism: Gender Values and Memory in the American Press in the Nineteenth and Twentieth Centuries

Janice Hume

Journalists use, and sometimes misuse, the term "hero" as a type of news frame, a tradition of highlighting extraordinary feats of individuals that dates back to the earliest newspapers and magazines. In the United States, journalistic references to heroism both increased and evolved as the press discovered new methods of newsgathering and reportage in the mid-nineteenth century.[1] Technological and cultural changes that gave way to a "mass" press encouraged the rise of human-interest journalism, which included stories about heroic figures. As such stories became more and more common, heroes and heroic attributes became increasingly egalitarian and more representative of the "everyday hero."[2] Yet they were not inclusive. Heroes in the nineteenth-century American press were predominantly white and male, and they represented values of nation building and westward expansion. National heroines were virtually nonexistent, yet the attributes of female heroism were part of press content. This essay considers the American heroine as portrayed in life and death on the pages of newspapers and magazines.[3]

The Revolutionary War patriot Nancy Hart serves as both exemplar and anomaly in the story of the mediated American heroine. According to press accounts and local lore, this hardy woman single-handedly captured a squad of British soldiers after they invaded her north Georgia cabin and forced her to cook a meal for them. When they sat to eat, she grabbed a

---

[1] Betty Houchin Winfield and Janice Hume, "The American Hero and the Evolution of the Human Interest Story," *American Journalism* 15, no. 2 (1998): 80–81.

[2] Ibid., 85–86.

[3] In this essay, I attempt to pull together the threads of media and gender analysis that have been woven through my research into American journalism history over the past two decades. Included are articles from *Journal of Popular Culture, American Journalism, Journalism History, Journalism & Communication Monographs,* and *Review of Communication,* as well as two books.

musket, demanded their surrender, and held them until help arrived, at which time they were either shot or hanged, depending upon the account. Hart's heroic deed probably happened in 1780, but newspaper accounts were not published until at least forty-five years later, when nostalgia for the Revolution was strong.[4] Newspaper articles in Georgia and South Carolina described Hart as a colorful character, a sharp shooter who was "remarkably well-limbed and muscular." One article noted: "Nothing was more common than to see her in full pursuit of the bounding stag." Yet the articles pointed out her more traditional feminine characteristics too, including her skill as a cook – she was "able to get up a pumpkin in as many forms as there are days in the week" – and her "profound knowledge in the management of all ailments."[5]

This regional heroine was introduced to a wider audience in 1848, when she was featured in an article by Elizabeth F. Ellet published in the highly successful and popular women's magazine *The Lady's Book*.[6] Ellet also included the article, with minor revisions, in the second of her three-volume collection, *The Women of the American Revolution*, published by Baker and Scribner, in New York, in 1849.[7] The newspaper accounts and Ellet's version of the story were reprinted almost verbatim in George White's *Historical Collections of Georgia*, published in 1854.[8] Thus, the original oral accounts of Hart's heroism found a larger audience in the press and a less ephemeral home when published in books that were handed down over the generations. Nancy Hart became the only women for whom a Georgia county is named, and her story is still celebrated today as part of history festivals near her home.[9]

---

[4] See E. Merton Coulter, "Nancy Hart, Georgia Heroine of the Revolution: The Story of the Growth of a Tradition," *Georgia Historical Quarterly* 39, no. 2 (1955): 118–151; and Janice Hume, "Press, Published History, and Regional Lore: Shaping the Public Memory of a Revolutionary War Heroine," *Journalism History* 30, no. 4 (2005): 200–209.

[5] George White, *Historical Collections of Georgia: Containing the Most Interesting Facts, Traditions, Biographical Sketches, Anecdotes, Etc., Relating to Its History and Antiquities, From its First Settlement to the Present Time* (New York: Pudney & Russell, 1854), 442–443.

[6] E. F. Ellet, "Heroic Women of the Revolution," *The Lady's Book*, October 1848, 201–202.

[7] E. F. Ellet, *The Women of the American Revolution*, vol. II (New York: Baker and Scribner, 1849), 227–233.

[8] White, *Historical Collections*, 442–443.

[9] Nancy Hart's story is included in the Battle of Kettle Creek Anniversary, held on the second weekend of February each year in Washington, Georgia, sponsored by the Georgia Society and Samuel Elbert chapter of the Sons of the American Revolution.

Why is Nancy Hart an anomaly in a discussion of heroic American women? First, she was known publicly, and by name, in an era when women were relegated to the domestic sphere.[10] Nor was Hart dainty, frail, or beautiful, but rather was described by Ellet as "vulgar" and "cross-eyed, with a broad angle mouth, ungainly in figure, rude in speech and awkward in manners."[11] She was described as "a honey of a patriot but the devil of a wife," another attribute that defied cultural expectations of women of the era.[12] Yet her participation in the Revolution, the foundational American story, allowed her feats to rise to public attention, and gave her a place in regional collective memory.

Media and Memory

The relationship between journalism and public memory has been the focus of a robust scholarly discussion over the past several decades. Serving an important cultural function, collective beliefs about the past inform a social group, community, region, or nation's present and future. "Representations of the past can be mobilized to serve partisan purposes," wrote Renee C. Romano and Leigh Raiford. "They can be commercialized for the sake of tourism; they can shape a nation's sense of identity, build hegemony, or serve to shore up the political interests of the state; and they can certainly influence the ways in which people understand their world."[13]

Memory scholars grapple with the methodological problem of how to study and interpret something as elusive as the way a society remembers its past. Many have done so by examining tangible memory sites and artifacts,

---

10 Molly Pitcher, the closest thing to a national heroine in the Revolution, was, according to scholars, probably a compilation of several women present at battles. According to legend, Pitcher took over her husband's cannon when he fell in battle. Pitcher was not her real name, but rather denoted the water pitcher she supposedly carried to soldiers in the field. See Janice Hume, *Popular Media and the American Revolution: Shaping Collective Memory* (New York: Routledge, 2014), 69–73.
11 Ellet, "Heroic Women of the Revolution," 201.
12 Ibid., 202.
13 Renee C. Romano and Leigh Raiford, "Introduction: The Struggle over Memory," in their edited, *The Civil Rights Movement in American Memory* (Athens, Ga.: The University of Georgia Press, 2016), xxi.

as well as other types of social and cultural traditions. Michael Schudson noted:

> Memory is social ... because it is located in institutions rather than in individual human minds in the form of rules, laws, standardized procedures, and records, a whole set of cultural practices through which people recognize a debt to the past (including the notion of "debt" itself) or through which they express moral continuity with the past (tradition, identity, career, curriculum.)[14]

Memory is also located in collectively created monuments and markers, "dedicated memory forms, cultural artifacts explicitly and self-consciously designed to preserve memory and ordinarily intended to have general pedagogical influence."[15]

Journalism too provides such a tangible memory site. Mass media, according to Carolyn Kitch, are "the primary means by which most people understand the past," a dynamic that does not apply just to contemporary times.[16] Arthur Shaffer studied how the history of the American Revolution was written prior to 1815, and noted that, "many Americans learned their history through newspapers and magazines."[17] He pointed to era periodicals such as the *Massachusetts Spy* and *Columbian Magazine* that printed works of the earliest U.S. historians. And those historians made liberal use of press sources in their books and published studies. The relationship between early American journalism and history was truly symbiotic and helped forge a patriotic narrative in critical nation-building years.[18]

Press stories do more than help readers recall simple facts about acts of heroism. They provide important clues about collective values as well. Barry Schwartz called for an understanding of two distinct aspects of remembering – chronicling and commemoration. "The events selected for chronicling are not all evaluated the same way. To some of these events we remain morally indifferent; other events are commemorated, i.e., invested

---

14 Michael Schudson, "Dynamics of Distortion in Collective Memory," in *Memory Distortion: How Minds, Brains, and Societies Reconstruct the past*, ed. D.L. Schacter (Cambridge, MA: Harvard University Press, 1995), 346.

15 Ibid., 347.

16 Carolyn Kitch, "'Useful Memory' in Time Inc. Magazines: Summary Journalism and the Popular Construction of History," *Journalism Studies* 7, no. 1 (2006): 94.

17 Arthur H. Shaffer, *The Politics of History: Writing the History of the American Revolution, 1783–1814* (Chicago: Precedent Publishing, 1975), 162.

18 Janice Hume, "Building an American Story: How Early American Historians Used Press Sources to Remember the Revolution," *Journalism History* 37, no. 3 (2011): 172–179.

with an extraordinary significance and assigned a qualitatively distinct place in our conception of the past. ... Commemoration celebrates and safeguards the ideal."[19] Hero worship is by definition a type of commemoration, and when the press shares publicly stories about heroes, those stories are amplified, legitimized, and afforded extraordinary significance. Jill Edy, who developed a typology of the ways journalists have used the past, wrote:

It has become cliché to assert that journalists write the first draft of history. Far less attention has been paid to who does the rewrites. Yet this "memory work" is extremely important. As our society continues to dissect itself into small, competing groups, our possession of a past in common may be one of the few things that bind us as a whole.[20]

Journalists in the nineteenth century used historical memory for context and placement, noting the country's origins, leaders, and wars, particularly the Civil War. During an era of increased magazine and newspaper circulation and a rise in feature stories, journalists connected the present with the past.[21] Michael Schudson noted the importance of such content. He called the newspaper a "remarkable institution" and "the most representative carrier and construer and creator of modern public consciousness." He wrote: "Few things are more characteristic and revealing of modern culture than the invention and changes in the ways it declares itself anew each day in the presentation of news."[22]

Heroism

Heroes serve a pedagogical role as both mirrors and teachers of mainstream cultural values. Nineteenth-century American poet and essayist

---

19 Barry Schwartz, "The Social Context of Commemoration: A Study in Collective Memory," *Social Forces* 6, no. 2 (1982): 377.
20 Jill A. Edy, "Journalistic Uses of Collective Memory," *Journal of Communication* 49, no. 2 (1999): 71.
21 See Betty Houchin Winfield and Janice Hume, "The Continuous Past: Historical Referents in Nineteenth-Century American Journalism," *Journalism & Communication Monographs* 9, no. 3 (2007): 121–174.
22 Michael Schudson, "Preparing the Minds of the American People: Three Hundred Years of the American Newspaper," *Proceedings of the American Antiquarian Society* 100, no. 2 (1990): 442.

Ralph Waldo Emerson provided a thoughtful explanation. Heroes, he wrote, mirror the ideal morals of the community. They are symbols of the highest aims of mankind, and serve as "mouthpieces of their age."[23] Twentieth-century scholars have presented the hero not so much as a great man, but as a cultural symbol. Daniel Boorstin wrote about heroes, saying, "We revere them not because they possess charisma, divine favor, a grace or talent granted them by God, but because they embody popular virtues. We admire them ... because they reveal and elevate ourselves."[24]

Unfortunately, the "relationship between hero and heroine is not clearly defined or understood," according to Marshall Fishwick.[25] Dixon Wecter illustrated the anonymity of women in the hero-worship of the United States by pointing to the bronze statue of the nameless pioneer mother – a municipal park staple. He wrote: "During the greater span of our national life ... the dominant ideal has been the perfect lady."[26] This is in line with Fishwick, who notes that heroic figures must "satisfy the emotional and psychological needs of admirers." Thus, in the nineteenth century, the very actions that might distinguish a woman as a "hero" if she were judged by male standards of morality, could simultaneously label her as unladylike, thereby making her an unfit symbol of the "heroine" for the women of her day. The mainstream reflected this incongruity with its lack of female icons.

Godey's *Lady's Book* Heroines

Heroic attributes of women were, however, part of media content in the nineteenth century and beyond. My study of the characteristics of heroic women in the years before and after the first U.S. women's rights convention, held in 1848 in Seneca Falls, N.Y., revealed changing cultural

---

23 See Barry Schwartz, "Emerson, Cooley and the American Heroic vision," *Symbolic Interaction* 8, no. 1 (1985): 106–107.
24 Ibid., 115.
25 Marshall Fishwick, "Prologue," in *Heroes of Popular Culture*, ed. Ray B. Browne, Marshall Fishwick, and Michael T. Marsden (Bowling Green, Ohio: Bowling Green State University Popular Press, 1972), 6.
26 Dixon Wecter, *The Hero in America* (Ann Arbor: University of Michigan Press, 1941), 476–477.

values related to gender.[27] The study focused on both fiction and non-fiction articles in *The Lady's Book*, a Philadelphia-based magazine founded in 1830 by Louis A. Godey that became the most esteemed and longest-running periodical of its day, reaching a circulation of 150,000 by the Civil War. The magazine is historically important for a variety of reasons, including its list of prominent contributors, popular success, and its influence on other American magazines.[28] It had much to say about the qualities of female heroism, even if it did not highlight many particular heroines.

In the years prior to the Seneca Falls convention, the *Lady's Book* women displayed "genius," but were likely – even required – to suffer as victims to achieve the status of "heroine." Their genius was not to be used to achieve accolades. Rather, it was to help women fulfill their duties as wives and mothers, or at least nurturers – roles of paramount importance. Heroines were women of Christian faith, known for self-sacrifice, and they were frail and melancholy.

Contributors to *The Lady's Book* were not blind to the fact that the descriptor "heroic" did not apply to women. As one article about the death of a pious woman noted:

> The great virtues, magnanimity and heroism, and the ambitious projects that convulse empires and strew the earth with desolated cities are blazoned on the false marble to win the admiration of succeeding generations, while the meek and unobtrusive worth and virtue and piety, and all those tender and endearing affections, which, if universal, would make an Eden of earth, leave no memorials behind them, have no monument, save that which is erected within the fond bosoms of those who have felt the sacred spirit of their presence in life.[29]

Virtuous women were to be quietly heroic, submissive and discreet – hardly qualities that would enable their reputations to be known beyond a family or to transcend a lifetime.

Fictional heroines were often victims of husbands, fathers, or brothers. They were pale and trembling; they nearly always wept or shrieked, and

---

27 The study included fiction and non-fiction articles in *The Lady's Book* in 1837, 1838, 1857, and 1858, based on era definitions of female heroism. In all, 696 articles were examined. See Janice Hume, "Defining the Historic American Heroine: Changing Characteristics of Heroic Women in Nineteenth-Century Media," *Journal of Popular Culture* 31, no.1 (1997): 1–21.

28 Frank Luther Mott, *A History of American Magazines 1741–1850* (Cambridge, MA: Harvard University Press, 1930), 351.

29 N.C. Brooks, "Ernestine," *Lady's Book*, April 1837, 149.

they often collapsed, senseless, in the face of bad news or danger. Even non-fiction articles characterized married women as living with "cares, anxieties, labour, watchfulness, and pain."[30] One article discussed the inherent danger, and thus heroic nature, of marriage:

> She promises to "love, honour and obey." Fearful promise! – to love and honour one, whom perhaps time and familiar intercourse will prove unworthy of regard, to obey him who perchance cannot command himself. And what heroic resolution does it sometimes require to enable the wife to keep this sacred promise?[31]

Ten years after the Seneca Falls women's rights convention, the "woman question" was often discussed in the press. Heroic women in *The Lady's Book* still exhibited characteristics of genius, self-sacrifice, and faith, but rather than being sorrowful victims, these women were now resourceful and brave. Melancholy no longer hung on their brows. Rather, nearly every one, both fictional and non-fictional, was described as cheerful. Women readers were instructed in one essay that, "truly good people are cheerful."[32] However, heroism was still a quiet virtue, "so large a part of many a woman's character, but for which she seldom had any acknowledgment made by others."[33] Indeed, fame remained a man's domain. One essay in 1857 noted that if a man was "talked about" because of his accomplishments, he had earned such fame, but if a woman was discussed, "it is blame to her."[34]

Godey's heroines in 1857 and 1858 were almost always well-educated, intelligent booklovers. They also had common sense, and did not let their intellectual pursuits harm their physical or emotional health. They could even take their intellect outside the home for some limited purposes. As one contributor wrote: "There is a voice in the girl's soul that is mightier than the voice of kindred, or of home, sending her out to do battle with the world, almost against her own will, and it is the voice of genius."[35] However, the domestic roles of wife and mother were still most important. Being single was labeled an "unnatural position," since the "true worth of a

---

30 B.Y., "Thoughts on the Happiness of Woman: As Connected with the Cultivation of her Mind," *Lady's Book*, November 1837, 204.
31 B.Y., "Thoughts," 205.
32 Mrs. A. E. Porter, "The Country Housewife," *Lady's Book*, April 1857, 365.
33 Meta Victoria Victor, "May: The Squatter's Daughter," *Lady's Book*, January 1857, 20.
34 "Editor's Table," *Lady's Book*, February 1857, 177.
35 Virginia B. Townsend, "The Lost Relatives," *Lady's Book*, October 1857, 307.

woman" could be judged only "within the circle of her domestic assiduity."[36]

Ladies' Home Journal Heroines

Women's heroic attributes had changed quite dramatically by the twentieth century, but some qualities remained the same. In another study of heroines, this one on the mass-circulating women's magazine *Ladies' Home Journal*, articles were pulled in sample years before and after the 1963 publication of Betty Friedan's *The Feminine Mystique*, considered to be the symbolic beginning of the modern women's movement. This resulted in 645 fiction and non-fiction articles from *Ladies' Home Journal*, which, in 1952, had the highest circulation of any women's interest magazine in the United States at more than 4.5 million.[37]

In 1952 and 1953, heroines were still defined according to their roles as wives and mothers, and the notion of heroism was mentioned infrequently. In fact, only one non-fiction article addressed the topic, and the only fictional character deemed "heroic" was a dog.[38] According to an article titled "Is There a Climate of Fear in America?" a true hero was a nonconformist who was willing to face persecution and death for his beliefs, such as Socrates, Jesus, Galileo, or Ghandi. "To be a nonconformist one must first be a *man* [emphasis in original]," the article noted. "Nonconformists have been the heroes of history and often its makers."[39] Far from being nonconformists, women featured in the magazine often spoke proudly about just how "average" they really were. Heroic women in the 1950s were "girls next door," wives, self-sacrificing mother/managers, and community housekeepers. Fictional heroines were described as kittens, children, "aimless and errant as the warm spring breeze," and innocent.[40]

---

36 F. R. Stauffer, "The Wife at Home," *Lady's Book*, January 1858, 43.
37 Janice Hume, "Changing Characteristics of Heroic Women in Midcentury Mainstream Media," *Journal of Popular Culture* 34, no. 1 (2000): 9–29.
38 Richard Sullivan, "Jupiter," *Ladies Home Journal*, January 1953, 32.
39 Dorothy Thompson, "Is There a Climate of Fear in America?" *Ladies' Home Journal*, September 1953, 11.
40 Elaine Greene, "Alice and Her First Four Men," *Ladies' Home Journal*, January 1952, 40; Eleanor Adams, "Slightly Lost and Found," *Ladies' Home Journal*, January 1942, 28; Leona S. Bruckner, "Triumph of Love," *Ladies' Home Journal*, January 1953, 38; Howard

In stark contrast to the heroines portrayed in *The Lady's Book* a century prior, the 1950s heroine was not defined by genius or education. Books would take her mind off of what was truly important in her life: marriage and family.

But in Cold War America, a type of political power and responsibility came with motherhood. As one article noted, "it will always remain true that the hand that rocks the cradle is the hand that rules the world. And it is in this sense that women must assume the job of making men who will know how to make a world fit for human beings to live in."[41] A similar duty came with the role of wife: to "influence and teach men to be more loving toward humanity."[42] Yet women were to do this without being bossy. As one fictional heroine explained: "I think the trouble with the American woman is that she has to do so many things, she gets turned into the boss of the family and hates it ... [because] she likes to be told firmly, but kindly, what to do."[43]

A woman's housekeeping skills were good for the community as well as the home. Women could clean up corruption by serving in local government, in part because they had more leisure time than their husbands. Another asset was their innate ability to crusade. As one article noted, "Temperamentally, most women make passionate crusaders when they are once aroused ... [because] a woman can get fighting mad when she sees that her home or her children are threatened ... and she will fight for other people's homes and children as well as for her own."[44] Thus, women occasionally stepped out of the domestic sphere, but their efforts were described in domestic terms: as housekeeping or shopping skills rather than as political acumen.

Ten years after publication of *The Feminine Mystique*, when the second-wave feminist movement was in full swing, *Ladies' Home Journal* portrayed heroic women as educated and intellectual. Books were important to both fictional and non-fictional women. One fictional heroine, for example, lugged "old-fashioned novels" home from the library until they "grew in

---

Rigby, "Left-Handed Daughter," *Ladies' Home Journal*, February 1952, 40; Kathryn Grohdahl, "Appointment in Hong Kong," *Ladies' Home Journal*, May 1952, 24.
41 Ashley Montague, "The Natural Superiority of Women," *Ladies' Home Journal*, July 1952, 36.
42 Ibid., 62.
43 Elizabeth Dunn, "The Incompetence of Candy," *Ladies' Home Journal*, October 1952, 44.
44 Millicent C. McIntosh, "Busy Women Have Enough time," *Ladies' Home Journal*, June 1952, 47.

heaps beside the bed."⁴⁵ A real-life woman read books "omnivorously" and swapped them with her husband "because we seem to like the same kind."⁴⁶

Women could, and did, find success outside the home in pursuits not described in terms of housekeeping and nurturing. The magazine launched its own "Women of the Year" awards in 1973, proclaiming: "This may be the age of the non-hero, but it is a time for heroines."⁴⁷ Yet right alongside this accomplished heroine were familiar categories of wife and mother. The magazine told every housewife and mother to declare herself "an unsung heroine and insist that [her] praises be sung loud and often."⁴⁸ Feminine roles of cook, nutritionist, cleaning woman, social and financial secretary, hostess, interior decorator, and child-care specialist were said to be worth more than $10,000 a year. The wife was valuable, and equal to her husband. A nonfiction article about former First Lady Mamie Eisenhower offered a symbolic declaration of her equality as a wife. While First Lady, she redesigned the dining area for state dinners so that she and the president could sit side-by-side at the head of the table.⁴⁹ Motherhood was essential too, though women were expected to want more. The mother/wife was "all of us – every woman," an article noted. "She is the nurturing force, spiritual and moral guide, comforter, wardrobe mistress, seamstress, caretaker, nurse, socializer, problem-solver, lullaby-singer, educator, adviser. To replace her completely is impossible."⁵⁰

Heroic women in 1972 and 1973, like the community housekeepers of the 1950s, were expected to live lives that would benefit those outside their family circles. They were socially conscious, committed to humanitarian causes but were less likely to be told that they should nurture the republic or save the country from external threat. Rather, volunteerism enabled women to enlarge their horizons beyond housework.

---

45 Rita Madocs, "Love is Something Between Two People Only," *Ladies' Home Journal*, May 1972, 52.
46 Evan Frances, "How America Lives," *Ladies' Home Journal*, February 1973, 54.
47 "*Ladies' Home Journal* Women of the Year 1973," *Ladies' Home Journal*, June 1973, 67.
48 Letty Cottin Pogrebin, "The Working Woman," Ladies' Home Journal, May 1972, 32.
49 J. B. West and Mary Lyn Kotz, "Ike and Mamie: Their White House Love Story," *Ladies' Home Journal*, August 1973, 118.
50 Pogrebin, "The Working Woman," 32.

The Uncomfortable Heroine

Both *The Lady's Book* and *Ladies' Home Journal* were geared for white, affluent American women, and their ideas about female heroism reflected the mainstream culture of their eras. Occasionally a woman broke out of the mold, however, and received press attention beyond the pages of women's magazines. Press coverage of temperance advocate Carry Nation, for example, provides clues about the cultural discomfort such women caused.[51] Nation became famous early in the twentieth century for smashing saloons with a hatchet in Kansas and at least five other states. Her motives included more than her disapproval of alcohol. As an article published decades after her death explained:

> Lost in the publicity of that time ... are the notable and abiding ethical tenets that Carry Nation espoused. Among them: women don't have to endure beatings by drunken husbands; women don't have to see the wages meant for their families spent elsewhere; men don't have to form clubs and cliques based on sex and race; ... homeless need a place to live; the young need sex education; alcoholism is a disease; smoking is bad for you; women have equal rights.[52]

Yet era news coverage was often critical. Writing in 1901, well-known Kansas journalist William Allen White called her "crazy as a bedbug" in January, and "a brave, fat old heroine" in February.[53]

Phillip I. Mittering has identified Nation as "one of the first personalities created by Americans to satisfy national anxieties and desires."[54] One reason was her "genius at self-promotion and her remarkably mediagenic personality," according to Frances Grace Carver, while another was the new journalism which, after the 1890s, focused on melodrama.[55] Part of the reason was also cultural: Nation fit a need for Americans who, in an

---

[51] Janice Hume, "Saloon-Smashing Fanatic, Corn-Fed Joan of Arc: The Changing Memory of Carry Nation in Twentieth-Century American Magazines," *Journalism History* 28, no. 1 (2002): 38–47.

[52] Irwin Ross, "Carry Nation: Saloon's Nemesis," *American History Illustrated* 2, no. 10 (1968): 13.

[53] See Robert Smith Bader, "Mrs. Nation," *Kansas History* 7, no. 4 (1984–85): 259. It cites the *Emporia Gazette* in Kansas for January 28, 1901, and February 11, 1901.

[54] Philip I. Mitterling, "Buffalo Bill and Carry Nation: Symbols of an Age," *North Dakota Quarterly* 50, no. 1(1982): 62.

[55] Frances Grace Carver, "With Bible in One Hand and Battle-Axe in the Other: Carry A. Nation as Religious Performer and Self-Promoter," *Religion and American Culture* 9, no. 1 (1999): 31.

era of great turmoil and uncertainty, "placed their faith and invested their wealth in emotion-packed personal symbols and rhetorical formulas."[56] As a result, Nation became a media sensation in an era where the press was already highly sensational. She became a recognizable figure; one who drew crowds and who elicited mixed responses. She sold souvenirs, including thousands of tiny hatchet pins, which followers wore on their lapels. And she was framed as a crackpot in both the regional and national press.

Nation's crusades were at least, in part, successful, which was evident in the traditional attempts to commemorate her life and works after her death. For example, her house in Medicine Lodge, Kansas, was dedicated as a memorial, and her grave in Belton, Missouri, was preserved as a monument in 1924, complete with a granite shaft bearing the line, "She Hath Done What She Could." Yet the press remembered Nation differently in different eras. In the late 1920s and early 1930s when prohibition was under fire (it was repealed in 1933), so too was Nation. Articles portrayed her as a frustrated, insane, hysterical, and shrieking fanatic.[57] An article in *American Mercury* called her a "corn-fed Joan of Arc" and said she probably was insane. Articles blamed her alleged shortcomings as a woman and wife, and her lack of traditional femininity for many of her problems. One speculated that her energies would have been better channeled if she had "romance and a home of her own in which she could have been happy and content."[58]

By the 1940s and 1950s, when prohibition was no longer an issue, articles were more bemused and nostalgic than critical. One said she was "incorruptible," a "born entertainer," and that "besides having humor, she was morally and fundamentally right."[59] An article in 1962 criticized her militant tactics, but also recalled "her good works, her kindness to the poor

---

56 Mitterling, "Buffalo Bill," 64.
57 As examples, see James L. Dwyer, "The Lady With the Hatchet," *American Mercury*, March, 1926, 324–331; Stark Young, "American Don Quixote," *New Republic*, November 23, 1932, 46–47; Herbert Asbury, "The Background of a Crusader: The Story of Carry Nation," *Outlook and Independent*, July 17, 1929, 442–478, July 24, 1929, 493–510, July 31, 1929, 527–559, August 7, 1929, 568–598, August 14, 1929, 620–638, August 21, 1929, 660–680, August 28, 1929, 701–706, and September 4, 1929, 21–39.
58 Asbury, "The Background," July 24, 1929, 495.
59 E. A. Braniff, "How I Ran Out on Carrie [sic] Nation," *Commonweal*, March 19, 1948, 558.

and unfortunate, her persistence in what she believed to be right, and her indomitable courage."⁶⁰

The Ideal Woman at Death

If the heroic woman in American history was to eschew fame and, instead, focus on her private, domestic duties as wife and mother, it follows that she would not be known outside her circle of family and friends. However, sometimes an everyday woman's "ideal" attributes were revealed publicly – not during her lifetime, but upon the occasion of her death.

A newspaper obituary informs readers about a death of interest to the community. It provides the "who, what, when, where" and sometimes "why" that any newspaper article would about breaking news. Yet the newspaper obituary does much more than report a death. It also provides a tiny synopsis of a life, and a commemoration; sharing publicly particular memories of the deceased. For the everyday citizen, it sums up memorable accomplishments and attributes, omitting, as private, that person's failures or culturally unacceptable traits of character. For the public figure, failures and flaws are sometimes included, albeit softened for an American audience that loves a happy ending and an uplifting conclusion.⁶¹

Historically, newspaper obituaries have included four framing categories: name and occupation of the deceased, cause of death, personal attributes of the deceased, and funeral arrangements. Though consistent through the centuries, each category reflects societal changes when examined over time. For example, historically, "occupations" for women were often listed as "wife," "consort," or "daughter," with women's first names often being omitted. Modern obituaries for women include their first names and list a variety of careers, reflecting major cultural shifts in ideas about their work and public role.

Evidence of changing gender values is also prevalent in details regarding the attributes of the deceased. It is apparent in the numbers of obituaries published – or, more accurately, in the obituaries left out of mainstream newspapers that found men's lives more worthy of com-

---

60 Alma Lutz, "Lady with a Hatchet," *Saturday Review*, November 3, 1962, 49.
61 Carolyn Kitch and Janice Hume, *Journalism in a Culture of Grief* (New York: Routledge, 2008), 93.

memoration than women's lives. One study found that, as late as the mid-twentieth century, Boston and New York newspapers displayed a clear pattern of masculine preference, giving "subtle confirmation of the greater importance of men" in American cities.[62] While the percentage of female obituaries has increased with each new generation, many women and others groups have still been ignored. For example, historically, mainstream newspapers appeared not to notice the deaths of the vast majority of African Americans. Children, the poor, and the socially outcast also failed to fit a cultural ideal that would allow them to be remembered publicly.[63]

Despite such exclusions, the obituary page serves a powerful cultural role, a type of commemoration meant for public consumption. Publication of an obituary for a mass audience constitutes a rare instance in a democracy when an individual can become part of collective thought, part of what a community might believe about the worth of a life. In addition, obituaries illustrate how the national memory of American cultural symbols is reflected in, and thus influences, the lives of individual citizens. For example, when references to the American heroes George Washington or Davy Crockett serve to illustrate characteristics of ordinary citizens generations after the passing of these icons, memories of those citizens are connected with American history and legitimized.

Memories of individuals can also influence the collective. Joseph A. Amato argues that "death causes people to tell stories" that can be "shaped by moral judgment, fashioned for the sake of argument, made buoyant by metaphor, or given meaning by the rituals of culture and the promise of religion."[64] Death stories, because of their powerful connection with cultural and religious rituals, fascinate and resonate in a society.

---

62 Robert Kastenbaum, Sara Peyton, and Beatrice Kastenbaum, "Sex Discrimination After Death," *Omega* 7, no. 4 (1976–77): 351.
63 Hume, *Obituaries*, 161.
64 Amato, Joseph A., "Death and the Stories We Don't Have," *Monist* 76, no. 2 (1993): 259.

Obituaries and Heroism

Nowhere is the connection between obituaries and collective memory so evident as when obits highlight American icons. During the early nineteenth century, the strongest symbols in American public memory were associated with the American Revolution – a shared national experience that served a political need for strength and unity. But, of course, those symbols did not remain constant, since memory serves needs of the changing present. Barry Schwartz traced what he called the "democratization of George Washington" between 1800 and 1865 and found that early recollections of Washington stressed his remoteness and "flawless virtue," while later memories reflected a hero worthy of a more egalitarian nation, showing Washington as "an imperfect man with whom common people could identify."[65] So, although Washington had not changed, the way he was remembered did. Thus, an obituary for Washington would be instructive in Washington's era, but subsequent obituaries that linked everyday citizens with Washington's memory would serve the needs of that particular generation. Later, the pioneer adventurer competed with Washington as a new cultural symbol, while the Industrial Revolution brought still more icons.

The Jacksonian Era

It is important to consider issues of inclusion when examining obituaries published in mainstream news media of any era. Not everyone's death was reported nor everyone's life remembered. And even among those commemorated, not every attribute or accomplishment was recorded for posterity. That is why for my book *Obituaries in American Culture*, the sample of more than 8,000 obituaries was gathered at turning points when the United States was becoming more inclusive; when more people were allowed into the political franchise by being given the right to vote. During the Jacksonian era, the political process became more open, with increased suffrage for white men, including the elimination of many voting restrictions, and the emergence of campaign techniques designed to win

---

[65] Barry Schwartz, "Social Change and Collective Memory: The Democratization of George Washington," *American Sociological Review* 56, no. 2 (1991): 221.

the support of new voters.⁶⁶ For this era, 658 obituaries published in two major news publications (*Niles' Weekly Register* and the *Daily National Intelligencer*) 10 years before and after Andrew Jackson's 1828 election to the presidency were examined.

In 1818, an erroneous notice of one American icon's death hints at the link between obituaries and heroic memory. The hero Daniel Boone supposedly "breathed out his last" in a deer lick "with gun in hand just in the act of firing," with the obituary noting that, "As he lived so he died."⁶⁷ Later, the periodical retracted the obituary, calling it a "fabrication," and then published an explanation, saying it was "probably framed for the purpose of introducing the fanciful incident of the heroic woodsman."⁶⁸ Daniel Boone, an extraordinary man, should not die an ordinary death.

Memories of other citizens not as famous as Boone also served as public examples of a worthy life, and a type of guide to achieve one. The *National Intelligencer's* obituary for the industrious, kind, and amiable lawyer, James B. Lane, said, "May his life be an example, and his death prove a warning voice, to the young, the thoughtless, the gay, and the dissipated."⁶⁹

In 1818, *Niles Weekly Register* published obituaries for thirty-eight men (88 percent) and five women (12 percent), while the *National Intelligencer* published obituaries for 143 men (73 percent), forty-seven women (24 percent), and seven children (3 percent). Military service was by far the most prominent occupation for men, but other occupations included doctors, ministers, a mason, a bank cashier, a surgeon's mate, merchants, academics, a newspaper editor, a printer, a museum proprietor, and planters. Neither publication listed occupations outside the home for women, who were nearly always identified by their associations with husbands, fathers, sons, or brothers. Scholars have pointed out that some women of the era were partners or assistants in their family businesses, others ran preindustrial cottage-based industries, and still others were teachers.⁷⁰ Were

---

66 Robert V. Remini, *Andrew Jackson and the Course of American Democracy, 1833–1845*, Vol. 3 (New York: Harper and Row, 1984), 6.
67 "Death of Col. Daniel Boone," *Niles Weekly Register*, September 19, 1818, 64.
68 "Chronicle," *Niles' Weekly Register*, November 7, 1818, 176; "Col. Boone," *Niles' Weekly Register*, December 26, 1818, 328.
69 "James B. Lane," *National Intelligencer*, August 27, 1818, 3.
70 Among the many discussions of early-nineteenth-century women and work are Mary P. Ryan, *The Cradle of the Middle Class: The family in Oneida County*, New York, 1790–1865 (New York: Cambridge University Press, 1981), 172–173; and Thomas Dublin, *Women at Work* (New York: Columbia University Press, 1979).

the women who died in 1818 not employed, or were their occupations simply not worth remembering publicly in a published obituary?

Participation in the American Revolution, still part of the remembered American national experience in 1818, was listed in half the male obituaries in the *Register* and in twenty-eight of the *Intelligencer's* death notices. Revolutionary service was mentioned more frequently than religious affiliation, and sometimes was the only attribute listed. Eight men were called heroes because of their service. In the obituary of patriot David Humphries, "one of the best men that ever lived," the *Register* lamented that in a few years there would be no revolutionary patriots left for posthumous notice: "Still the consolation is left that so many have lived to see such glorious fruits from their toils, privations and hazards, and to behold their country rapidly getting the bone of manhood, respected abroad, and happy at home, beyond any other on the globe."[71] Any kind of association with George Washington was worthy of mention in 1818. Benjamin Walker was listed as an aide-de-camp and friend to Washington, and, as Walker's obituary stated, that relationship was "epitaph enough. Would you add more?"[72]

The pioneer-adventurer was another important icon in the nineteenth century, as several obituaries reflected. Perhaps the most prominent example was the one for General George Rogers Clark, called in both publications the "Father of the Western Country." As the *National Intelligencer* wrote: "With his little band of Spartans he is seen piercing the gloom of the sequestered forests, illuminating them in quick succession with the splendor of his victories and early inviting his countrymen to a residence his courage and skill purchased for them."[73] Both publications also printed an obituary for a man whose first name was unknown but who fit the "adventurer" mold. A "Mr. _____ Lilly," said to have died at the advanced age of 115, was compared with Boone and described as a settler who supported himself through hunting "chiefly by his gun." And as both obituaries noted, "It is worthy of remark that this very old man never owned or had a bed in his house."[74] For these publications, Lilly's worth as

---

71 "General David Humphries," *Niles' Weekly Register,* February 28, 1818, 15.
72 "Benjamin Walker," *National Intelligencer,* January 23, 1818, 3.
73 "George Rogers Clark," *National Intelligencer,* March 12, 1818, 3.
74 "Longevity," *Niles Weekly Register,* February 28, 1919, 16; "Longevity," *National Intelligencer,* February 1, 1818, 15.

a symbol of a woodsman, of a frontier figure, and of longevity were more important for his obituary than was an accurate record of his name. Personal attributes most often listed in male obituaries were associated with nation building (patriotism, bravery, gallantry, vigilance, boldness, merit as an officer) or with service (honesty, skill, industry, devotion to duty, public esteem, ardor, integrity, good sense, and zeal). Some, though fewer in number, were associated with relationships, including hospitality, benevolence, kindness, and gentlemanly deportment. Only rarely were attributes of a good father and husband mentioned.

Former first lady, Abigail Adams, was the only well-known woman whose death was recorded in these two newspapers. Remembered in 1818 for her association with her husband and father, she also "had a distinct view of public men and measures and had her own judgment upon them, which she was free to disclose to her friends but not eager to defend in public circles."[75] However, most women were not remembered for their vigor or their political views. Rather, they were described as patient, resigned, obedient, affectionate, amiable, pious, gentle, virtuous, intelligent, educated, tender, innocent, and useful. Women were much more likely than men to be described in terms of Christian sentiments and innocence. The obituary for Sarah English serves as a good example of those published for women in 1818. Mrs. English was "as intelligent as she was good. Not at all ambitious of worldly show, she chose to be useful rather than gay. Her domestic concerns were managed with the most admirable economy exhibiting at the same time a degree of comfort and neatness not to be surpassed – that she might give greater extensiveness to her labors of charity."[76]

Obituary coverage of Americans in the mainstream press did become more egalitarian in the twenty years surrounding Jackson's election to the presidency. Although women still were likely to be included in 1838 based on their associations with men, their numbers did increase by 13 percent. More men, too, were commemorated in 1838 without having been military heroes or known public servants. However, this new inclusiveness did not benefit Native Americans or African Americans. If members of these groups were remembered at all, it was for their subjection to the dominant culture. Attributes of women also changed. They became less obedient and

---

[75] "The Late Mrs. Adams," *Niles Weekly Register*, November 14, 1818, 200; "The Late Madam Adams," *National Intelligencer*, November 7, 1818, 2.
[76] "Sarah English," *National Intelligencer*, September 22, 1818, 3.

more admirable, as was nineteen-year-old Mary Rose, who "left an impression neither time nor circumstance could efface."⁷⁷ Women were sometimes described for their intelligence, dignity, and benevolence, but, just as in 1818, they were also praised for modesty, piety, and their unobtrusive nature. One woman's obituary lamented the brevity of life, but also encapsulated the admirable woman's cultural role: "Within the short period of a year she was a bride, a beloved wife and companion, a mother, a corpse! 'Early bright, transient, chaste as morning dew. She sparkled, was exhal'd, and went to heaven.'"⁷⁸

The Civil War

The Civil War was the most dramatic event of the nineteenth century and arguably remains one of the most important cultural and political influences in American history. America emerged from the war not merely as a confederation of states but as a nation with a strong central government, and powerful roots in the industrial era. In the mid-nineteenth century, the right to vote was increasingly linked with the rights of the citizen, and the Civil War not only incorporated the African American male into the political culture, but also "introduced two new concepts into constitutional law: the principles of national citizenship and equal protection under the law."⁷⁹ And though it would be 1920 before women's suffrage was constitutionally secured, the Civil War era rhetoric emphasizing citizen rights helped inspire the postwar movement for women's rights.⁸⁰

Drawing from sample years before and after the Civil War, 1855 and 1870, 3,670 obituaries in major regional newspapers were examined. Included were obituaries published in the first week of each month in the *New York Daily Times*, the *New Orleans Picayune*, and the *Baltimore Sun*. In 1855, only 8 percent of news obituaries published in the *New York Daily*

---

77 "Mary Rose," *Daily National Intelligencer*, July 8, 1838, 3.
78 "Emeline Elizabeth Morgan," *Daily National Intelligencer*, May 5, 1838, 3.
79 Donald W. Rogers, "Introduction – the Right to Vote in American History," *Voting and the Spirit of American Democracy: Essays on the History of Voting Rights in America*, ed. Donald W. Rogers (Chicago: University of Chicago Press, 1991), 10.
80 Ibid., 11.

Times were for women, while 34 percent of death notices were for adult women. In the *Picayune*, 6 percent of news obituaries recalled women's lives, and 25 percent of death notices were for adult women. Finally, in the border city of Baltimore, 14 percent of news obituaries were for women, and 30 percent of death notices were published in the *Sun*.

Participation in the American Revolution was still worthy of notice in 1855, as was any connection with Washington and the founders of the nation. For example, Conrad Bush, despite the fact that he lived to be 102, was noted just for his service in the Revolution, his "personal acquaintance" with Washington, and the fact that he lived on land "received from the Government for services rendered his country during the war."[81] Elderly Mary Channell was eulogized on the front page of the New Orleans newspaper simply for being, as a child, "one of the choir of singers that welcomed Gen. Washington upon his visit to Boston."[82] Peter Van Antwerp was remembered because he had cast "his first vote for Jefferson." In short, the worth of these everyday citizens' lives was their connections to the Founders.

Men's occupations were in military, business, public service, and religious work and reflect a growing emphasis on technology. They included clergymen, merchants, judges, military officers and infantrymen, manufacturers, newspaper editors, railroad engineers, attorneys, craftsmen, and legislators. Women were noted for being wives or daughters.

Newspapers in 1855 were likely to list both public and private attributes of men in their obituaries. Those published public virtues assured readers that the deceased man was highly esteemed, active, intelligent, scholarly, manly, gallant, courteous, of strong character, just, honorable, religious (Christian), generous, vigorous, and patriotic. He also possessed oratory skills. His more private attributes were modesty, gentleness, integrity, usefulness, hospitality, and faithfulness. Southern men were more likely to be recalled as "true gentlemen" and less likely to be noted for patriotism. Characteristics of women portrayed in obituaries from 1855 were decidedly different from men. Women were remembered for being Christian, gentle, kind, amiable, loving, pious, obliging, honest, faithful, beautiful, talented, warm, and happy.

Obituaries became a bit more inclusive after the Civil War, although most people commemorated in 1870 were still upper and middle class.

---

81 "Death of a Veteran – Conrad Bush," *New York Daily Times*, June 2, 1855, 5.
82 "Death of a Venerable Lady," *New Orleans Picayune*, March 1, 1855, 1.

More women were remembered, and business attributes gained in importance for men, as did qualities attainable by everyman, such as honesty, industry, generosity, energy, and kindness. Women were still remembered for their associations with men, and for being gentle and nurturing. However, after the war, each newspaper included a scant few obituaries of women because of their professions, indicating a small step toward the inclusion of women in the world outside the home. Examples included physician and women's suffrage activist Charlotte Lozier and author Anna Cora Mowatt Ritchie.[83]

Occasionally, a woman of color was recalled because she died in an unusual way, because she lived for a long time, or because she provided an example of submission to the dominant culture. Victorie Simon Mercier, "a colored woman" had, according to her obituary, "reached the patriarchal [sic] age of 111 years. ... She remained active and sensible to the last. On Friday last she walked a distance of three squares."[84] In Baltimore, Dolly Robinson, "a colored woman," was remembered for her loyalty to her mistress in Syracuse, New York: "The most remarkable feature of her character was her resolute persistence in maintaining the same relations to her mistress as she held to her Virginia master; so that in spite of the laws of New York ... in the very dust and smoke of the underground railroad, she lived and died in the property of our most excellent and benevolent lady friend."[85]

A New Century

As the United States moved from the nineteenth century to the twentieth, the nation's social structures shifted, affecting the lives and the character of citizens. By the end of the 1920s, Americans had changed spiritually, culturally, economically, and politically. The new century ushered in a more consumptive and less religious America, and with it came a dramatic, substantive change in the democracy. Seventy-two years after women

---

83 "Death of Dr. Charlotte Lozier," *New York Times*, December 5, 1870, 5; "Funeral of Mrs. Dr. Lozier," *New York Times*, January 6, 1870, 5; "Death of Anna Cora Mowatt Ritchie," *Baltimore Sun*, August 1, 1870, 2.

84 "Longevity," *New Orleans Picayune*, October 3, 1855, 2.

85 "Death of a Slave in Syracuse," *Baltimore Sun*, April 2, 1855, 1.

gathered at Seneca Falls, New York, to hear radical calls for women's property rights and suffrage, ratification of the Nineteenth Amendment in 1920 finally affirmed women's right to vote. With the advent of the industrial age and the suffrage movement, women in the 1920s embraced new ideas about their public behavior. But T. J. Jackson Lears argues that women's domestic roles were still the most prominent. He notes that women became the target of advertisers who described their products, i.e. household goods, as deliverers not only of an ordered life, but also of "authentic experience."[86]

For this era, 4,163 obituaries published in the *New York Times, Chicago Tribune,* and *San Francisco Chronicle* during the first week of each month in 1910 and 1930 were examined. In 1910, women represented only 15 percent of the *Times* news obituaries, 18 percent in the *Tribune* and 18 percent in the *Chronicle*.

Obituaries in 1910 reflected a culture that valued men, money, and industry. Most women were identified by associations with husbands, fathers, brothers, or sons. Upon death, these women were commemorated less for their own personal attributes than for their husbands' business accomplishments. Elizabeth Schack, for example, was remembered for being the widow of Otto Wilhelm Christian Schack, former secretary of the New York Stock Exchange, and for being the daughter-in-law of a member of a private stock-exchange firm.[87] Another woman's male association was more distant. As her obituary noted, "Mrs. Albert E. Plant, whose husband is the first cousin of the late Henry B. Plant, the railroad and steamship owner, was killed this morning by the express train from New York City."[88]

Unlike nineteenth-century obituaries, notices in 1910 did not describe a deceased woman as gentle, kind, obliging, honest, or faithful. In fact, the articles seldom listed character traits at all. Rather, women were described as "well known," "prominent," or "wealthy." An exception was in the *San Francisco Chronicle*, when many women were remembered for their pioneer spirit. A few women in each newspaper were remembered for being

---

[86] For a discussion of these turn-of-the-century changes, see T. J. Jackson Lears, "Roots of Antimodernism: The Crisis of Cultural Authority during the Late Nineteenth Century," in his *No Place of Grace: Antimodernism and the Transformation of American Culture, 1880–1920* (Chicago: University of Chicago Press), 4–58.
[87] "Elizabeth Inez McCarty Schack," *New York Times*, March 7, 1910, 9.
[88] "Mrs. A. E. Plant Killed," *New York Times*, Sept. 5, 1919, 1.

educators, nurses, authors, and for their philanthropic and temperance work.

What about the occupations and attributes of men who died in 1910? Obituaries in all three newspapers offered stark gender contrast. Men were commemorated for their hard work, wealth, power, education, and memberships in male associations and fraternal organizations. The fact most often listed for men in 1910 was the number of years worked. Hundreds of occupations were listed, including company founders, bank presidents, industrialists or manufacturers, wealthy merchants, brokers, or powerful political figures.

Just as with women in 1910, character traits for men were seldom mentioned, but were implied based on long lists of professional accomplishments and associations. For example, a work ethic and loyalty to employers were valued: a large number of obituaries described men who had spent ten to fifty years in the same profession, even with the same company. Many men were retired, but their obituaries assured readers that they labored right up until their health failed. Eighty-two-year old Joshua Crosby remained at work until the Saturday before he died.[89] Professor Samuel Sanford, "worth several million dollars," worked "from sheer enjoyment."[90]

Twenty years later, a decade after the Nineteenth Amendment secured women the right to vote, women's obituaries made up only 18 percent of those published in the New York Times and 17 percent in the Chicago Tribune. The *San Francisco Chronicle's* numbers were higher at 32 percent. However, the substance of those obituaries had changed significantly. More working women were represented, and not just the familiar educator, author, or nurse. Obituaries recalled a female racehorse trainer, owner of a confectionary manufacturing company, and assistant chief of a microanalytical laboratory at the Department of Agriculture's Bureau of Chemistry, and many others. A number of women were remembered for their political influence and reform efforts in health, labor, women's rights, and social causes. Wealth was still an important attribute, but women in 1930 were remembered more for charity and philanthropy, for giving their money away.

For men in 1930, at the beginning of what would be a long Great Depression, the attribute listed most often was the number of years spent

---

89 "Captain Joshua W. Crosby," *New York Times*, April 7, 1910, 11.
90 "Samuel S. Sanford Dead," *New York Times*, January 7, 1910, 9.

at work, even at a particular corporation, including long lists of career promotions and appointments. Many were company founders or held upper-management positions, and they were described often as "prominent" or "well known." They, too, were known for their philanthropy. In 1930, newspapers also highlighted a man's ingenuity; perhaps a reflection of increasingly desperate financial times. A number of men were remembered as inventors. A few African Americans were remembered in the 1930s for their own accomplishments rather than for longevity, a unique cause of death, or a connection with a patriotic symbol, including a pastor, an attorney, and a politician.

For women, links with historical memory included family lineage with male icons such as Abraham Lincoln, the Marquis de Lafayette, Thomas Jefferson, Daniel Boone, and George Washington. One woman was remembered for being a "pioneer woman," but also for being the granddaughter of an officer in Washington's army. Membership in the Daughters of the American Revolution, a society for women who could trace their ancestry back to revolutionary days, was often included. Connections with historical memory also included participation in shared American experiences, such as wars, the Gold Rush of 1849, and westward expansion with references to the routes or trails they had taken.

Newspapers highlighted men for their associations with Buffalo Bill Cody, General George Armstrong Custer, General William Tecumseh Sherman, General Robert E. Lee, and Mayflower pilgrims. In *The San Francisco Chronicle*, the descriptor "pioneer" was used repeatedly in men's obituaries, including pioneer residents, a pioneer clothier, pioneer harness maker, and pioneer banker. A link with a patriotic symbol could warrant inclusion of an African American. For example, Moses Webb was described in the Chicago Tribune as "an old negro who is said to have been the last survivor of the eight 'contrabands' who led the horses attached to the hearse at the funeral of Abraham Lincoln. ... Webb was born a slave in 1825."[91]

---

91 "Lincoln Funeral Aid Dies," *Chicago Tribune*, December 2, 1910, 8.

Conclusion

Throughout American history it has been extraordinarily difficult for an ordinary woman to achieve the status of hero, or to be known publicly by name for an act of heroism. The press, as a reflector of cultural values, shares at least partial responsibility for this, while offering a unique window into the nation's gender divide. Male heroes were remembered for feats that were active, public, and nationalist, being most often connected with the nation's founding, subsequent wars, westward expansion, and industrialization.[92] As methods of journalistic storytelling evolved, those male heroes became more egalitarian, more "everyman," and their stories were told to mass audiences. Women's lives were deemed less worthy of commemoration. They were valued for attributes that would not measure up to a mainstream definition of male heroism. The ideal woman was patient, resigned, and obedient in the nineteenth century and a community housekeeper through the mid-twentieth century. Like Mrs. Sarah English in 1818, she was "not ambitious of worldly show." Occasionally a woman would break the established pattern. The Georgia Revolutionary War heroine Nancy Hart, for example, was part of the foundational American story. Yet even her story was colored by the era's cultural expectations for women. Carry Nation stepped out of her prescribed role and became a type of cartoon character, criticized for her unfeminine ways and called a "fat old heroine."

A woman's "genius" was celebrated in the nineteenth century when it helped her fulfill important duties at home. Scholars have noted how female participation in the Revolution, and the memory of it, influenced generations of American women to become "republican mothers" – women whose patriotic duty was to teach their sons to be good citizens. This idea has been credited with inspiring women's education even while relegating them to the home.[93] Intellect was not valued as a heroic female characteristic in the 1950s. Heroines were girls-next-door who became wives, mothers, and nurturers of their communities. They comforted a society longing for safety as the nation came to grips with the Cold War.

---

92 Winfield and Hume, "The Continuous Past," 155.

93 For a discussion of the idea of Republican motherhood, see Linda Kerber, *Women of the Republic: Intellect and Ideology in Revolutionary America* (Chapel Hill: University of North Carolina Press, 1980); Mary Beth Norton, *Liberty's Daughters: The Revolutionary Experience of American women, 1750–1800* (Boston: Little, Brown, 1996).

Men, back from service in World War II, had returned to the private work force and, thanks to the G.I. Bill, back into the college classroom. The economy had shifted from a wartime emphasis to that of domestic production, and advertisements for household goods peppered the pages of American magazines. The American wife and mother was an important consumer of household products. She reflected the nation's hope for safety and prosperity.

If heroines were scarce, how did the "ideal" American woman serve as a role model? One way was through her newspaper obituary which often reinforced the nation's gender divide. What was worthy of remembering about a woman in death was decidedly different from that of a man, and the ideal female attributes would not serve to lift a woman onto a heroic pedestal. Often, women were not remembered by name in their own obituaries, but rather by relationships with husbands, fathers, and sons.

Were newspapers and magazines hero makers? They did amplify and magnify stories of heroism, but only as far as mainstream culture allowed. They legitimized rigid gender roles that kept most women out of the public sphere, and skewed the image of those women who did venture outside the home. History and memory construct identity, and they also enable hegemony.

These findings, of course, reflect a point of view of the dominant culture. The American press included many more voices than just that of the mainstream. The African-American press, and newspapers and magazines published by abolitionists, suffragists, and radicals likely had different notions of the value of the individual life and the definition of an everyday American heroine. Much more work needs to be done to bring those different stories to light.

Heroic Ordinariness after Cavell and Capra: Hollywood Cinema and Everyday Heroism in the Interwar Period and World War II

Matthias Grotkopp

The Hero as the Ordinary

The hero, so the idiom goes, comes to save the day. But what is that "day"? Does it not mean the "everyday," the lives and livelihood of unheroic ordinary men and women? And does this not imply that the hero has to come again and again in order for "the day" to be saved? By this logic, the coming of the hero itself turns out to be an everyday occurrence; turns out to be ordinary.

What may sound like a short Kafkaesque parable concisely describes the specific turn that I want to give the discussion of the "everyday hero." The aim is to describe the heroic and the everyday neither as the mutually exclusive terms some might take them to be, nor as a simple resolvable dialectic. Rather, they have to be regarded as irresolvable but equally indispensable antinomies of democracy and modern life – just like the antinomies of consensus and disagreement, of freedom and security, or of freedom and equality.[1]

My goal is to formulate an idea of the importance of the ordinary as a "heroic ordinariness." In order to do this, I want to present a short analysis of a film by Frank Capra: *Meet John Doe* (USA 1941).[2] This film is part of a series of films by Capra that are not only films with heroes in the sense of protagonists, or films about heroes, but films about the making and the unmaking of a specific kind of ordinary hero. A central reference point for me is Stanley Cavell's philosophy of moral perfectionism and the way he formulates the task to rediscover the ordinary as a meaningful space of

---

1 See Oliver Hidalgo, *Die Antinomien der Demokratie* (Frankfurt: Campus, 2014).
2 *Meet John Doe*, directed by Frank Capra (1941; Burbank, CA: Frank Capra Productions / Warner Bros., VCI Video Collection International, 2011), DVD.

public and political action.[3] The following disclaimer should therefore not be a surprise: I will not concern myself with heroism as the doing of exciting, extra-ordinary deeds like saving lives by risking one's own life. John Price and others have investigated this kind of heroism in fine-grained analyses of rewards, medals, memorials and other measures of public appreciation for death-defying courage. Price, for instance, defines everyday heroism as "acts of life-risking bravery, undertaken by otherwise ordinary individuals, largely in the course of their daily lives and within quotidian surroundings."[4]

The striking insight these studies provide is that the public recognition of this kind of action, and therefore their very existence as a valid category of human action, has emerged only recently; that is, in the course of the nineteenth century. That is why it would be wrong to try to integrate this phenomenon into an a-historical, universal definition of heroism per se.[5] And this certainly has to mean that the conditions that make this understanding of everyday heroism perceptible and meaningful are related to broader historical shifts in the cultural, social, and political discourses, as well as to shifts in media technologies, media practices, and poetics.[6] It is to these underlying conditions at a very specific time and place upon which I will focus. My working definition for everyday heroism, or – in order to maintain this distinction for the moment – heroic ordinariness, would be the service to a moral ideal of everyday life, the defense of this moral ideal against dangers from the outside, as well as from its very own antinomies, and its predisposition to corruption. What is important to me is that this

---

[3] Stanley Cavell, *Cities of Words: Pedagogical Letters on a Register of the Moral Life* (Cambridge, MA: Harvard University Press, 2004); Andrew Norris, ed., *The Claim to Community: Essays on Stanley Cavell and Political Philosophy* (Stanford: Stanford University Press, 2006).

[4] John Price: *Everyday Heroism: Victorian Constructions of the Heroic Civilian* (London: Bloomsbury, 2014), 2.

[5] Silke Meyer, "Helden des Alltags: Von der Transformation des Besonderen," in *Die Helden-Maschine: Zur Aktualität und Tradition von Heldenbildern*, ed. LWL-Industriemuseum (Essen: Klartext-Verlag, 2010), 33.

[6] Lance Strate, "Heroes and/as Communication," in *Heroes in a Global World*, ed. Susan J. Drucker and Gary Gumpert (Cresskill, NJ: Hampton Press, 2008), 26. Strate claims that "the most dramatic shifts in conceptions of the hero have been associated with innovations in communication such as the invention of writing and printing, and the development of the electronic media." Strate applies this idea to long-term historical shifts like the transition from mythic to historical heroes and to the contemporary celebrity cult, but one can also use it as a searchlight for changes and differentiations on shorter time spans.

service does not happen in contrast to everyday life – like the idea of heroism as the exceptional implies – but has to be embedded in it.

There is a little diabolical question that immediately shows how the two phenomena are connected: "Why has saving lives in itself become publicly praiseworthy?" And I think that this question can only be perceived as scandalous or even oddly ridiculous in a secular context in which political community is not based on mythical origins, ethnic essentialisms, or doctrines, but on "life, liberty and the pursuit of happiness"[7] for each and everyone, everyday. Heroic ordinariness would be a specific kind of everyday heroism that is positioned on the extreme end of the scale of what counts as "action," making it less about corporeal agency and more about service to a sense of commonality.[8]

If every form of heroism is a cultural mode of communication[9] or address, then one needs to ask: What does this kind of everyday hero communicate, what problems does he address, and what is it that he makes thinkable? My proposition is that he makes us aware of those dangers to democracy, freedom, and everyday life that come from their very own conditions. He makes us aware of the way that the institutions of democracy – commerce, media, political parties, law, freedom of speech and of art, and so on – have in themselves tendencies or possibilities to subvert democracy, and that the everyday is not a realm of mindless repetition from which extraordinary actions stand out, but that it is the realm in which democracy and freedom have to be won, have to be deserved, again and again and again.

The United States in the 1930s: Heroism, Democracy, and the Age of Mass Media

This leads me to the specific context and object of my study: A series of films by Frank Capra from the 1930s and their inquiry into the condition

---

7 Thomas Jefferson et al., *The Declaration of Independence*, 1776, National Archives and Records Administration, http://www.archives.gov/exhibits/charters/declaration_transcript.html.

8 Selwyn W. Becker and Alice H. Eagly, "The Heroism of Women and Men," *American Psychologist* 59, no. 3 (2004): 163–178.

9 Strate, "Heroes and/as Communication," 19– 45.

of democracy. There were a lot of factors for the way heroism in particular, and political subjectivity in general, changed in the United States of America between the two World Wars.[10] These years were a critical time for the nation's self-understanding as a democracy; from the Red Scare, to the economic crisis, and the New Deal. Not only the idea of an inherent connection between technological progress and democracy was questioned, but also the role of mass media and mass entertainment in a democratic public sphere was reconsidered.

In the context of these uncertainties, it became equally questionable how far hero-worship in the classic sense – that means a worship of the military and political leaders like George Washington and Abraham Lincoln – could still be consistent with democracy and a valid form of expressing social and political values. For instance, the historian, Dixon Wecter tried to defend this tradition in his 1941 book, "The Hero in America,"[11] by claiming that these American heroes were chosen by the people rather than by an elite and that they had certain qualities that made them more common and less extraordinary.[12] The achievements of American heroes were a question of character and attainability "open to everyman's comprehension."[13]

However, Wecter also observed with concern that not only American democrats but also Fascism and Communism used the idea of the common man as a heroic type. If the everyday hero, the idealization of ordinary men and women could be seen as something that seems inherently democratic, it could also be misused to undermine democracy, when the common man became "the collective ideal of the little man."[14] The hero-tyrant dressed up in plain clothes or the uniform of the foot soldier embodied not an invitation to self-realization and acknowledgement of the everyday but, rather, the invitation to give up individuality: "He is the triumphant sublimation of a million inferiority complexes."[15] Here the "everyday hero" intersects with another prominent figure of the political imagination of the early twentieth century: the masses. Wecter

---

10 On the idea of a social equalization of heroism through the fallen troops of the First World War, see Meyer, "Helden des Alltags," 34.
11 Dixon Wecter, *The Hero in America: A Chronicle of Hero-Worship* (New York: Scribner, 1941).
12 Wecter, *The Hero in America*, 11.
13 Ibid., 486.
14 Ibid., 7.
15 Ibid.

concluded his typology of American heroes with a double warning. First, he cautioned against the growing sense of disillusionment and cynicism; of anti-heroism. But, at the same time, he remained suspicious of the way heroes are made in the modern age: "Above all others, newspapers and newsreel and radio and the mechanisms of ovation have such power in making or breaking the idol of the moment, that fresh irony has been given to the old saying, 'Heroes are not born but made.'"[16]

This brings me to an important aspect of the context I am concerned with: the critical condition of democracy and the media as it has been discussed in the 1920s and 1930s. Nowhere has this crisis been as tangible as in the so-called Lippmann-Dewey-Debate. While I will not go into the details of that debate[17] – which was far less antagonistic than some accounts suggests – I want to quickly show where it connects to the question of heroism and everydayness. The disagreement between Walther Lippmann and John Dewey, formulated by the first in his books *Public Opinion* (1922)[18] and *The Phantom Public* (1925)[19] and by the latter in his response *The Public and its Problems*, written in 1927,[20] can be summed up in these questions: If the masses are so susceptible by the media, how do you achieve a democratic public that is aware of its own interests? Is the ideal of a participatory democracy unrealistic? And should one instead rely on experts in government to solve the nation's problems and on experts in the media to communicate these decisions? If so, how do you then make the government and the media responsive to the general public?

The problem was less whether experts for the complexity of economic, social, and diplomatic affairs were necessary, but, rather, how to keep their activity legitimate. In other words, how do you make sure that experts remain experts of the everyday?

Whereas Lippmann took this latter problem to be a second-order question regarding the overall necessity of an expert-led democracy, it was Dewey's main concern. He struggled with ways to make ordinary people experts of their own needs and positions: not by sticking to the Enlightenment ideal of the universally informed citizen since this was

---

16 Ibid., 488.
17 Sue Curry Jansen, "Phantom Conflict: Lippmann, Dewey, and the Fate of the Public in Modern Society," *Communication & Critical/Cultural Studies* 6, no. 3 (2009): 221– 245.
18 Walter Lippmann, *Public Opinion* (New York: Harcourt, Brace and Co., 1922).
19 Walter Lippmann, *The Phantom Public* (New York: Harcourt, Brace and Co., 1925).
20 John Dewey, *The Public and its Problems* (New York: Holt and Company, 1927).

prevented by the quantity of information, the new quality of social and political complexities, and the sheer plurality of publics, but by instilling the right attitudes and habits in order to stop the descent into political apathy. According to Dewey, this was "the primary problem of the public: to achieve such recognition of itself as will give it weight in the selection of official representatives and in the definition of their responsibilities and rights."[21]

But then again, the means of this education are themselves open to grave abuse. According to Benjamin, the arts as an *education sentimental* of the public can just as easily be transformed into a totalitarian aestheticization of politics.[22] And this was precisely what Lippmann and Dewey were both concerned about yet drew different conclusions from. As Dewey noted: "The same forces which have brought about the forms of democratic government ... have also brought about conditions which halt the social and humane ideals that demand the utilization of government as the genuine instrumentality of an inclusive and fraternally associated public."[23] Indeed, this is the common thread that connects this debate and the figure of the everyday hero as he is presented in Capra's films: They are reactions to the historical experience of a close encounter between democracy and totalitarianism at a moment when state propaganda and a tendency towards fascism seemed to become a viable option.

Frank Capra's Heroes (out) of the Ordinary

The films in question are *Mr. Deeds Goes to Town* (USA 1936), *Mr. Smith Goes to Washington* (USA 1939), and *Meet John Doe* (1941), even though I will base my argument mainly on the last one. While one could include other films by Frank Capra in order to highlight the same reoccurring principle ideas and conflicts, these three form a cohesive trilogy. On the surface, these films are simple fairytales about innocent, common men who are used and misused by a corrupt elite, but then achieve self-awareness and triumph over evil. They are exemplary of Hollywood's portrayal of politics

---

21 Ibid., 77.
22 See Walter Benjamin, *The Work of Art in the Age of Mechanical Reproduction* (London: Penguin, 2008 [1936]).
23 Dewey, *The Public and its Problems*, 109.

as a struggle for personal integrity and for the reconciliation of the public and the private spheres.[24] And even though ideological critique may ridicule this conflation, these films make politics matter for their audience; they make palpable "that there was a right way, or at least a livable way, to conduct political life."[25] In this sense, one has to allow for the rhetorical pathos of a series of films that was explicitly meant to strengthen the movie-going public against the temptations of fascism.

Viewed as such, they become much more complex than escapist sentimentalism: They are explorations of modes to publicly express "America" and democracy.[26] The three films investigate the way the life of ordinary American citizens can be endangered by their society's own institutions and conditions. The institutions of law and the practices of juridical, social, and aesthetic judgment are the primary concern of *Mr. Deeds Goes to Town*; professional politics and the question of representation is at the center of *Mr. Smith Goes to Washington*; while *Meet John Doe* focused on the media industry and the controllability of seemingly grassroots movements.

The beginning of *Meet John Doe* immediately interweaves the question of media power and the – today one would say precarious – working conditions of ordinary people: Barbara Stanwyck plays Ann Mitchell, a journalist who loses her job after D. B. Norton (Edward Arnold), a rich man with political ambitions, bought the newspaper for which she was working. As a final act of defiance, in her last piece for the paper she fakes a letter from an anonymous unemployed man, John Doe, who announces that he would commit suicide on Christmas Eve out of protest against the state of civilization. Because of the strong reactions to this fake letter, she and her editor (James Gleason) have to produce a face and a body for this fictional character, and choose the unemployed baseball player, Long John Willoughby (Gary Cooper).

For different reasons, the journalist, her editor, and the owner of the paper all want to make the most out of the attention this "letter of intent" has created. This culminates in a speech on the Radio, written by Mitchell,

---

24 Harry Keyishian, "Heroes in American Political Film," in *The Hero in Transition*, ed. Ray B. Browne and Marshall W. Fishwick (Bowling Green, OH: Bowling Green University Popular Press, 1983), 219– 220.
25 Ibid., 227.
26 Raymond Carney, *American Vision: The Films of Frank Capra* (Cambridge: Cambridge University Press), 281– 282.

and held by Long John, who in the process of reading this speech "becomes" the character "John Doe" invented by the words. Across the country, spontaneous "John Doe Clubs" emerge, in order to promote neighborly values. This again prompts the tycoon to use these clubs as a base for his political ambitions of forming a fascist dictatorship. When he is made aware of being "mixed up with skunks," Long John wants to use one of his public appearances to denounce the whole thing, but is silenced and exposed as a fake. As a result, when Christmas arrives, "John Doe" wants to fulfill his promise (which he never made) and commit suicide, but he is stopped by Mitchell, who has fallen in love with him, and by a group of faithful John Does.

The central objective of the film, as most critics and scholars see it, is the parallel creation of the figuration "John Doe" as a hero and the (re-) creation of Gary Cooper as the star of this film.[27] This is nowhere as apparent and openly acknowledged by the film than in the scene of the big radio broadcast at its center (0h 39m 45s – 0h 52m 27s). While preparing backstage, Mitchell tells Long John that his task is to think of himself as "the real John Doe." She uses the word "real," even though it is clear that he does not exist (although a previous scene showed her character referring to her deceased father as a kind of co-author of her speech). What therefore seems absurd is, on the other hand, the ordinary business of "actors": Barbara Stanwyck is simply giving acting instructions to her colleague Gary Cooper. She asks him to do what he normally does: play a fictional character. Not only does this hint at the fictional and performative nature of heroism, which is not only achieved by the hero but imposed on him by his environment.[28] One could also claim that this shows how becoming someone – impersonating an identity – is something that is within the realm of what everybody does all the time, and that, therefore, becoming a hero is also an attainable kind of identity performance.

The act of reading the script is then not only filmed as the process in which the character Long John becomes more and more at ease with reading the script the journalist wrote for him, but also as the process in

---

27 Ibid., 347.
28 See Stanley Cavell, "North by Northwest," in *Cavell on Film*, ed. William Rothman (Albany: State University of New York Press, 2005 [1981]) 43. Cavell writes about another actor (Cary Grant) and another film (*North by Northwest*) but the structure he describes can be applied to a lot of films that are self-conscious about the relationship between stars and their roles.

which Gary Cooper more and more acts like Gary Cooper – the top-earning movie star of his time who starred as 'Wild Bill Hickok' in *The Plainsman* (dir: Cecil B. DeMille, USA 1936), or as a multi-millionaire womanizer in *Bluebeard's Eighth Wife* (dir: Ernst Lubitsch, USA 1938), and who won an Oscar as best actor the same year for his role as the war hero *Sergeant York* (dir.: Howard Hawks, USA 1941). Historically speaking, one could claim that the choice of Cooper – who was mostly known for his roles in Westerns – further demonstrates that heroism of the common man has, in the age of mass media, been firmly connected to the heroism of popular entertainment genres, as opposed to the heroic traditions of mythologies, political arenas, or battlefields.[29]

The complexity of this parallel creation is emphasized by the fact that, of all the different media technologies that are traversed in the course of the film's narrative, the moving pictures themselves are left "out of the picture". The audience is encouraged to identify the hero-creating performance of Cooper and of the film's expressive qualities as an integral part of the acts of staging and manipulating that are shown in the film's plot. Throughout the delivering of the speech, Cooper is, with only slight variations, framed in the same frontal, slightly low angle medium shots. What is gradually enhanced is firmness of diction, assurance of bodily posture, timing of accents and pauses. This is in contrast to the beginning, when his voice is always breaking, his hands are shaking and disrupting the microphone, and he is repeatedly looking to the side of the stage for support from Mitchell or looking for the emergency exit, where his friend "The Colonel" (Walter Brennan) beckons him to leave. But not only the performance of Gary Cooper changes, the performance of the film does so as well by giving increasingly more time and space to the impact of the speech on the audience in the hall, on Mitchell and the impressed editor, and finally to the audience listening on the radio. It is as if his self-assurance is the direct product of their perception and of their communal agreement to his agreeableness. Everybody seems to be united in unanimous approval of the content and the style of the speech: praising the resilience and the strength of character of the "little punks," praising team-work and charity, calling on others to live the "spirit of Christmas" the whole year, invoking "a tidal wave of goodwill that no human force could stand against it."

---

[29] John Dean, "U.S. and European Heroism Compared," in *Heroes in a Global World*, ed. Susan J. Drucker and Gary Gumpert (Cresskill, NJ: Hampton Press, 2008), 74– 75.

However, the moment in which the ideal of the average man as a political utopia achieves full embodiment is not only the moment in which he ceases to be average, but also the moment in which the tycoon Norton realizes his potential to mobilize support for political causes. Having secretly observed the euphoric reaction of his domestic staff, who firmly approve of the message, Norton realizes the malleability of public opinion.

There are two analytical studies within the film: The first shows how heroism is a question of perception that can be written, produced, and directed, while the second transforms this into a study of taking heroic responsibility for everyday life. The fact that, of all the different media *within* the film – from newspapers and billboards, to public appearances and radio broadcasts – film itself is absent, can, of course, be interpreted as proposing that film as art, as opposed to film as media, is an exception from these structures of staging and manipulating. But as I have already claimed above, it can also be taken as pointing towards the fact that the film *Meet John Doe* puts itself in question and asks its audience: How is it possible, that a very specific somebody like Gary Cooper, with his singular appearance, can convincingly play a "John Doe"; i.e. can be a credible anybody?

The answer given in the scene of the casting (0h 14m 23s – 0h 17m 04s) is simple: It is possible due to the right music, and the right editing and timing. The moment of Cooper's entry is accompanied by a suggestion of pastoral music, as opposed to the mickey-mousing effect accompanying the candidates before him. It is also longer than the ones before him and his face is intercut with Stanwyck's approving look, asking the editor – and us – to agree with her aesthetic judgment. When Stanwyck tells the editor, "Look at that face, it's wonderful, they'll believe him," she means as much the people in the film as the audience of the film. In this sense, the film is very pessimistic and optimistic at the same time, because it shows that there is no exception, no "outside," to the media technologies that produce identities; that "John Doe" as well as "Gary Cooper" are empty signifiers to which star- or hero-making technologies like framing and editing moving images are attached. As Carney notes: "There is no one there, only a series of images or masks. Doe is an absence at the centre of the events in which he nominally stars."[30]

---

30 Carney, *American Vision*, 363.

But at the same time that the star system is criticized because it is just a technology that seems to contradict the democratic values of equality[31] and because it mixes attainable fame with unattainable desire,[32] the star also becomes comprehensible as the perfect expression of these values. The idea of the "star" in the Classical Hollywood era was neither the absolutely exceptional, nor the reproducibly stereotypical, but something oscillating between the two. Cavell uses the term "type" to describe Hollywood personalities as reconciliations of the competing claims of individuality and sociality. Their social features, and the reoccurring costumes and behaviors, did not determine the types, but, at the same time, they were not completely independent from these: they were "individualities that projected particular *ways* of inhabiting a social role."[33] For the audience, they indicated the mutable ways of positioning oneself to the possibilities and the limits of becoming and being acknowledged as an ephemeral, singular projection of selfhood (within a plurality of roles and eccentricities) which is central to any democratic imagination of the political. The star or type therefore can be regarded as a form of thinking self-education and self-development. As Cavell saw it: "Their singularity made them more like us – anyway, made their difference from us less a matter of metaphysics, to which we must accede, than a matter of responsibility, to which we must bend."[34]

And that brings up the second analytical study of the film: the study of responsibility. As a political allegory, the false promise of fascism and the horror of repression are easily deciphered by the contemporary audience. In the scenes that feature the rich tycoon, D. B. Norton, one can immediately see how well Capra was prepared for his next task: After the USA entered the war, he prepared a series of government information films for the soldiers that were sent to fight. Especially the first parts of this *Why we fight*-series (1942 – 1945), called *Prelude to war* (1942) and *The Nazis Strike* (1943), were propagandistic information films that were – more than anything else – based on analyzing, re-editing and thus exposing German and Italian propaganda films of the 1930s and more specifically

---

31 Ibid., 307.
32 See Philip Drake, "From Hero to Celebrity: The Political Economy of Stardom," in *Heroes in a Global World*, ed. Drucker and Gumpert, 438– 440.
33 Stanley Cavell; *The World Viewed: Reflections on the Ontology of Film. Enlarged Edition*, (Cambridge, MA: Harvard University Press, 1979), 33 [emphasis in the original].
34 Ibid., 35.

the infamous works of Leni Riefenstahl.[35] The first screen appearance of Norton (0h 28m 0s – 0h 28m 30s) shows him on horseback presiding over a choreographed parade of a paramilitary motorcycle-brigade that eerily resembles the geometrical aestheticization of war machinery in the fascist imagery.

But there is another, more implicit but also much more urgent, warning: the central nemesis of Capra's films is not evil intent, but the danger of escapism or moral disengagement. As Carney points out, Long John Willoughby is the poster child of the citizen as Walter Lippmann imagined him: "One could say that he is the perfect modern democrat, willing to obey the majority vote, the perfect unprincipled pragmatist, with no convictions apart from what opinion polls and advisers tell him."[36] His companion "the Colonel," who is constantly at his side during the first half of the film protesting against all the claims that are made upon John, does not fare much better. His protest could, at first, be confused with Ralph Waldo Emerson's or Henry David Thoreau's gesture of radical retreat from society as a mode of criticism and expression of society's insufficiency.[37] However, quite the contrary is the case: He simply embodies disenchanted indifference. And even though John is sometimes momentarily moved by the words that are put into his mouth, what he and his friend want more than anything else is to have no engagement in society of any kind.

The object of the film is not the evil of political repression, but – using Hannah Arendt's famous term – "the banality of evil";[38] i.e. indifference as the refusal to think for oneself and the inability to judge one's company. As Arendt saw it:

Out of the unwillingness or inability to choose one's examples and one's company, and out of the unwillingness or inability to relate to others through judgment, arise the real *skandala*, the real stumbling-blocks which human powers cannot remove

---

35 For a detailed comparative analysis of Capra's and Riefenstahl's propaganda aesthetics, see Hermann Kappelhoff, "Kriegerische Mobilisierung: Die mediale Organisation des Gemeinsinns. Frank Capras Prelude to War und Leni Riefenstahls Tag der Freiheit," *Navigationen. Zeitschrift für Medien- und Kulturwissenschaften* 9, no. 1 (2009): 151–165.
36 Carney, *American Vision*, 357.
37 See Cavell, *Cities of Words*.
38 Hannah Arendt, *Eichmann in Jerusalem: A Report on the Banality of Evil* (New York: Viking Press, 1963).

because they were not caused by human and humanly understandable motives. Therein lies the horror and, at the same time, the banality of evil.[39]

Thus, the dystopian prospect of everyday life is not repression, but an everyday life without ideals and dreams. As Carney put it: "The real horror of the film is thus not a vision of the repression, but of blankness and vacancy."[40] In other words, Capra is warning against an everyday life where freedom and repression would be indistinguishable. The "little man", the everyday person, cannot be the traditionally idealized pillar of moral values as long as he does not accept responsibility for his everyday existence and the people he encounters. That is the true meaning of the film's title as I would interpret it: John Doe or Gary Cooper becomes the protagonist or hero of the film only through those that meet him. Heroism or heroic ordinariness thus becomes a form of encounter. Again, we can see how everyday heroism is not a continuation of universal ideas about what constitutes a hero (something superior or even superhuman, for example[41]) or traditional heroism because it lacks one of the latter's basic characteristics, which demands that "members of a society are separated from their culture heroes by time, space, and social class, and therefore know their heroes only through stories, images, and so on."[42] For a large part of *Meet John Doe* this seems to be true. The members of society are related to John only by media technologies and acts of staging, but the film transforms these into scenes of direct encounter and mutual acts of acknowledgement which then are presented as the genuine ordinary heroism.

The end of the film is exemplary for this transformation: The mediated John Doe is exposed as a fake and the film refuses to give him any kind of satisfactory resistance or even triumph. He only receives consolation and moral support from those that he was abused to betray: the ordinary people. A lot of people, including Capra himself,[43] have complained that the ending – or, rather, the endings, since there were at least five different

---

39 Hannah Arendt, "Some Questions of Moral Philosophy. 4th Session," cited in Ronald Beiner, "Hannah Arendt on Judging," in Hannah Arendt: *Lectures on Kant's Political Philosophy*, ed. Ronald Beiner (Chicago: University of Chicago Press, 1982), 113.
40 Carney, *American Vision*, 369.
41 Christian Schneider, "Wozu Helden?," in *Die Helden-Maschine: Zur Aktualität und Tradition von Heldenbildern*, ed. LWL-Industriemuseum (Essen: Klartext-Verlag, 2010), 20.
42 Strate, "Heroes and/as Communication," 23.
43 Frank Capra, *The Name above the Title: An Autobiography* (New York: Macmillan, 1971), 338–339.

ones[44] – is somewhat unsatisfactory because it does not really deliver a solution to the critique of the media institutions, nor to the potential dysfunctionality of the common man. Least of all could he present "John Doe" as the heroic answer to the social and political problem posed by "John Doe," the corruptible protagonist inclined to indifference and conformism. But is this failure really only caused by the film's ideological tensions and ambiguities; its "strange mixture of demagoguery and attacks on demagoguery" as a form of "confusion"?[45]

I would counter this simple tale of failure by turning it into a tale of Freudian faulty action. That means that failing to make John Doe the hero of the film in a classical sense – challenging the corrupt system as had Mr. Deeds and Mr. Smith in the previous films – is the heroic, sacrificial gesture of the film itself. While both the hero as extraordinary agent and the conformism of the common man have to be distrusted, neither can be dispensed with since they are both sources or mechanisms – quintessential antinomies – of democratic imagination. And they are both corruptible into forms of totalitarian absolutisms. The hero "John Doe" only attracts heroic qualities through the realm of the media but, he himself is incapable of heroic action. The real heroes are those "John Does" that represent him (rather than he is representing). The real heroes are those ordinary citizens that want to continue the dialogue of society with itself: the citizens that "John Doe" meets, that can be spoken to by him, and than can speak for him in the sense that they take responsibility for their words and deeds as everyday expressions of a political community. As Poague noted: "Even in its failures and hesitancies, the conclusion of *Meet John Doe* is more usefully understood – *not* as Capra's quick and easy cure to social dysfunction or disaster – but as 'figuring' (as standing for, as working out) the problem of authorship or language."[46]

The film asks how it is possible to create a free personality for which one can take responsibility and claim authorship, when the conditions of that creation are always already predetermined by media technologies and when the myth of this free personality can always be converted into a marketable commodity or worse. (Incidentally, this idea of marketability

---

[44] Carney, *American Vision*, 371,
[45] Joseph McBride, *Frank Capra: The Catastrophe of Success* (New York: Simon & Schuster, 1992), 431.
[46] Leland Poague, *Another Frank Capra* (Cambridge: Cambridge University Press, 1994), 47– 48 [emphasis in the original].

has become one of the central arguments in the second half of the twentieth century for claims that "heroism" has been replaced by "celebrity."[47] This claim can be countered by the fact that, while there may be ordinary heroes, there is no such thing as ordinary celebrities – only vulgar ones.[48]) Heroic ordinariness is a form of accepting the fact that there is no innocent, immediate outside of media technologies, and at the same time a form of insisting against simple determinism. Heroic ordinariness, as the film presents it, is simultaneously exposing heroism and posing it as resistance. It presents heroism as taking responsibility for one's personal fantasies of selfhood: not only a "product of communication,"[49] but also a mode or a process of multiple, conflicting ex- & re-communications.

The unspectacular but fundamentally new answer of *Meet John Doe* to the problem of the hero as media product is to refuse to exempt the hero from the ordinary and to transfer stardom/heroism from the singular star/hero to the plurality of everyday singularities that he represents or rather expresses. It claims that it is vital to risk expressing one's dreams of singularity, one's ideas of heroes, even if they can be abused for sinister ends.

In a scene close to the end of the film, John tries to accuse the tycoon of abusing the John Doe movement, (1h 39m 19s – 1h 48m 26s) but he is held back and prevented from talking to the people first by crowds of people that want to talk to him, then by the audience singing an anthem, as well as by a priest leading the audience in prayer. After he is dragged away from the microphone and makes it back, the wires are cut. It would be much too simple and very much against the film's ambiguities to claim that "the film metaphorically equates the hordes of ordinary citizens, the state, and the church as cooperating, interlocking forms of repression,"[50] since, at the same time, they are also the very institutions that make the life of the community possible and livable – and I would propose that here Capra includes the arts and the cinema itself. The fact that they are also the sources of the greatest dangers to the political community makes it so

---

47 Strate, "Heroes and/as Communication," 23–26. Drake, "From Hero to Celebrity," 437. See also Daniel J. Boorstin, *The Image: A Guide to Pseudo-Events in America*, (New York: Atheneum, 1978).
48 A pun on the strong connotation of *"ordinär"* as "vulgar" in German.
49 Strate, "Heroes and/as Communication," 21.
50 Carney, *American Vision*, 347.

much more necessary to take responsibility for them and to engage in them.

Heroic ordinariness is not about life and death, but about defending the ordinary as the realm of personal dreams and fantasies that intersects with our public dreams and fantasies – with movies about heroes for example. It is, I would claim, a question of conceiving action in the public sphere in a way that makes everyday heroism of the life-saving kind possible or at least perceivable in the first place. It can further be regarded as a melodramatic kind of heroism that participates in the highly political struggle of recognizing the ordinary, the everyday, as an exciting place in which to act.[51] It is a kind of heroism that makes heroism its own reward in the strongest sense. It is a kind that considers heroism not as a given but as an achievement.[52]

Stanley Cavell's Political Philosophy of the Ordinary as Heroic

As it turns out, the question of everyday heroism, as I would like to propose it, is based less on an idea of what constitutes heroics than on a political philosophy of the everyday. Referring to Stanley Cavell's works on the ordinary and the political as conversation (or conversation as the political), I would claim that Capra's film works on the production of "heroism" and "ordinariness" as categories of the public sphere. According to this view of public action, ordinary men, women, and children are not heroic because of their deeds and their contributions to society. However extraordinary those deeds may be, what makes them heroic is the fact that the doers resist the urge to be set apart from their fellow beings because of them. As Cavell noted: "No amount of contribution is more valuable to the formation and preservation of community than the willingness to contribute."[53]

---

51 Peter Brooks, *The Melodramatic Imagination. Balzac, Henry James, Melodrama, and the Mode of Excess* (New Haven/ London: Yale University Press, 1995 [1976]), 6, 13– 14.
52 See Dean, "U.S. and European Heroism Compared," 75.
53 Stanley Cavell, "What Photography Calls Thinking," in *Cavell on Film*, ed. William Rothman (Albany: State University of New York Press, 2005 [1985]), 133.

If it really is true that "we desperately need to live heroically,"[54] then Capra's heroic ordinariness is the lesson that teaches us to live heroically together; to share heroism within the ordinary. And if trying to define heroism always implies defining the evil that heroism battles, then the opposite of everyday heroism is not cowardice or weakness but a refusal of the ordinary: the will to extraordinariness and its logical counterpart, the disenchanted fall into indifference and cynicism.[55] Cavell reformulates the Kantian stance on moral as a question of choosing to view human community as possible or to view it as nonexistent in this way: "This takes moral as the will to exempt oneself, to isolate oneself, from the human community."[56] Heroic ordinariness means to accept to be judged by others; to be subjected to their acknowledgement or rejection.

Again, this idea is strongly connected to the life-saving everyday heroism whose evil counterpart is the fragility of mere life as an endangered existence in modern, secular societies: Saving a life in this context means to save it as a public life worth living; as the representative saving of everybody's right to speak and to be heard.

Frank Capra's *Meet John Doe* shows the creation of a "star" or a "hero" out of an ordinary person. And it – as well as in the other films I have mentioned – shows that becoming a hero is not a special gift, but expresses something very general; something absolutely common. It expresses "a stance toward whatever endowment you discover is yours, as if life itself were a gift, and remarkable."[57] Heroism denotes the promise or the necessity to become aware of the public responsibilities of everyday private actions and private sensibilities; the necessity to balance our everyday obligations with the most valued claims of political ideals. In this sense, the dialectic between heroism as a stabilizing, conservative force[58] and, at the same time, as a challenge to the concrete establishment[59] is kept in suspense because heroism becomes the challenge to the corruption of authorities in the name of the spirit they were supposed to embody.

---

54 Strate, "Heroes and/as Communication," 19.
55 See the papers by William Graebner and Martin Lüthe in this volume.
56 Stanley Cavell, *Pursuits of Happiness: The Hollywood Comedy of Remarriage* (Cambridge, MA: Harvard University Press, 1981), 80.
57 Stanley Cavell, *In Quest of the Ordinary: Lines of Skepticism and Romanticism* (Chicago: University of Chicago Press, 1988), 114.
58 Roger R. Rollin, "The Lone Ranger and Lenny Skutnik: The Hero as Popular Culture," in *The Hero in Transition*, ed. Browne and Fishwick, 33.
59 Meyer, "Helden des Alltags," 31.

Finally, one could argue that what John Doe is trying to become in his final stage is the most current embodiment of the everyday hero as I have tried to describe in these pages: the whistleblower. This figure presents us with another step in the "evolution" of heroism away from extraordinary action by the extraordinary few and towards the preservation of moral causes by the many within ordinary life. How do we identify wrongs in our societies? How do we maintain the conditions of participation and acknowledgement? These are heroic tasks. But the community of heroes is open to everybody and it is created only by the will to contribute to it – everyday.

Everyday Socialist Heroes and Hegemonic Masculinity in the German Democratic Republic, 1949–1989[1]

Sylka Scholz (translator Simon Ward)

Introduction

This study of everyday heroism in the German Democratic Republic (GDR) begins with the analysis of one of the Republic's iconic heroic images.[2] This photograph, created barely a year before the founding of the state on October 7, 1949, shows the miner Adolf Hennecke. Hennecke was seen as the prototype of the socialist "hero of labor" and embodied, as I argue here, the hegemonic masculinity of the GDR. The photograph was taken on October 13, 1948 and shows the miner at work. In this shift, which subsequently became legendary, he accomplished "387 per cent" of the work norm.[3]

---

1 For the purposes of this book project, this contribution expands on my earlier publications on this topic. See Sylka Scholz, "Sozialistische Helden: Hegemoniale Männlichkeit in der DDR," in *Postsozialistische Männlichkeiten in einer globalisierten Welt*, ed. Sylka Scholz and Weertje Willms (Münster: Lit, 2008), 11–35; Sylka Scholz, "Vom starken Helden zum zärtlichen Vater? Männlichkeit und Emotion in der DDR," in *Die Präsenz der Gefühle: Männlichkeit und Emotion in der Moderne*, ed. Manuel Burotta and Nina Verheyen (Bielefeld: Transcript, 2010), 203–229.

2 Scholz, "Sozialistische Helden," 11–35.

3 Silke Satjukow, "Früher war das eben der Adolf .... Der Arbeitsheld Adolf Hennecke," in *Sozialistische Helden: Eine Kulturgeschichte der Propagandafiguren in Osteuropa und der DDR*, ed. Silke Satjukow and Rainer Gries (Berlin: Christoph Links, 2002), 118.

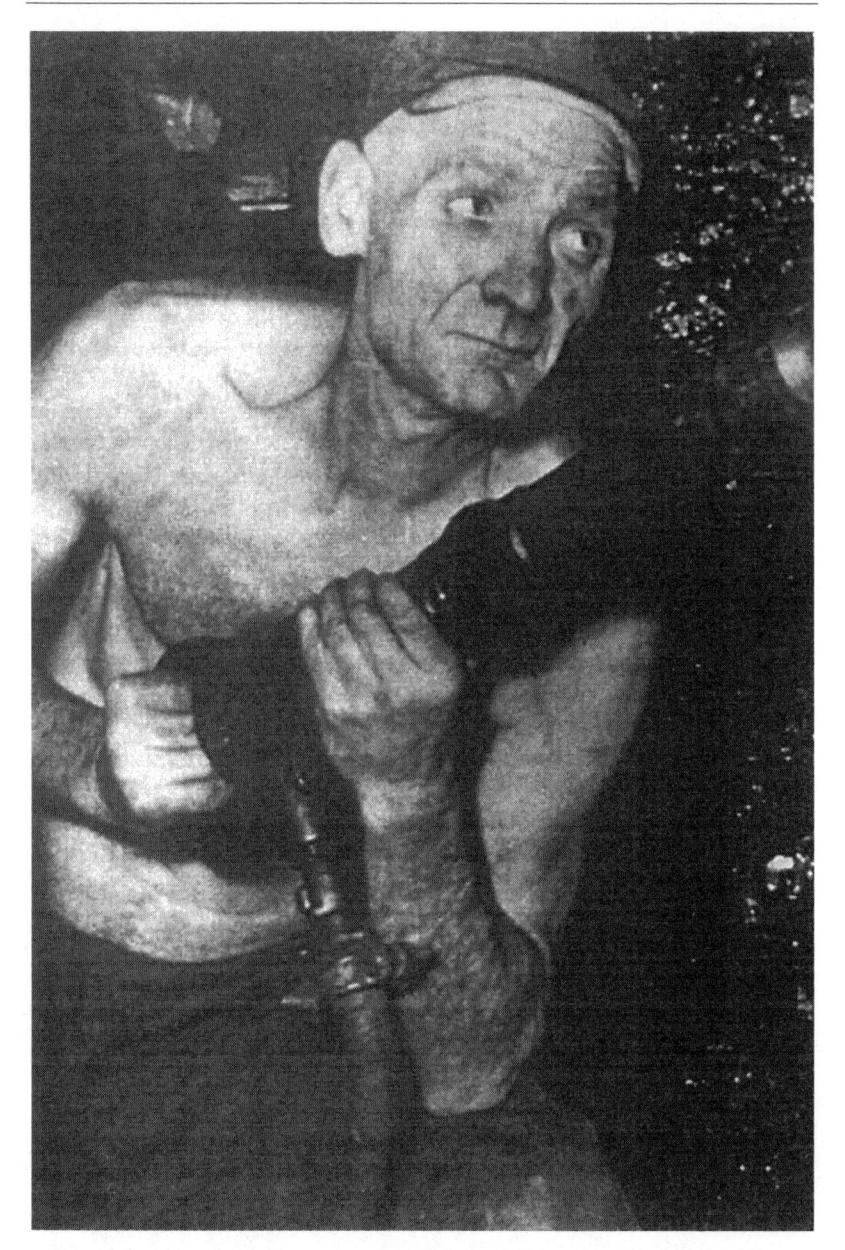

Figure 1: The "heroic photograph" of Adolf Hennecke.

In *Sozialistische Helden. Eine Kulturgeschichte der Propagandafiguren in Osteuropa und der DDR*, ed. Silke Satjukow and Rainer Gries (Berlin: Christoph Links 2002), 119.

The composition of the image focuses on the man's upper body, and dynamism is created by the direction of the tool moving from bottom left to upper right. Stability is generated through the left arm supporting the bent left leg, enabling the drill to bore into the coal. The center of the image is dominated by the left hand, which is covered in black coal dust. Hennecke is wearing a cap and looking up at the coal seam. His gaze can be interpreted as focused, but also as abstractedly directed towards a better future. The photograph appears to claim that a humble, and no longer young, worker (Hennecke was already 43 years old) can exceed performance targets. It is precisely the painful leanness of the body, bearing witness to the post-war hunger years, that may well have given the image credibility for his contemporaries. The party leadership of the German Socialist Unity Party (SED) admittedly bungled the staging of this heroic act, which unintentionally proved beneficial for the presentation of the hero himself. The reception committee of comrades and schoolchildren turned up late, so that the miner had already showered. He thus had to put his dirty work attire back on for this oft-reproduced photograph.[4] Highlighted by the camera's flash, his freshly-showered skin glows brightly against the background of the coal – the "black gold" – which also contributes to the powerful effect of the image.

This image glorifies hard, physical industrial labor, placing at the center the worker's dirty, laboring hand, which is extended by the machine. Man and machine seem to be molded together. At the same time, and this is emphasized in texts about the heroic deed, this expert has brains,[5] since such high productivity was only possible with very good forward planning. Characteristics such as discipline, creativity, and strength are combined in this proletarian ideal of masculinity which is founded on a powerful emphasis on the body, and an association between masculinity and the machine.

This image of the worker-hero Hennecke demonstrates typical aspects of the construction of heroism in the GDR: from the outset, the leadership of the GDR state used the humble man (and humble woman) from the working class for their propaganda purposes. As will be demonstrated, such images served both as a means to encourage the population to participate in the construction of the Socialist state, as well as to legitimize the political elite. Those who participated fully in the project of state

---

4 Ibid., 118.
5 Ibid., 122.

construction were idolized. Anyone, male or female, could become a hero in the GDR. This also means that heroism in the GDR was not grounded in acts of civilian courage, such as the selfless rescuing of people in emergencies, as John Price describes them in his fundamental study of everyday heroism.[6]

Socialist hero culture thus differs significantly from the model of heroism in Western European and North American countries. The aim of this article is to illuminate the specific aspects of heroism as they operated in a Socialist country. A central aspect is the significance of gender, and particularly masculinity, in the production of Socialist heroes. To begin with, I will present R. W. Connell's theory of hegemonic masculinity, and demonstrate how it can be used for the analysis of Socialist states. In the second step, I approach the question of how heroes were "made" and who made them, through the communication model of Satjukow and Gries.[7] This model is expanded through the inclusion of the GDR's film production, in which real everyday heroes were set alongside fictional heroic figures, a process which served both to strengthen but also undermine the ideology of the hero. The third step analyses selected constructions of heroic figures. The analysis focuses on *Heroes of labor* (Helden der Arbeit) since, in the GDR, gainful employment was seen as the place where the individual should both emancipate him- or herself, and also participate in the construction of a new and more just society. Based around the mass-media construction of the "real" heroes of socialism and the promotion of this hero-type in popular feature films in the 1950s through fictional characters, this analysis draws out both the differences and similarities. The crisis of socialist propaganda from the 1970s onwards brought with it an increased critique of the heroic figure. The article's fourth section illustrates how this ideological crisis manifested in feature films of that time, then ends with the conclusion and further questions raised by this contribution on the issues of images of everyday heroism in the GDR.

---

6 John Price, *Everyday Heroism: Victorian Construction of the Heroic Civilian* (London: Bloomsbury, 2014).

7 Silke Satjukow and Rainer Gries, "Zur Konstruktion des 'sozialistischen Helden.' Geschichte und Bedeutung," in *Sozialistische Helden*, 15–34.

The Concept of Hegemonic Masculinity and its Applicability to Socialist Societies

Over the past 30 years, R. W. Connell's concept of "hegemonic masculinity" has established itself as central to research into the social construction of masculinity and masculine ascendancy.[8] As is well known, Connell's model emerged in the 1980s in relation to feminist and neo-Marxist theories. Connell understands his model as part of a theory of gender relations.[9] The core of Connell's theory of masculinity is determined by his appropriation of Gramsci's concept of "hegemony." Hegemony indicates (as in Gramsci's analyses of class relations in Italy) a social ascendency achieved through "a play of social forces that extends beyond contests of brute power into the organization of private life and cultural processes."[10] This affirmation of dominance is produced in the cultural sphere – through the production of commonly shared patterns of interpretation, norms, and values. Connell shifts the concept of class dominance to the domain of masculinity. "The social ascendancy of the masculine gender is founded in the symbolic and institutional connection of masculinity and authority."[11] Masculinity is constructed through two sets of relationships: "to women and subordinated masculinities."[12] Its relationship to femininity is determined by dominance and subordination. For Connell, this is the "main axis of masculine power."[13] At the same

---

8 R. W. Connell, *Gender and Power: Society, the Person, and Sexual Politics* (Stanford: California University Press, 1987); R. W. Connell, *Der gemachte Mann: Männlichkeitskonstruktionen und Krise der Männlichkeit* (Opladen: Leske und Budrich, 1999). Within the framework of this contribution, I do not have the space to incorporate all critical reflection on the concept of hegemonic masculinity in the field of masculinity studies. See Sylka Scholz, *Männlichkeitssoziologie. Studien aus den sozialen Feldern Arbeit, Politik und Militär im vereinten Deutschland* (Münster: Westfälisches Dampfboot, 2012). There is, nevertheless, a consensus in masculinity studies around the fundamental ideas that there are varying conceptions of masculinity, that we have to assume a plurality of masculinities, and regarding the association between masculinity and structures of power and dominance. This article also shares this consensus of opinion.

9 R. W. Connell, "Zur Theorie der Geschlechterverhältnisse," *Das Argument* 36 (1986): 330–344.

10 Connell, *Gender and Power*, 184.

11 Michael Meuser, *Geschlecht und Männlichkeit. Soziologische Theorie und kulturelle Deutungsmuster* (Wiesbaden: VS/Springer, 2006), 162. [Translator's translation]

12 Connell, *Gender and Power*, 186.

13 Connell, *Der gemachte Mann*, 94.

time, masculinity is determined by the relationships that men have to other men. This is the conjugate axis of masculine power. Hierarchically ordered, different constructions of masculinity are in competition in society. Only one historically concrete form of masculinity is hegemonically dominant, and all others exist in a specific relationship to this form. These relationships can be determined by "hegemony, dominance/subordination, and complicity on the one hand, and marginalization and empowerment on the other."[14] In this context, Connell refers to complicit, marginal, and subordinate masculinity. These categorizations should, however, not be understood as specific types of masculinity, but rather as a way of analyzing the relations between different forms of masculinity.

It is also important to recognize that Connell does not regard masculinity as a personality characteristic, but rather as something that is produced through social praxis and interactions amongst men, and between men and women. Above all, hegemonic masculinity functions as a cultural pattern of orientation. Connell assumes that hegemonic masculinity is shaped in society's centers of power: the state, the military, and the economy. Within these institutions, the respective elites shape hegemonic masculinity, even if they do not necessarily have to embody it.[15]

Connell's concept can be applied to the Socialist situation.[16] The specificity of Socialism as a variant of modern societies[17] consists in the fact that there was always a clear power center – the Politburo of the respective Socialist Unity Party and the political and bureaucratic power structure connected with it. The power of the Politburo was legitimized through its roots in the working class and the Communist resistance against the Nazis.[18] This elite significantly influenced the development of

---

[14] Ibid., 102.
[15] Michael Meuser and Sylka Scholz, "Hegemoniale Männlichkeit – Versuch einer Begriffsklärung aus soziologischer Perspektive," in *Männer – Macht – Körper. Hegemoniale Männlichkeiten vom Mittelalter bis heute*, ed. Martin Dinges (Frankfurt: Campus, 2005), 211–228.
[16] See Sylka Scholz, *Männlichkeiten erzählen. Lebensgeschichtliche Identitätskonstruktionen ostdeutscher Männer* (Münster: Westfälisches Dampfboot, 2004); Scholz and Wilms, *Postsozialistische Männlichkeiten in einer globalisierten Welt*.
[17] See Peter Wagner, *Soziologie der Moderne* (Frankfurt: Campus, 1995).
[18] See Thomas Ahbe and Rainer Gries, "Gesellschaftsgeschichte als Generationengeschichte. Theoretische und methodische Überlegungen am Beispiel der DDR," in *Die DDR aus generationsgeschichtlicher Perspektive*, ed. Annegret Schüle, Thomas Ahbe, and

the culture of the GDR. Wolfgang Engler neatly describes the GDR *in toto* as a "society of workers,"[19] in which culture and design were also shaped by the tastes of the working class. The one-party state functioned as a leveler – cultural identities, religious connections, and traditional family structures were dissolved. Since the state also organized the allocative activities, social differences were increasingly leveled out. The economy was subordinated to political goals, centrally planned, and directed according to strategic political aims (the planned economy). Three main political ideas determined the planned development of society: first, the idea of ordered and reliable social development and (scientific-technical) progress; second, the idea of social equality and justice; and third, the idea that gainful employment was the most important model for social integration and contained the emancipatory potential to level out existing social differences.[20] Social differences between the genders were expressly to be dismantled. The almost total integration of women into the workforce was typical for gender relations in the GDR – something that was made possible by a corresponding system of public childcare provision and other welfare measures. The integration of women into the workforce was seen as evidence of the gender equality that all Socialist countries sought. Nevertheless, in the economic sphere, numerous gender inequalities remained, such as the imbalanced allocation of leadership positions or unfavorable differences in salary between men and women.[21]

Despite the hailing of gender equality, the political leadership in the GDR state was male-dominated. On the one hand, key roles were occupied by men, as were most of the leading positions in the economic sphere. On the other, the interests of men and specific, masculine ways of seeing and interpreting the world were privileged. As a result, there was no change in the masculinely-coded social and cultural dominance of the labor

---

Rainer Gries (Leipzig: Leipziger Universitätsverlag, 2006), 475–573; Scholz, "Vom starken Helden zum zärtlichen Vater."

19 See Wolfgang Engler, *Die Ostdeutschen. Kunde von einem verlorenen Land* (Berlin: Aufbau, 1999).

20 See Irene Dölling, "Zwei Wege gesellschaftlicher Modernisierung. Geschlechtervertrag und Geschlechterarrangements in Ostdeutschland in gesellschafts-/modernisierungs- theoretischer Perspektive," in *Achsen der Differenz. Gesellschaftstheorie und feministische Kritik II*, ed. Gudrun-Axeli Knapp and Angelika Wetterer (Münster: Westfälisches Dampfboot, 2003), 73–100.

21 See Hildegard M. Nickel, "Mitgestalterin des Sozialismus – Frauenarbeit in der DDR," in *Frauen in Deutschland 1945–1992*, ed. Gisela Helwig and Hildegard M. Nickel (Bonn: Bundeszentrale für politische Bildung, 1993), 233–256.

sphere over the sphere of biological reproduction.[22] Instead, that masculine dominance was reinforced by a Socialist utopia of labor, which contained the idea that the independence and emancipation of the individual could only be achieved through gainful employment. This was based on the modern principles of instrumental reason such as economic rationality, calculability, and the management of labor. Any human dimension that could not be integrated into this form of labor, such as generativity, emotionality, and sexuality were excluded from the labor sphere. Since, at the same time, the state officially supported the emancipation of women, albeit only in terms of their integration into the workforce, there was a "tense relationship between masculine hegemony and feminine emancipation."[23] This tension was characteristic for gender relations in the GDR overall.

The Mass Media's Construction of Socialist Heroes

In all socialist states such as the GDR, a pantheon of heroic figures, so-called socialist heroes, served as a means of communicating socialist ideology and legitimizing the party's hold on power.[24] This celestial hall of fame was based on a socialist heroism-theory that was developed in the 1920s around writings by Nietzsche, Marx, Gorki, and Lunatscharski: as in earlier times, the Socialist hero should represent moments of enlightenment in what was perceived as the grey light of day, and thus function as a pedagogical role model, as well as a figure of identification and integration. What was new in the GDR was that anyone could become a hero. It was, however, no accident that socialist heroes were mostly male, since masculine dominance was legitimized through this pantheon by the creation of hegemonic masculinity. The aforementioned tension between male hegemony and female emancipation found its expression in the construction of a few Socialist heroines. However, these were also – like women in general – only superficially equal to their male counterparts.

---

22 See Susanne Stolt, *Zwischen Arbeit und Liebe. Eine empirische Studie zum Wandel der Geschlechterbeziehungen in Ostdeutschland nach der Wende* (Kassel: Uni Press, 2000).
23 Scholz, "Männlichkeit erzählen," 48. [Translator's translation]
24 See Satjukow and Gries, "Zur Konstruktion des 'sozialistischen Helden.'"

According to Sajukow and Gries, "the successful communication of a heroic figure only took place when the masses accepted this idol."[25] The construction of a hero was a one-way communication process between the powers-that-be and the population – something dictated to the people by the state and the SED. When addressing the populace, the political elite communicated messages that were intended to legitimize their power; a process in which the mass media played an important role. Citizens came across these hero figures in a variety of contexts: as workers, as members of parties and organizations, as students, and as private citizens. In this process, the meaning of socialist heroes became diversified. Over the course of time, the state, the media, and the populace "agreed upon the essential qualities of the heroic,"[26] and thus, in consort, created these hegemonic figures. This then led to the legitimization and consolidation of the political and implicit masculine dominance by a hegemonic culture in Gramsci's terms.[27] This culture was based on negotiation and consensus-building between the political elite and the population.[28] Yet, where there were deviations from the hegemonic ideal and when provocations arose, there was often a shift, and violent response. Despite an awareness of this, we still do not have a precise analysis of the conditions under which hegemony and violence relate to the maintenance of elite ascendancy.

Alongside those heroic figures that were based on real persons, the ideology of heroism was also disseminated through fictional heroes in feature films and television programs. Film production in the GDR was state-run through the DEFA (Deutsche Film AG), which had been founded in 1946. The DEFA can be read as a key element in the mass media network of the GDR. Following Stalin, whose thoughts influenced early film policy in the GDR, film's job was "to educate the workers in the spirit of Socialism."[29] And yet, the politics of film in the GDR were more

---

25 Ibid., 33. [Translator's translation]
26 Ibid. [Translator's translation]
27 See Sabine Kebir, *Antoni Gramscis Zivilgesellschaft. Alltag, Ökonomie, Kultur, Politik* (Hamburg: VSA-Verlag, 1991).
28 See Thomas Lindenberger, "Die DDR nachdem das Tor zum Westen geschlossen war," in *50 Jahre Mauerbau. Vorgeschichte und Folgen*, ed. Hans-Joachim Veen und Franz-Josef Schlichting (Erfurt: Stiftung Ettersberg, 2011), 37–51.
29 Cited in Dagmar Schittly, *Zwischen Regie und Regime. Die Filmpolitik der SED im Spiegel der DEFA-Produktionen* (Berlin: Christoph Links, 2002), 9. [Translator's translation]

complex than might be expected.[30] While the state sought to promote its ideology in feature films through the use of various control commissions, it often came up against the resistance of film makers on the one hand, and an uninterested public on the other. This led to permanent slippages in film policy which allowed film makers to continue to make aesthetically-valuable and internationally-successful films throughout the history of the GDR. Overall, the DEFA's feature film production[31] was an amalgamation of schematic propaganda films, contemporary entertainment products, and outstanding artistic creations.

Heroes of Labor: Embodiments of Hegemonic Masculinity in the GDR

In contrast to other socialist countries, the figure of the war hero had little significance in the GDR; due, of course, to the experiences of National Socialism. After the Second World War, militaristic constructions of masculinity were discredited with populations in both East and West Germany.[32] The men of the political elite may have held onto militarized conceptions of masculinity, since they had been socialized in militarized workers' associations and in the anti-fascist resistance.[33] They did not succeed – despite great efforts to stage it[34] – in creating a political leader hero from their own ranks. Throughout the history of the GDR, this role was embodied by the workers' leader Ernst Thälmann, who had been murdered by the National Socialists. In the 1950s, "a slick, artificial figure was shaped, through omissions and additions, which the SED held on to until 1989 with very few modifications."[35] A large contribution to this process was made by the feature films *Ernst Thälmann – Sohn seiner Klasse*

---

30 See Ralf Schenk eds., *Das zweite Leben der Filmstadt Babelsberg: DEFA 1946–92* (Berlin: Henschel 1994); Schittly, *Zwischen Regie und Regime*.
31 There is an overview of DEFA feature film production in Schenk, *Das zweite Leben der Filmstadt Babelsberg*.
32 See Scholz, "Männlichkeit erzählen."
33 See Scholz, "Vom starken Helden zum zärtlichen Vater."
34 See Rainer Gries, "Die Heldenbühne der DDR. Zur Einführung," in *Sozialistische Helden*, 84–100.
35 See Anette Leo, "Deutschlands unsterblicher Sohn. Der Held des Widerstandes Ernst Thälmann," in *Sozialistische Helden*, 101–114. [Translator's translation]

(*Ernst Thälmann – Son of his Class*, 1954) and *Ernst Thälmann – Führer seiner Klasse* (*Ernst Thälmann – Leader of his Class*, 1955).[36] Yet, because his status was inviolable and unattainable, Thälmann was less useful as an identification- and orientation-figure for large parts of the population in the everyday world of the real existing heroes (and heroines) of labor.

While political leader heroes and war heroes belonged to a long tradition with which socialism associated itself, as a type, the hero of labor and reconstruction was a genuine socialist invention. Historically, proletarian masculinity was one of the subordinate forms of masculinity. This transformation in hegemonic masculinity was accompanied by an idolization of labor which connected back to traditions in worker culture. Naturally, it required considerable orchestration to establish this new type of hero. To illustrate this, I will begin with the aforementioned Adolf Hennecke as the prototype of the hero of labor, before going on to discuss selected DEFA feature films. The role model for this type of hero came from the Soviet Union: in 1935, the miner Alexej Stachanow had produced not merely the usual ten to twelve tons but 102 tons of coal in one work shift and brought to life the activist movement named after him.[37] The state leadership of the GDR wanted to create a corresponding hero of labor in order to solve legitimization problems, and chose the miner Adolf Hennecke for this purpose.[38] Hennecke was known as an experienced miner; he had joined the German Socialist Unity Party (SED) in 1946 and had been a qualified instructor for the party since 1947. In spite of his support for the party, he was cherished by his fellow miners, and was therefore an advantageous choice to embody the message of the party and the state at a difficult moment for the GDR– the political elite in the Soviet Union had rejected the Marshall-Plan in 1948, the populace was unsettled, and productivity was low. While the workers demanded: "First more food, then more work," the party instead declared: "More production, proper distribution, and better living-standards."[39] In the wake of the Soviet Stakhanovite-movement, many factories already had activists who surpassed their norms, but their deeds did not manage to convey the

---

36 *Ernst Thälmann – Führer seiner Klasse*, directed by Kurt Maetzig (1955; Potsdam-Babelsberg: DEFA, 2004), DVD. Filmanalysen finden sich in Schenk, *Das zweite Leben der Filmstadt Babelsberg*.
37 See Rosalinde Sartorti, "Helden des Sozialismus in der Sowjetunion. Zur Einführung," in *Sozialistische Helden*, 35–44.
38 See Satjukow, "Früher war das eben der Adolf."
39 Ibid., 116.

message. As a result, in October 1948, the state, the party, and the company deliberately staged an act of heroism.

On that Wednesday, October 13, 1948, Hennecke traveled down to the mine shaft and produced a remarkable yield: 287 percent above the usual productive norm. Hennecke's shift at the coalface acquired an iconic status unlike that of any other representation of heroism, and was consistently reproduced in the GDR. This staging of heroism had the desired effect: an activist movement emerged under Hennecke's leadership, which only two years later comprised 150,000 members.[40] At the same time, Hennecke was criticized as a "norm-breaker" and "scab." From the beginning, the new heroic ideal not only had its supporters amongst the general public, but also its opponents. If, for some, Hennecke became a conduit for complaints, someone who could represent[41] the workers' interests to the state leadership, from others he received letters that ranged from protests to death threats.[42] Right up to the end of the GDR, the state leadership maintained the heroic narrative it had constructed and reproduced. The "idea of the everyday hero" was duplicated not only "in public discourses, compositions, images and books,"[43] but also in feature films. It was the mission of the sole film company in the GDR, the DEFA, to concern itself with everyday life in a socialist society, rather than simply making escapist entertainment. The actors and actresses represented the common man or woman and showed how anyone could become an everyday hero in the contemporary conflicts of mundane life. In DEFA-films, both men and women acted as heroes of labor, although a specific role was ascribed to the heroines: the disciplining of the male heroes. This aspect will be examined in detail through the feature film *Das kleine und das große Glück (The Major and the Minor Happiness)*,[44] and thereafter related to other films.[45]

---

40 Ibid, 121.

41 Ibid., 125.

42 Ibid.

43 Ibid., 132.

44 *Das kleine und das große Glück,* directed by Martin Hellberg (1953; Potsdam-Babelsberg: DEFA), copy available as a DVD from the Defa-Stiftung in Berlin.

45 The following film analyses were produced as part of the work of the SFB project "Transzendenz und Gemeinsinn in privaten Lebensformen" (Transcendence and Community Spirit in Personal Relationships) at the TU Dresden (2008–2013), led by Professor Karl Lenz und myself. For the method of film analysis involved, see Sylka Scholz, Michel Kusche, Nicole Scherber, Sandra, Scherber and David Stiller, "Das Potential von Filmanalyse für die (Familien-) Soziologie. Eine methodische Betrachtung und das Beispiel der Verfilmungen zu *Das doppelte Lottchen*," *Forum für qualitative*

This 1953 film, directed by the well-known Martin Hellberg, is considered to be the first official love film made by the DEFA.[46] It sparked a broad debate in the media, including much discussion about the figures of the heroes. The love story between the young brigade[47] leader Erika Brandt and the foreman Karl Schwalk takes place at a fictive road construction site in Kleinfurt, which is part of the Socialist reconstruction project (see Figure). The construction site suffers from a shortage of material, technology, and experts. At the beginning of the film, only the youth brigade has expert support, in the figure of foreman Schwalk. The rest of the film's plot deals with how it succeeds in completing the road construction on time, despite the difficult conditions.

Figure 2: Press photo from the feature film, Das kleine und das große Glück, in Defa-Pressedienst, ed. Defa-Studie für Spielfilme (Potsdam-Babelsberg: Pressestelle 1953), 4.

Sozialforschung 15, no. 1 (2014) http://nbn-resolving.de/urn:nbn:de:0114-fqs1401157. The sample is based on the research questions of the project, which examined the change in the conceptions of love, living, and gender from the 1950s to the present in a comparison between East and West Germany. Since these aspects are very closely connected to the heroic figures of labor and reconstruction, the method is appropriate for this article. Students at the TU Dresden also participated in the film analyses, and they and other colleagues involved in the project are to be thanked at this point for their contributions to discussion about the films.

46 "Das kleine und das große Glück," DEFA-Pressedienst, no. 4 (1953), Newspaper Archive of the Film University Babelsberg, KONRAD WOLF.

47 On youth policy, and the institution of the youth brigades, see Peter Skyba, *Vom Hoffnungsträger zum Sicherheitsrisiko. Jugend in der DDR und Jugendpolitik von 1946–1961* (Köln: Böhlau, 2000); and Ulrich Mählert and Gerd-Rüdiger Stephan, *Blaue Hemden – Rote Fahnen. Die Geschichte der Freien Deutschen Jugend* (Opladen: Leske und Budrich, 1996).

The film's title already indicates the socially-desired way of life: private and collective happiness are identical with one another. Private happiness is only considered legitimate if it coincides with the interests of the collective. Erika Brandt is framed as an enthusiastic heroine of state reconstruction, embodying the ideal of engaged youth desired by the state and the party. In this context, we can see a specific gender constellation in the socialist project: young women embody socialist construction, but it is men who take on the work of the expert and the leader, and represent the ideal hero. This didactic constellation is also visible in the film's image composition (see Figure 3).

Figure 3: Still from the feature film, Das kleine und das große Glück (timecode 00:35:37) directed by Martin Hellberg (1953; DDR: DEFA).

Erika may be in love with the foreman, but she consistently rejects his advances. The construction project is the priority; only once it has been completed can she enter a romantic relationship. The foreman, who is visibly older than Erika, develops over the course of the film from a "daredevil" who has fleeting female relationships, into a "devoted partner." In his role as a hero of construction and labor, he also has to transition from being a fiery risk-taker, into a fully convinced Socialist. These two transformations are linked with each other in the film – in this plotline, the fusion of public and private happiness is put into (filmic) practice. As a hero of construction, he initially acts in a risky fashion: in order to win a competition with the other brigade involved in the project, the new road is not sufficiently bedded in, and crumbles during a stress test. It is this event that triggers his development, which succeeds with Erika's support. In the end, the road is complete and the protagonists become a couple.

Erika's femininity functions as a "projection surface for the construction of a new masculinity that corresponds to the new situation."[48] This is possible because she is represented as a woman without her own backstory; as pure, innocent, and without any responsibility for what happened during the war. Schwalk, by contrast, fought in the Second World War and wears a paramilitary uniform. His initial encounters with Erika reveal aggressive masculine patterns of behavior, and it is only by means of this female figure that the protagonist can develop a masculinity "which is appropriate to the times – respectful towards women, reliable in personal relationships ... [and] unconditionally, unselfishly committed to the cause."[49] Schwalk thus becomes the ideal "architect of Socialism" to whom the female figure, in contravention of Socialist ideology, is subordinated.

Participation in the project of the construction of a Socialist society is framed as "the major happiness" in the film. Various scenes of marching and celebration illustrate how the individual becomes part of a large, happy socialist community. The fate of "minor happiness" in socialism remains underdetermined in the film, and the end is left strangely open (see Figure

---

48 Irene Dölling, "Das kleine und das große Glück, Himmel ohne Sterne – Kommentar zu den beiden Filmen aus geschlechtersoziologischer Perspektive." Unpublished typescript of a talk given in the context of the workshop on "Transzendenz und Gemeinsinn in privaten Lebensformen" (Dresden: Technische Universität, 2010), 8. [Translator's translation]
49 Ibid., 9. [Translator's translation]

4). While both protagonists are included within the frame, gazing together towards the future, a final kiss, which has a central meaning within the genre of the love story,[50] is missing – just as there is neither a declaration of love nor a marriage proposal. The fact that both protagonists lack individual characteristics can be understood as a result of the equation of the two levels of happiness. They thus appear as "lifeless mouthpieces of the politically correct"[51] and, as such, are not useful as figures of identification.

Figure 4: Press photo from the feature film, Das kleine und das große Glück, in Defa-Pressedienst, ed. Defa-Studie für Spielfilme (Potsdam-Babelsberg: Pressestelle 1953), 1.

---

50 See Annette Kaufmann, *Der Liebesfilm. Spielregeln eines Genres* (Konstanz: UVK, 2007).
51 Dölling, "Das kleine und das große Glück," 9.

A fierce, emotionally-charged debate opened up in the GDR's newspapers around this first romantic genre film. The debate reveals how heroism and love in Socialism were discursively negotiated. According to his autobiographical account, the director Martin Hellberg attempted to commit suicide due to its lack of success.[52] The criticism of the film directed itself towards both its content and its aesthetic strategies. Two different lines of discourse can be discerned in the newspaper articles. The first line of argument used by the largest percentage of the reviews, start from the assumption that the fundamental concern of the film – the connection of public and private happiness – is correct, but has not been sufficiently translated into film. The criticisms address the casting of the main figures. The actor playing Schwalk was said to be "an arrogant, conceited, tall-booted loudmouth";[53] a "show-off";[54] and, for one particularly disappointed reviewer, "an arrogant squirt."[55] The audience reportedly laughed at Schwalk in solemn scenes.[56] The character of Erika did not fare any better: in *Neues Deutschland* she was characterized as a "little, petty-bourgeois goose."[57] The central romantic scene was criticized in many reviews as "terribly embarrassing ... [and] a sort of love scene by a river, like the kind we know from the film *One Summer of Happiness*, albeit now translated into German, a very "German" and bad translation."[58] The Swedish film *One Summer of Happiness* was well-known in the GDR, due to the openness of the border at the time. Simultaneously, the DEFA films also came to the attention of the West. *Spiegel* magazine's hatchet job claimed that the DEFA-Film already had a new unofficial title: "One

---

52 See Martin Hellberg, *Mit scharfer Optik. Erinnerungen eines Filmmenschen* (Berlin: Henschelverlag, 1982).
53 "Das kleine und das große Glück," *Neues Deutschland (ND)*, November 28, 1953, Newspaper Archive of the Film University Babelsberg KONRAD WOLF.
54 "Kein ausgesprochener Glücksfall. Zu einem neuen DEFA-Film," Weltbühne, November 25, 1953, Newspaper Archive of the Film University Babelsberg KONRAD WOLF.
55 "Erwartungen nicht gerechtfertigt. Leser schreiben zu dem DEFA-Film 'Das kleine und das große Glück,'" *Neues Deutschland (ND)*, December 5, 1953, Newspaper Archive of the Film University Babelsberg KONRAD WOLF. [All translator's translation]
56 "Kein ausgesprochener Glücksfall," *Weltbühne*, November 25, 1953, Newspaper Archive of the Film University Babelsberg Konrad Wolf.
57 "Das kleine und das große Glück," *Neues Deutschland (ND)*, November 28, 1953, Newspaper Archive of the Film University Babelsberg KONRAD WOLF. [Translator's translation]
58 Ibid. [Translator's translation]

Summer of Shoveling."[59] A second line of argument is evident in the GDR reception. It is one which is quantitatively less visible but, in my opinion, very important as it places the central premises of the film in question: "Why is true love between two people only the minor happiness?"[60] Here, the desire for individual, private happiness is articulated, along with the insistence that the fate of the individual, and not the "type," be placed at the heart of the matter. This implicitly questions both the construction of heroism and the "total disappearance of the individual within society," as Katrin Sell describes it in her analysis of the film.[61]

If one compares this construction of heroism with that in two further DEFA-films of the 1950s, one sees that all these films invest in the connection between individual, romantic happiness and the construction of a socialist society, although one can also identify differences in the emphasis given to "major" or "minor" happiness in each case. In *Roman einer jungen Ehe* [Story of a Young Marriage], produced in 1951-1952,[62] and made by the well-known DEFA-director Kurt Maetzig, the construction of the socialist state is represented with considerable pathos and given pseudo-religious dimensions. The film tells the story of the romantic relationship between two actors, the East German Agnes and the West German Jochen. Agnes expresses her support for the Socialist state by staging an evening of culture for workers on the Stalinallee – the state's prestige building project. A little later she plays an important role in the topping-out ceremony on a section of the Stalinallee known as the Weberwiese. In these scenes, Agnes becomes the proclaimer of a new socialist era and praises Stalin in a poem (see Figures 6 and 7).[63]

---

[59] "Ost-Erotik. Sie schippte nur einen Sommer," *Der Spiegel*, January 6, 1954, Newspaper Archive of the Film University Babelsberg KONRAD WOLF. [Translator's translation]

[60] "Ist es wirklich das kleine Glück," *Film*, December 12, 1953, Newspaper Archive of the Film University Babelsberg KONRAD WOLF. [Translator's translation]

[61] Katrin Sell, *Frauenbilder im DEFA-Gegenwartskino* (Marburg: Tectum, 2009), 159. [Translator's translation]

[62] *Roman einer jungen Ehe*, directed by Kurt Maetzig (1951; Potsdam-Babelsberg: DEFA, 1999) VHS-Video.

[63] The text of Kuba's poem reads "Auf dieser Straße ist der Frieden in die Stadt gekommen. Die Stadt war Staub, wir waren Staub und Scherben und sterbensmüde .... Sagt, wie soll man Stalin danken? Wir gaben dieser Straße seinen Namen." [On this street, peace has come to the city. The city was dust, we were dust and rubble and dead tired .... Tell us, how should we thank Stalin? We gave this street his name." – translator's translation] (Roman einer jungen Ehe 00:75:28–00:77:06).

Figure 5: Still from the feature film, Roman einer jungen Ehe *(timecode 01:15:56) directed by Kurt Maetzig (1952; Potsdam-Babelsberg: DEFA, 1999).*

Figure 6: Still from the feature film, Roman einer jungen Ehe *(timecode 01:34:06), directed by Kurt Maetzig (1952; Potsdam-Babelsberg: DEFA, 1999).*

The interpretation of the poem makes it clear that the German people have the Soviet leader (Stalin) to thank for their "resurrection," and they effectively owe him a debt of gratitude. Instead of the heavenly father, we now have Stalin, who is cinematically enthroned through references back to Christian topoi and symbols. The reconciliation between the pair of lovers at the end of the film is based on the same logic as before: the "minor" happiness between Agnes and Jochen can only thrive when both of them are integrated into the burgeoning Socialist community. As with *Das kleine und das große Glück*, the film's reception was rather muted, with the heroic figures being seen as too declamatory and too far removed from everyday reality.[64]

Following the death of Stalin in March 1953, and the introduction of the "New Political Course" by the Socialist Unity Party in June of the same year, the solemn representation of construction becomes less prominent, while film policy also becomes less restrictive. The film, *Berlin – Ecke Schönhauser* (*Berlin – Schönhauser Corner*),[65] directed by Gerhard Klein, is recognized as an example from this "thaw period" in film policy[66] and, for Ralf Schenk, is "one of the most important contemporary DEFA films of the 50s."[67] In this film, which belongs to the "street film" genre, the protagonist, Dieter, expresses his right to individuality. The film's plot is concerned with young people trying to find their way in post-war Berlin and defending themselves against state authority. Dieter is a construction worker, and considered to be hard-working and conscientious, as is seen in a sequence with an unexploded bomb at the construction site. He is, however, irritated by Socialist ideology and discusses this critically with his brother who is a policeman. Dieter wants to do a good job, but he is also interested in music and fashion. As such, this figure is cinematically constructed as an East German James Dean.

---

64 See Schenk, *Das zweite Leben der Filmstadt Babelsberg*.
65 *Berlin Ecke Schönhauser*, directed by Gerhard Klein (1956; Potsdam-Babelsberg: DEFA, 2005), DVD.
66 Schittly, *Zwischen Regie und Regime*, 97.
67 Schenk, *Das zweite Leben der Filmstadt Babelsberg*, 127.

Figure 7: Still from the feature film, Berlin Ecke Schönhauser (timecode 00:06:09) directed by Gerhard Klein (1956; Potsdam-Babelsberg: DEFA, 2005).

The protagonist is in love with Angela, a young worker, and the film shows how they tentatively get to know each other (See Figure 7). The plot is focused on the conflicts among the male members of the street gang. In one of these fights, Dieter and his friend appear to kill one of the other youths, and they run away to West Berlin to avoid prison. From the very beginning, Dieter considers their escape to have been a mistake: he longs for Angela, and when his companion dies in an accident at the refugee camp, he returns to East Berlin and gives himself up to the police. The sergeant, who is a point of connection for the youths throughout the film, demonstrates a paternalistic understanding for Dieter's situation. The sergeant explains to him that the other youth is not dead, sending him home to Angela with the words "Start again, my boy."[68] The viewer knows that Angela is expecting a child. The individuals' romantic relationship is placed at the forefront of the new beginning and thus has its own justification. The construction of the hero here is significantly lacking in socialist pathos. What remains is a young man who feels himself to be

---

68 Quote from *Berlin Ecke Schönhauser* (01:18:18–01:18:20).

responsible for his work and, indeed, in the scene with the unexploded bomb, shows himself to be closely related to the civilian construction of heroism that one sees in the West. Moreover, through his clothing and his rather relaxed manner, Dieter corresponds to a contemporary Western idea of masculinity. Critics and audiences were persuaded by the representation of the everyday lives of young people and, in its first three months, the film had attracted "more than one and a half million viewers." [69] In this form, the construction of the hero of labor struck a chord with young people and offered itself as an icon of identification, not least through its orientation towards western youth culture, as expressed in the clothing and music tastes of its protagonists.

Overall, film policy after the death of Stalin was responsive to shifts in political direction.[70] Periods of openness would be followed by more restriction ones in quick succession; something that is visible in film production and their construction of heroic figures. This led to different emphases being placed on "major and minor happiness," as well as schematic or more differentiated representations of the heroes of labor. By the end of the 1950s, this type of hero, particularly in its most schematic form, as with the real figure of Adolf Hennecke, had had its day. According to Gries, such heroes of labor and reconstruction were too crudely drawn to be effective.[71] Above all, the message of delayed consumer gratification in the present, for the goal of a future communist society, was not sustainable in the long term. The hero of labor as a type was particularly important for the generation that had been born in the 1930s and 40s.[72] After all, that generation could turn enthusiasm for work into a way of cutting itself free from the complicated National Socialist past. The message about the hero of labor complemented, of course, what they had been taught under National Socialism about contributing as fully as possible to the community.[73] Despite the diminishing acceptance of the socialist hero of labor amongst the population, the party leadership nevertheless held on to this heroic model throughout the whole period of the GDR's existence. As a result, state honors for "heroes of labor" ("Held der Arbeit") and "collectives of socialist labor" ("Kollektiv der sozialistischen

---

69 Schenk, *Das zweite Leben der Filmstadt Babelsberg*, 131. [Translator's translation]
70 Schittly, *Zwischen Regie und Regime*, 91.
71 See Gries, "Die Heldenbühne der DDR."
72 See Abbe and Gries, *Gesellschaftsgeschichte*.
73 Ibid.

Arbeit") were still being handed out in large numbers right up to the end of the GDR's existence.[74] Beginning in the mid-1950s, the hero of labor was gradually replaced as an icon by the collective sports hero,[75] a figure who, in contrast to the hero of labor, can be found in both East and West Germany. As has been pointed out,[76] in the GDR, sport was a matter for state and party, and was considered "an important political weapon"[77] in the struggle between Capitalism and Communism. The GDR correspondingly supported sports both for the whole population and for elite athletes. For the state and the party, sports victories symbolized the superiority of the socialist system and contributed to the international recognition of the GDR. Sportsmen were therefore officially considered to be "diplomats in tracksuits."[78] The prototype of this kind of hero was the cyclist Gustav-Adolf Schur, who was born in 1931. According to Rainer Gries, "Täve" Schur's successes, which included two amateur world championship victories in 1958 and 1959, are part of the development of sportsmen into collective heroes in the 1950s[79] – something that can also to be seen in West Germany and Austria. In all three countries which emerged from the Third Reich, sportsmen allowed for the recalibration of the nation's broken self-esteem. The message that accompanied the victories of Schur, but also those of the Austrian skier Tony Sailer and the West German football team at the World Cup in 1954 declared: *we* are someone once more.[80] The athletic successes achieved by these heroes were equated with economic performance and, as such, the whole population could share in these victories. There was, however, a significant difference between East and West: while western sports stars embodied an individualistic masculine performance ethos (every man for himself), –the Eastern sports heroes represented the ethos of collective performance (one for all and all for one). In the cycling world championship of 1960, Schur, the team captain,

---

74 See Alf Lüdkte, "Helden der Arbeit – Mühen beim Arbeiten. Zur mißmutigen Loyalität von Industriearbeitern," in *Sozialgeschichte der DDR,* ed. Hartmut Kaelble, Jürgen Kocka, and Hartmut Zwahr (Stuttgart: Klett-Cotta, 1994), 188–213.
75 Gries, "Die Heldenbühne der DDR," 94.
76 See Scholz, "Sozialistische Helden."
77 See Norbert Rossbach, "'Täve'. Der Radsportler Gustav – Adolf Schur," in *Sozialistische Helden,* 133–146. [Translator's translation]
78 Ibid., 135.
79 Gries, "Die Heldenbühne der DDR," 94.
80 Ibid., 95.

allowed his teammates to go ahead while he guarded their Belgian opponents, thus ensuring victory for the GDR. According to the official propaganda, he represented the image of collectivity and embodied, so to speak, the "new human being"[81] while, at the same time, becoming a symbol of the successful integration of the generation that had been in the Hitler Youth.

The Crisis of the Socialist Hero of Labor: A Crisis of Hegemonic Masculinity?

In the early 1970s, a crisis in state propaganda, combined with a crisis of its socialist heroes, was already becoming visible.[82] One of the reasons for this was increasing disappointment among the population regarding their unfulfilled consumer desires, the lack of sufficient housing, and the absence of individual prosperity. An expression of this crisis is the fact that, with one exception, no new socialist hero figures were being produced. Only Sigmund Jähn, the first German in space, functioned according to the model established around the Soviet cosmonauts:[83] "as a

---

81 Ina Merkel, "Modernisierte Gesellschafts – 'Bilder' in den DDR-Printmedien der fünfziger Jahre," in *Biographien in Deutschland*, ed. Wolfgang Fischer-Rosenthal and Peter Alheit (Opladen: Leske und Budrich, 1995), 173.

82 Satjukow and Gries, "Zur Konstruktion des 'sozialistischen Helden.'"

83 There is no space here to go into more detail on the heroic type embodied by the cosmonauts – a type established in the Soviet Union in the 1960s (see Scholz, "Sozialistische Helden"). It should, however, be briefly noted that these were far more popular than the sports heroes. In 1961, Yuri Gagarin became the first human in space, and two years later, as part of the tenth manned [sic] space-mission, Valentin Tereschkowa became the first woman in space. These spectacular journeys into space enabled the Russian cosmonauts to symbolize the superiority of the socialist order: "Whoever controlled the earth's orbit, to them also justifiably belonged the earth." [Translator's translation] (Gries, "Die Heldenbühne der DDR," 98). The cosmonauts were "heroes of technology" who were celebrated by the populations of all socialist countries. Precisely Valentina Tereschkowa , often described as "Venus of the Star City," was a "heroine of modernity" for many girls and women (Monika Gibas, "Venus im Sternenstädtchen. Walentina Tereschkowa. Heldin der Moderne in der DDR," in *Sozialistische Helden*, 147). Tereschkowa was evidence of female emancipation and served as an identification figure for the younger female generation, given that she had succeeded in the male-dominated world of technology. The ambivalence of gender relations in socialism becomes evident when one considers that Valentina Tereschkowa

hero in an era without heroes."⁸⁴ Thanks to Jähn's extraordinary feat, the model of disseminating the socialist hero stilled seemed to work: Jähn was a modest man, the ambitious son of a proletarian father, an excellent pilot and officer, a friend and teacher of young people, as well as a convinced Communist. In addition, for the first time in the history of the GDR, it was possible to ascribe national identity to the heroic figure. Jähn was therefore honored as the first German in space. Apart from this exception, the idea of the "everyman hero" had established itself by the 1970s and 1980s. As a result, "minor" heroes were to be found everywhere: heroic foremen, heroic policeman, heroes of labor, and successful athletes – none of whom managed to radiate the charisma of earlier heroes and were thus not useful in legitimizing the political system. Quite the opposite, in fact: "They revealed not only the decline of the concept of the hero but also the ongoing decline of the GDR socialist state."⁸⁵

This crisis of the socialist hero was also evident in artistic productions with the stagnation of the socialist system being a theme of many feature films. Filmmakers often endeavor to produce films that function as "seismographs of social conditions."⁸⁶ The right to "minor" private happiness and to a space for individual freedom are central themes of the so-called "woman's film" of this period, where female protagonists stand at the center of the plot. Typical for this is *Solo Sunny*, directed by the well-established Konrad Wolf, and first distributed in 1980. This film, about a young singer who lives in the alternative district of Prenzlauer Berg in Berlin, proposes a counter model to that of the heroine of labor. As part of her search for an alternative way of living beyond the conventions of marriage and motherhood, Sunny has left a secure, but mundane, job at a factory in order to be a singer for a dance band. Sunny and similar female figures, as analyzed by Elke Schieber, "refuse the iron law of society which

---

could take up this masculine-coded role of cosmonaut, but remained excluded from the military complex, in contrast to Gagarin who held a high military rank. There is no independent construction of femininity in terms of "conquering space"; she is neither the partner nor the (little) sister of Gagarin (see Scholz, "Sozialistische Helden"). Part of this construction is that her feminine and erotic qualities are consistently emphasized (see Gibas, "Venus vom Sternenstädtchen"), and thus hierarchical gender differences covertly reinforced.

84 Gries, "Die Heldenbühne der DDR," 99. [Translator's transition]
85 Ibid., 100. [Translator's translation]
86 Elke Schieber, "Anfang vom Ende oder Kontinuität des Argwohns. 1980-1989," in *Das zweite Leben der Filmstadt Babelsberg: DEFA 1946-92*, ed. Ralf Schenk (Berlin: Henschel 1994), 268. [Translator's translation]

places work at its very center" and they become for the audience the "embodiment of a vitalistic life principle."[87]

Such alternative constructions of the heroic figure do not emerge in the "men's films" of the 1980s. The directors found themselves in a generational conflict with those who had founded the socialist state and now occupied the main positions of power, from which they set the guidelines for film production. Even if younger filmmakers fundamentally agreed with the socialist state project, it was still frowned upon for them to offer any criticism of existing conditions. There was massive state intervention in film production, which occasionally led to the cancellation of production or the banning of distribution.[88] The feature film *The Architects*,[89] made in the years 1989 and 1990, symptomatically draws the crisis in socialist ideology generally together with that of the socialist hero figure in particular. As Schieber has noted, "like no film before it, Peter Kahane's and Thomas Knauf's *Architects* describes the hopes, travails, and resigned attitude of the generation of 40-year-olds in the GDR."[90]

This film enables one to see whether the crisis of hero construction is also to be read as a crisis of hegemonic masculinity. This is not to describe it as a crisis of masculinity in general but, rather, as a crisis about the operation of power. According to Connell, this crisis becomes visible when the model of hegemonic masculinity is no longer consensually accepted by the majority and, thus, violence has to be employed to ensure its position.[91] As a result, other constructions of masculinity emerge in competition to the dominant ideal of the times.

The Architects is an "allegorical representation of the final failing of a political utopia as seen from within the GDR."[92] Officially greenlighted as a DEFA project in 1988, the start of filming was pushed back from February 1989 to October 1989 so that the film was being made during the period of political upheaval that led to the fall of the Berlin Wall. The film tells the story of a group of architects, both male and female, all of whom

---

87 Ibid., 305. [Translator's translation]
88 See Schenk, *Das zweite Leben der Filmstadt Babelsberg*; Schittly, *Zwischen Regie und Regime*.
89 *Die Architekten*, directed by Peter Kahane (1990; Potsdam-Babelsberg: DEFA, 2008), DVD.
90 Schieber, "Anfang vom Ende," 305. [Translator's translation]
91 Connell, *Der gemachte Mann*.
92 Klaus Finke, "Utopie und Heimat. Peter Kahanes Film 'Die Architekten,'" in *DEFA-Film als nationales Kulturerbe?*, ed. Klaus Finke (Potsdam-Babelsberg: Beiträge zur Film- und Fernsehwissenschaft, 2002), 53. [Translator's translation]

are about to turn forty, and none of whom have yet been able to complete any significant architectural projects. Indeed, some of them have already left the profession. After a conversation with his former professor at the latter's birthday party, the protagonist, Daniel Brenner, unexpectedly gets the chance to design the so-called "subsequent buildings" (cinemas, restaurants, cultural buildings, supermarkets, etc.) in a new residential area, within the framework of a youth project. This group of architects hopes to finally be able to give concrete form to their ideas of a *Heimat* (a place with a true sense of "home"). The conflict between these no-longer-young architects – who are under pressure to prove themselves as the next generation – and their superiors can be read as a conflict about hegemonic masculinity mediated through the figure of Daniel in particular. This is a generational conflict in which older men of the first generation who built the GDR, occupy leading positions, and determine the fate of the building collectives are pitted against younger, highly-qualified men who were not able to turn their own ideas into reality since their career paths were blocked by the older males. As Bourdieu might describe it,[93] women are excluded from this masculine power game. The female architects are, as the operations manager says in a key moment of dialogue, not equal players due to their maternal obligations.[94]

---

93 See Pierre Bourdieu, "Männliche Herrschaft," in *Ein alltägliches Spiel. Geschlechterkonstruktion in der sozialen Praxis*, ed. Irene Dölling and Beate Krais (Frankfurt: Suhrkamp, 1997), 153–217.

94 In the actual words of the scene from which this figure is taken: Daniel: Seven is a good number. Director: If you are referring to the Seven Samurai, Colleague Brenner, I can only see three heroes here. Franziska: Women don't count then? Director: I am utterly convinced that you are highly qualified architects, but you know as well as I do that for young women there are certain contradictions between their concern with work and with family planning. (*Die Architekten*: 01:12:44–01:14:18).

Figure 8: Still from the feature film, Die Architekten (timecode 00:13:43) directed by Peter Kahane (1990; Potsdam-Babelsberg: DEFA, 2008).

Daniel embodies the conflict between hegemonic and subordinate masculinity. He has risen to be the leader of a team and yet, at the same time, he is merely a member of this youth collective. This is indicated in the composition of Figure 8, with Daniel positioned alongside the operations manager, while at the same time being part of the semi-circle of members of the brigade that has formed itself around the manager. Due to this double bind position, Daniel has to continuously prove himself to the management, which represents state and party. Through the film's use of Georg Friedrich Handel's *Messiah* on its soundtrack, Daniel is ascribed the role of savior.[95] The group's design may win first prize, but their plans will only be completed if they make considerable compromises. The need for these changes is attributed to economics, but they are, above all, politically motivated, as the conflict surrounding the artistic designs for the new housing area illustrates. The proposed sculptures engage critically with the state's founding myths of anti-fascism and female emancipation, and are therefore rejected by the management. Increasingly, members of the brigade drift away in resignation and, finally, the entire project is

---

95 See Bettina Mathes, "Mit der Heimat verheiratet? Die Architekten von Peter Kahane," in: *Die imaginierte Nation. Identität, Körper und Geschlecht in DEFA-Filmen*, ed. Bettina Mathes (Berlin: DEFA-Stiftung, 2007), 42–71.

mothballed. Thanks to Daniel's intervention at the Central Committee of the Free German Youth (FDJ), the project is taken up again and Daniel has to take on the implementation of a structure that barely resembles the original design. He receives state recognition for his work and seems to have a promising career ahead of him. In the course of what he sees as another failure in his professional life, the protagonist also loses his spouse and daughter, who leave the GDR – a country that has long ceased to be a homeland for the divorced wife. In contrast to the 1950s, here private and collective professional happiness are connected with one another in a negative fashion: the collapse of the political socialist utopia and the separation of the family go hand-in-hand, while at the same time, the image of the emancipated woman is deconstructed. The film shows that, in contrast to official ideology, women are prevented from having professional success on the basis of their gender. Seeing neither the possibility of a professional nor a private future for herself, Daniel's wife chooses flight into a capitalist country as a way out. In contrast, the figure of Renate, a female architect colleague of Daniel's, once again represents the model of the supportive woman – yet even she too is no longer able to stop the protagonist's failure.

After a year and a half of project development, the ceremonial opening of the construction site takes place – although, by now, Daniel is already a broken figure. On the same day, he receives a phone call from his daughter, who has travelled to West Berlin with her school class. They agree to stand on opposite sides of the Brandenburg Gate in order to see each other across the Iron Curtain. This plan fails because the distance between them is too great. Drunk, Daniel runs to the new construction area and, to the sound of Handel's Messiah, hides under the stage set up for the construction ceremony, and remains lying there, as if dead. Through the attempt to measure himself against hegemonic masculinity and not betray his own ideals at the same time, Daniel is crushed – his mental and physical breakdown symbolizing the collapse of the hegemonic masculinity of the socialist hero of labor.

It is not only the protagonist who fails: the history of the film's production and reception mirrors this failure. When the film was shown in cinemas in May of 1990, it was already too late to intervene in the debate about necessary political change in the GDR, for this had occurred during the filming. As a result, the film only attracted 5,000 paying customers. The failure of the protagonists also connect with the real situation, given that we are dealing precisely with filmmakers, as well as actors and actresses, who were members of what the political scientist Joyce Mushaben, has called the "blocked generation." [96] Their projects having faced huge obstacles in the 1980s, Kahane and the other directors who belonged to this fourth generation had to work as assistant directors for many years. Ironically, those film projects that they were able to bring to fruition around the time of the *Wende* no longer spoke to a public preoccupied with other challenges. In relation to Connell's approach, it is clear that, within this particular socialist constellation, the younger generation may have rejected the hegemonic masculinity of the socialist hero of labor, but they could not develop any competing alternatives through the medium of film.

Conclusion

If we read the socialist hero figure as the embodiment of hegemonic masculinity, it is possible to specify what constituted masculine ascendancy in the GDR. The proletarian idea of masculinity, which was constructed to legitimize male dominance, revealed itself to be of limited use in the long run. A proletarian or workers' culture may still have existed until the end of the GDR, but proletarian-inflected hegemonic masculinity increasingly lost its dominant status.[97] It remains to be determined how far other artistic spheres, such as the differing music scenes and various counter culture, developed other forms of masculinity, and to what extent these competed with the official forms. It was specific to the conditions of power in the GDR that both men and women were governed by the state and the party. Nevertheless, women seem to have been more bound up with the state right until its demise. They may have been subordinate to the patriarchal, paternalistic state, but welfare policy enabled them to break away from their personal dependence on men and husbands, and to live economically independent, if modest lives.[98] The cohesive function of hegemonic

---

[96] See Joyce M. Mushaben, *From Post-War to Post-Wall Generations* (Boulder, Co: Westview Press, 1997).
[97] See Holger Brandes, "Hegemoniale Männlichkeit in Ost- und Westdeutschland," in *Postsozialistische Männlichkeiten in einer globalisierten Welt*, ed. Sylka Scholz and Weertje Willms (Münster: Lit, 2008), 59–77.
[98] See Dölling, "Zwei Wege"; Brandes, "Hegemoniale Männlichkeit."

masculinity gradually diminished with each new generation, resulting in diminishing professional and financial benefits for older males. [99] The relationship between masculinities in the 1980s can be described as the subordination of the majority of men to a small political elite that gradually lost its legitimacy. If we follow this argument through, then the collapse of the political structures of the GDR in autumn 1989 was also the result of the crisis of its hegemonic masculinity.

In terms of this volume and the question of everyday heroism, it should be pointed out that, in reflecting upon the history of the GDR as it appears in newspapers, books and especially films, a new type of hero has been constructed: the peaceful demonstrator of the autumn of 1989 who brought about the collapse of the GDR. This construction legitimizes the reunification of Germany and provides East Germans with a different model of heroism and figure of identification. An example of this is the 1995 feature film *Nikolaikirche*,[100] directed by Frank Beyer. The film narrates the events around the political transformations at the Nikolai Church in Leipzig. These new heroes seem to offer a much easier association with the construction of civilian everyday heroism. The extent to which they also connect with the hegemonic construction of masculinity in West Germany, which is much more determined by bourgeois cultural traditions, will have to be left to future analyses.

---

99 Compare the analyses in Scholz, "Männlichkeit erzählen."
100 *Nicolaikirche*, directed by Frank Beyer (1995; Berlin: Provobis und WDR, 2009), DVD.

Everyday Heroes in Germany: Perspectives from Cultural Anthropology

Silke Meyer

"To speak of the heroic is to risk sounding a little dated."[1] The intellectual and academic milieu has long preferred an "anti-heroic" position, and postmodernism does not care much for master narratives that are intended to entertain and instruct. In his "World in Pieces," Clifford Geertz states that "there are just events, persons, and passing formulas, and those inconsonant."[2] Brave and powerful heroes are simply out of fashion. According to Herfried Münkler, we live in a post-heroic age.[3]

However, popular and everyday culture does not seem to be concerned with these academic assessments of the validity or significance of heroism. Here, we can witness a boom of heroic terms. So-called heroes and their medial aesthetics permeate cinema and television productions, computer games, and advertising. The term "hero" functions as a mode of generating attention,[4] and as Simon Wendt has pointed out in his introduction, "heroism" cannot simply be substituted by rather vague terms such as "civic courage." Still, those who make it through the day, to work, to the

---

1 Mike Featherstone, "The Heroic Life and Everyday Life," *Theory, Culture & Society* 9, no. 1 (1992): 159.
2 Clifford Geertz, "The World in Pieces: Culture and Politics at the End of the Century," in *Available Light: Anthropological Reflections on Philosophical Topics* (Princeton: Princeton University Press, 2000), 218–263, here 222.
3 Herfried Münkler, "Heroische und postheroische Gesellschaften," *Merkur* 61, no. 8/9 (2007): 742–752. For a more detailed discussion, see Herfried Münkler, *Der Wandel des Krieges: Von der Symmetrie zur Asymmetrie* (Weilerswist: Velbrück Wissenschaft, 2006). Münkler argues that in postwar Western societies, the readiness to suffer and to make sacrifices for the community has eroded. In a nuclear age, it has become hard to image that the world could be saved by one person sacrificing him- or herself. However, if society is no longer interested in war heroism, this does not prove that the heroic figure as such has exhausted its usefulness. Münkler's argument can just as well be read as evidence for pluralization of the heroic.
4 Ralf von den Hoff, et. al, "Das Heroische in der neuen kulturhistorischen Forschung: Ein kritischer Bericht," *H-Soz-Kult*, July 28, 2015, 2, http://hsozkult.geschichte.hu-berlin.de/forum/2015-07-001.

supermarket, or to the gym are lauded as "heroes." In 2008, for instance, the German supermarket-chain Edeka took out a full-page advertisement in the German weekly *Die Zeit* to thank their employees for "saving the world, always and every day as the friendly hero from next door." Edeka explicitly refers to the fact that these "heroes" reside "not in Hollywood but in Uttrichshausen, Pfullendorf, Husum and 10,000 other locations,"[5] all of which are small and medium-sized German towns that are neither glamorous nor well known. Other examples also abound. In advice books, the compass or logbook for breaking a routine, finding new ways, and making the world a little better is called "the heroic principle."[6] The German Red Cross asks people to donate blood under the heading "heroes like you and me."[7] An amateur German soccer magazine is called *Us Heroes*, and a German TV series portrays soccer teams of lower ranks and their battles against each other under the title "Heroes of the District League."[8] In Germany, heroism even became a state affair in 2008, when the country's President and the Körber foundation called for a youth essay competition on "Heroes: Worshipped, Misjudged, Forgotten."[9]

We can infer that there is no time without its heroes, and our contemporary society is no exception to that rule. The heroic figure is a manifestation of social values and norms, and, therefore, a dynamic, culturally and historically specific phenomenon.[10] Heroic figures reflect, surpass, and challenge the social norms of their environment and can be read as desires, ambitions, and aspirations of a social group during a specific time. The discursive creation of a hero is an act of boundary work

---

5 All translations are my own.
6 For example, Cristián Gálvez, *Logbuch für Helden. Wenn Männer neue Wege gehen* (München: Knaur, 2014); Franz Mittermair, *Neue Helden braucht das Land. Persönlichkeitsentwicklung und Heilung durch Rituelle Gestaltarbeit. Das Handbuch für die "große Heldenreise"* (Blaufelden: Eagle Books, 2011); Nina Trobisch and Thomas Schildhauer, *Heldenprinzip. Kompass für Innovation und Wandel* (Berlin: Verlag Universität der Künste, 2012); Angelika Höcker, *Business Hero. Eine Heldenreise in sieben Etappen* (Offenbach: GABAL, 2010); and Paul Rebillot and Melissa Kay, *Die Heldenreise. Das Abenteuer der kreativen Selbsterfahrung* (Wasserburg: Books on Demand, 2011).
7 https://www.facebook.com/drkblutspendedienste/videos/176038145746287/.
8 See http://www.wir-helden-magazin.de/ and https://de.wikipedia.org/wiki/Helden_der_Kreisklasse.
9 See Geschichtswettbewerb des Bundespräsidenten, Körber-Stiftung: Helden – verehrt – verkannt – vergessen, http://www.koerber-stiftung.de/uploads/tx_smskoerberimport/gelbe_seiten_2008-2009.pdf.
10 See Katalin von Horn, "Held, Heldin," *Enzyklopädie des Märchens*, ed. Rolf Wilhelm Brednich et al., vol. 6 (New York and Göttingen: de Gruyter, 1990), 721–745.

in which the line between the ordinary and the extraordinary is constantly being negotiated. Heroes belong to the realm of the extraordinary while, as liminal figures, they reaffirm the boundaries of social norms. Who is declared a hero (and when) is determined by his or her relationship to society and in demarcation to counter-figures.[11] Revolutionaries are today's villains and tomorrow's heroes, or vice versa. Heroes are often born too early, misunderstood and unappreciated in their time, or even considered outlaws in their social system. As Giesen notes: "what is demonic terrorism for one community is revered as heroic martyrdom by another."[12] Rebels and revolutionaries, geniuses and innovators, alternate between being insider and outsider and thereby simultaneously challenge and affirm the social system. From an anthropological point of view, it is worth repeating that heroic figures are cultural constructions and can be read as compact, time-specific representations of people's anxieties, hopes, and dreams.

Hero Typologies from a Historic-Anthropological Point of View

Because of its cultural and historic specifics, the phenomenon of heroism cannot be reduced to types. However, these specifics have not always been the focus of attention in heroism studies which undertake an academic examination of "the heroic." Especially early anthropological, psychoanalytical, and historical research on the topic was characterized by the search for universal criteria of the hero. In this view, heroes are archetypes rather than social constructions, and the analysis of them focused on universal patterns. In his lecture "On Heroes, Hero Worship and the Heroic in History" (1841), Thomas Carlyle drafted such a typology of 1. the prophet (Mohammed), 2. the poet (Dante and Shakespeare), 3. the priest (Luther and Knox), 4. the author (Johnson, Rousseau, Burns) and 5. the king or regent (Napoleon and Cromwell). While Carlyle's examples are influenced by his puritan thinking, his catalogue reveals a desire to construct ideal categories rather than pursue a historic popular cult of

---

11 See Bernhard Giesen, *Zwischenlagen. Das Außerordentliche als Grund der sozialen Wirklichkeit* (Weilerswist: Verlbrück, 2010), 67–69.
12 Bernhard Giesen, *Triumph and Trauma* (Boulder: Paradigm Publishers, 2004), 1.

personalities. The heroes' role here is to provide moral orientation and social solidarity.[13]

The Viennese psychoanalyst, Otto Rank, and the U.S. mythologist, Joseph Campbell, penned further contributions to hero typologies. Both refer to Jung's concept of archetypes. Campbell is known for his idea of the monomyth (first published in 1949) in which he propagated a universal pattern of the heroic, stating that "whether the hero be ridiculous or sublime, Greek or barbarian, gentile or Jew, his journey varies little in essential plan. Popular tales represent the heroic action as physical; the higher religions show the deed to be moral; nevertheless, there will be found astonishingly little variation in the morphology of the adventure, the characters involved, the victories gained."[14] The morphology of the heroic journey is shaped by thresholds: the hero departs his environment, faces a number of adventures – after initially refusing them – and passes an ordeal that resembles an initiation. Eventually, he returns to society as a refined and mature adult. The recurrent symbols in the heroic story are, according to Campbell, products of the human psyche, stemming from a universal system. Campbell claims to have detected a grammar of symbolic enigmas in the types of the Warrior, the Lover, the Conqueror, the World Savior, and the Saint.

A different hero model, provided by Lord Raglan in 1936, included the different narrative traditions of heroic biographies and thus illustrated the constructivist character of the hero. With 21 exemplary stories, Raglan demonstrated that the narrative patterns were variants of the classifications, which the folklorists Antti Aarne and Stith Thompson had established in their index of folkloristics titled *The Types of the Folktale: A Classification and Bibliography*.[15] Despite the abundance of variations, Raglan stuck with the hypothesis that a blueprint of the folk hero actually existed

---

13 See Thomas Carlyle, *On Heroes, Hero Worship, and the Heroic in History* (1841), (Berkeley and Oxford: University of California Press, 1993); for further analysis see Jens Nordalm, "'Der gegängelte Held. 'Heroenkult' im 19. Jahrhundert am Beispiel Thomas Carlyles und Heinrich von Treitschkes," *Historische Zeitschrift* 276, no. 3 (2003): 647–676.

14 Joseph Campbell, *The Hero with a Thousand Faces*, 3rd edition (Novato: New World Library, 2008), 30.

15 The first version was published in Helsinki in 1961 in the series *Folklore Fellows' Communications* 184. An update is provided by Hans-Jörg Uther: *The Types of International Folktales. A Classification and Bibliography. Based on the System of Antti Aarne and Stith Thompson* (Helsinki: Suomalainen Tiedeakatemia, 2004).

and could be deciphered through a study of its variants.¹⁶ In a similar line of argument, the U.S. folklorist Orrin Klapp devised a complex system of the folk hero's characteristics, such as an extraordinary birth, lonely childhood with challenges to prove bravery, selflessness, vision, as well as an early and unjustified death. As historic figures he named – rather provocatively – Adolf Hitler, Mahatma Gandhi, and Franklin D. Roosevelt.¹⁷ An assertive critic of hero typologies with universal patterns is the U.S.-folklorist Alan Dundes. In his famous study about the historic figure of Jesus Christ (first published in 1976), he mostly objects to the methodology of hero research and its lack of empirical evidence. In Dundes' view, especially Joseph Campbell abstains from concrete evidence. Consequently, he sees Campbell's monomyth model as remaining abstract and formalistic, stating that, "Joseph Campbell ... tries to delineate a 'monomyth' which might apply to heroes from all cultures. However, Campbell's pattern is a synthetic composite which he fails to apply in toto to any one single hero. Campbell's hero pattern ... is not empirically verifiable, e.g. by means of inductively extrapolating incidents from one given hero's biography."¹⁸ Dundes refutes Campbell with his own analysis of the story of Jesus Christ. Here, he manages to show how theologians and religious scholars realign themselves according to narrative patterns in reconstructing the historical figure, Jesus of Nazareth. He further applies different hero patterns, such as those by Raglan and Otto Rank, to the story of Jesus Christ and analyses variants as cultural differences. For example, marriage and family in the Mediterranean are shaped by oedipal behavior: Jesus therefore does not marry a princess but his celibacy symbolizes how the father suppresses his son. As Dundes sees it, this suppression is eventually overcome by the virgin birth, stating:

So Jesus has it both ways: he is the dutiful son obeying a distant, powerful father, but he becomes one with that father – just as boys growing up in circum-

---

16 Fitzroy Richard Somerset Raglan, "The Hero: A Study in Tradition, Myth and Drama, Part II," in *In Quest of the Hero*, ed. Robert Segal (Princeton: Princeton University Press, 1990), 3–86.
17 See Orrin Klapp, "The Creation of Popular Heroes," *The American Journal of Sociology* 54, no. 2 (1948/49): 135–41.
18 Alan Dundes, "The Hero Pattern and the Life of Jesus," in *In Quest of the Hero*, ed. Robert Segal (Princeton: Princeton University Press, 1990), 187–188. The intertextuality of the Jesus narrative is pointed out by Henrike Maria Zilling, *Jesus als Held. Odysseus und Herakles als Vorbilder christlicher Heldentypologie* (Paderborn: Ferdinand Schöning, 2011). Intertextuality, it is important to emphasize, does not mean ahistorical heroic types.

Mediterranean households have to learn to progress from a close and prolonged association with protective mothers to a world of men dominated by elders to a time finally when they themselves become distant fathers to their own children as they seek virgin wives and attempt not to become cuckolded (like Joseph).[19]

Even if one does not want to follow Dundes in every step of his oedipal interpretation, his analysis of hero patterns as a manifestation of cultural specifics is still innovative and empirically grounded at the same time.

Hero Narratives

Heroes need poets who tell their tales; that is to say, in general, they are products of discourse. A folkloristic approach is therefore based on narrative analysis of the cultural and historic specifics of heroic stories, and not on universal criteria of the heroic. These differences are evident in adaptations of historic biographies in legends, ballads, songs, novels, children's stories, poems, and myths. Researching the appropriations and cultural translations of heroic stories and their political and ideological exploitation in myth-making provides an especially fruitful approach to study the making of the hero.[20] For example, social bandits are turned into heroes by the narrative structure of their story. They do not start out as deviants but as victims of social injustice. Thus, the quest to make amends for injustice becomes a central structural element in the plot. Accordingly, the social bandit robs the rich to give to the poor, and he kills only to defend himself or to take revenge. He meets challenges with exceptional bravery and wisdom, he is firm in his beliefs, and sometimes he is even gifted with supernatural talents, like the ability to become invisible. After passing a series of tests, he returns to society as an honorable member where he is met with respect and support. His early death as a young man is often caused by treason. The historian Eric J. Hobsbawm, for instance, has interpreted narrative material like autobiographies, legends, and songs to show how in the nineteenth and early twentieth century, social bandits were worshipped as noble rebels.

---

[19] Dundes, "The Hero Pattern," 216. In the U.S., Dundes received much criticism for questioning the historic figure of Jesus Christ in his folkloristic interpretation.
[20] See von den Hoff, et. al, "Das Heroische in der neuen kulturhistorischen Forschung," 50.

Here it is important to note that the narrative approach is not based on historic facts, but on historic representation. The stories do not provide details about the socio-economic conditions and everyday routines of their protagonists. However, with a contextual reading, the narratives can be seen to present images of the heroic that mirror the social values of an epoch or a milieu. Heroes originate through attribution and labeling, and can thus be interpreted as significant indicators for popular beliefs rather than for historic realities.[21] In oral or written representations, we do not find accounts of deviant deeds but of the hopes and desires of those people who revered them. As Blok points out: "The 'social bandit' as conceptualized and described by Hobsbawm is … a construct, stereotype, or figment of human imagination. Though such constructs may not correspond to actual conditions, they are psychologically real, since they represent fundamental aspirations of people."[22]

When seen as reflecting the self-image of a social group and as the projection of their hopes and ambitions, the relationship of heroes to authorities and morality becomes significant. Heroes often challenge an earthly, man-made law in favor of a transcendental and superhuman order of good and evil. Heroic stories address moral problems and their culturally specific solutions. While a social bandit hero like Robin Hood might act against the law, it is a temporary and corrupted law, enacted by the evil Sheriff of Nottingham. Robin Hood always obeys the true law of his King, Richard I. That is why the rebel is transformed into a loyal servant of the king when Richard I returns to England. The moral of the rebel's story is thus a conservative one and ultimately affirms the traditional order by producing conformity, albeit through deviation.[23] The social bandit does not oppose the king as a divine or moral institution of power, but only the contemporary spokesperson of that authority. Over time, the character of Robin Hood takes on different forms: he is a murdering highwayman in medieval ballads or a pious Christian worshipping the Virgin Mary; a simple man or, from the seventeenth century onwards, a nobleman. The tales represent him as a national hero saving

---

21 Wolfgang Seidenspinner, "Der Mythos vom Sozialbanditen," *Geschichte in Wissenschaft und Unterricht* 49, no. 11 (1998): 698.

22 Anton Blok, "The Peasant and the Brigand: Social Banditry Reconsidered," *Comparative Studies in Society and History* 14, no. 4 (1972): 400.

23 Niklas Luhmann, "Die Autopoiesis des Bewußtseins," in *Soziologische Aufklärung 6. Die Soziologie und der Mensch* (Wiesbaden: VS Verlag für Sozialwissenschaften, 2008), 86.

England from the Norman invaders, or as a philosophical agent of natural law. Even when read as a universal need to identify with a higher power, the tales of Robin Hood show how different the forms of identification can be.[24]

In the endeavor of "getting the story right," the biographies of characters are twisted and changed. Privateer Klaus Störtebeker, whose deeds include murder, rape, arson, and other atrocities, is framed with the legend of a rebel who "took from the rich to give to the poor" ("Het rich lüd wat wegnahm un arm lüd wat gäbn").[25] According to different legends, Störtebeker gave a poor woman in Rügen some pieces of gold on the back of a rag, and he paid the rents of tenants in Hagen and in Bobbin.[26] Supernatural powers are also present in the stories about his death, when he made a deal in his trial that the number of men he could walk past after being decapitated would be spared. In one version, as he passed the fifth man, the hangman threw a log between his legs. In another version, he came as far as the eleventh man and stumbled there.[27]

Contemporary cinematic productions pick up elements of the heroic story to frame their protagonists as heroes. Mel Gibson, director of Hollywood's *Braveheart*, added the loss of William Wallace's father and the murder of his bride to the plot to justify the protagonist's turn to violence.[28] In another example, the German press reinterpreted the story of Arno Funke, a.k.a. Dagobert, who blackmailed several department stores in the 1990s and caused financial damage of more than a million Euros. Despite his purely egoistic motives and his willingness to use violence, the press stories turned him into a folk hero who cunningly fled from the police through the sewer system or by bike. What remains of his

---

24 See Kevin Carpenter, *Robin Hood. Die vielen Gesichter des edlen Räubers/The many faces of that Celebrated English Outlaw*. Exhibition catalogue (Oldenburg: Bibliotheks- und Informationssystem der Universität Oldenburg, 1995).
25 See Wossidlow-Archiv Rostock, B VII 18 (recorded in 1924), quoted after Maya Zumdick, *Störtebeker. Ein sagenhafter Held der Meere* (MA thesis, Münster University, 2004), 1.
26 See Leander Petzoldt, *Historische Sagen. Von der Antike bis zur Gegenwart* (Wiesbaden: Marix Verlag, 2008), 305–306.
27 *Die Sage vom Störtebecker. Alterthümer, Geschichte und Sagen der Herzogthümer Bremen und Verden*, ed. Friedrich Köster (Stade: A. Pockwitz, 1856), 86–87 and Friedrich Sundermann and Ludwig Frahm, *Klaus Störtebeker in Sang und Sage* (Reinfeld, 1885).
28 Silke Meyer, "Heldenmythen. Inszenierung von Geschichte im Spielfilm," in *Historizität. Vom Umgang mit Geschichte*, ed. Andreas Hartmann, Silke Meyer and Ruth-Elisabeth Mohrmann (Münster: Waxmann Verlag, 2007), 69–83.

biography is a tongue-in-cheek tale of a gentleman gangster who manages to beat the system, i.e. the police. Biographies are turned into hero stories by using narrative patterns and topoi of the heroic. With a different emphasis, but through a similar mechanism, winter athletes are constructed as heroes in the Austrian press. Structural elements connected to their sometimes long and tiresome path to success are their humble, often poor origins, a love of nature, the mountains, and a simple and down-to-earth lifestyle represented by their use of dialect.[29]

Having it Both Ways: Everyday Heroes

Ski racers possess a specific athletic talent, but in stories about them, the emphasis is placed mostly on their endurance, diligence, and discipline – one might say on the hardship of everyday life. Since the mid-twentieth century, those civic qualities have been raised to be heroic qualities. This is evidenced by the fact that those who diligently helped to reconstruct Germany after World War II, peace and civil rights activists, whistleblowers, fire fighters, and others in the helping professions have all been called heroes. When media campaigns look for everyday heroes today, normal people are selected and praised for social behavior which seems natural and self-evident: they help their neighbors, they care for the elderly and for those in financial need, they organize the local library, they give blood, and they never give up in the battles of everyday lives. The German charity Caritas launched a campaign in 2008 under the title: "These are what heroes look like" (*So sehen Helden aus*). The different portraits of young people all carry a caption with a short biography. Thus, Kerstin is a hero because she did not let bad childhood experiences break her and now leads a normal life. Imran is a hero because he taught himself German and fights for his rights without violence. Other heroic deeds are going back to school, continuing to look for a job, or finishing a job training. Heroism is here associated with backbone and willpower rather than with martyrdom, acquittal, and obedience.

---

29 Reinhard Johler, "Warum haben Österreicher keinen Bedarf an Nationalhelden? Hiesige Anmerkungen zu "Les héros nationaux: construction et déconstruction," *Österreichische Zeitschrift für Volkskunde* 100, no. 2 (1997): 185–222.

Figure 1: Billboard used by the German charity Caritas for the 2008 Campaign "So sehen Helden aus" ("These are what heroes look like"). Photograph: Silke Meyer

An empirical study among teenagers echoes these findings. When asked for their heroes and heroines in 2006, the boys and girls between the ages of 15 and 17 from a German high school answered in two ways. Firstly, they named athletes because they were "real cool," because they "had made it," and because they "never give up." Secondly, they referred to male members of the family: "my Dad, because he is always there for us," "my

Granddad, because he helps with my homework and knows about life."[30] If coping with everyday life qualifies people to be heroes, we need to ask ourselves how the ordinary and the extra-ordinary are negotiated in contemporary society. First of all, can ordinary Dads and Granddads or famous athletes be considered heroes? If we accept that every time period and society creates and declares its own heroes, and that structural change is a possible, if not an integral element of the heroic,[31] then anthropological hero research can only argue inductively. Hence, those figures described as heroic should be analyzed as such. Moreover, it is important to note that the media campaigns did not use the words "role model," "ideal," or "star," but opted for "heroes" instead, while the youth from the survey did not hesitate to call their family members "heroes." Thus, this evidence for a structural change within heroism needs to be explored in greater detail.

According to the historian George L. Mosse, the transformation of the heroic began with the cult for dead soldiers during World War I. Death on the battlefield and in the trenches was reinterpreted in a national frame: soldiers had become martyrs who sacrificed themselves on the altar of the nation. Consequently, German war cemeteries after 1915 were turned into national memorials with oak groves, sculptures, and pictures of "Jung-Siegfried."[32] What was significant was the lack of rank in remembering the dead in public. Every dead soldier was a hero that had fallen for the Fatherland. The community of the trenches had become a community of dead heroes. This process of democratization is also indicated in the simple cross of stone or iron, or in commemorative plaques that list the names of all the dead soldiers from a particular town or village. The most prominent symbol for the common man who has given his life for his nation is the tomb of the Unknown Soldier. Representative of the collective, an everyman is worshipped as a hero. At the same time, the production of myths opened up countless ways of identifying with the heroic soldiers:

---

30 What needs to be noted is the gender of everyday heroes: although there is no logical reason that these figures need to be male and, in the survey, I explicitly asked for "heroes" and "heroines," the discourse of masculinity still dominates the heroic. While this attribution can be explained as the hegemonial social discourse, we need to consider its consequences in researching the heroic; see von den Hoff et al., "Das Heroische in der neuen kulturhistorischen Forschung," 80–82.
31 See Michael Naumann, *Strukturwandel des Heroismus. Vom sakralen zum revolutionären Heldentum* (Königstein: Athenäum, 1984), 41–54.
32 George L. Mosse, *Gefallen für das Vaterland. Nationales Heldentum und namenloses Sterben* (Stuttgart: Klett-Cotta, 1993), 93.

patriotic literature and songs, postcards and films, board games and toys brought the war home from the battlefields into living rooms. Not only did this process trivialize war, it also contributed to making everyday life heroic.[33] The everyman and, thereby, every man could be a hero as long as he stood by his beliefs and lived up to his ideals. Also, in the German context, the discourse around the hero's body and the reality of war invalids after both World Wars have reinforced the changing semantics of heroes and victims. Whereas war heroes of the nineteenth century were those who survived with their physical integrity and honor intact, this perception changed with the cruel reality of the World Wars. In the twentieth century, traumatized soldiers have been ascribed an aura of the extraordinary.[34]

While I see the changing interpretations of death, war, and nationalism as important steps in the transformation of the heroic towards everyday heroism, there is more to the making of everyday heroes than the democratization of martyrdom. The young boys from my study named "coolness" as one of the criteria why they thought of sport stars as heroes. Here, I would argue that "coolness" as a heroic quality goes back to the modern heroes Walter Benjamin described in his late 1930s fragmentary analysis of Charles Baudelaire's poetry. Baudelaire presents the modern hero in the urban characters of the flaneur and the dandy. These figures truly envision "mode-éternité" but the vision comes at the price of a radical convulsion of identity. The dandy does not stand out due to his beliefs and moral character but, on the contrary, due to his distance from such notions. As Walter Benjamin notes in his study of Baudelaire, an important element in the dandy's manner is not to please anybody.[35] These modern heroes turn their lack of social engagement, ideals, and convictions

---

33 Ibid., 155–191. Counter-figures in this discourse were pilots like Manfred von Richthofen and Gabriele D'Annuzio: they offered an alternative to mass dying on the battlefields and gave fighting a sense of the individual. Plus, the air war techniques could be charged with images and figures from the heroic antiquity like Icarus; see Fernando Esposito, "'Über keinem Gipfel ist Ruh.' Helden- und Kriegertum als Topoi medialisierter Kriegserfahrungen deutscher und italienischer Flieger," in *Der Erste Weltkrieg im Alpenraum. Erfahrung, Deutung, Erinnerung*, ed. Hermann J.W. Kuprian and Oswald Überegger (Innsbruck: Universitätsverlag Wagner, 2006), 73–90.

34 Sabine Kienitz, *Beschädigte Helden. Kriegsinvalidität und Körperbilder 1914–1923* (Paderborn: Ferdinand Schöningh, 2008).

35 See Walter Benjamin, "Charles Baudelaire. Ein Lyriker im Zeitalter des Hochkapitalismus," in *Gesammelte Schriften* 12, ed. Rolf Tiedemann and Hermann Schweppenhäuser, 2nd edition (Frankfurt am Main: Suhrkamp, 1978), 600.

into a virtue and play a role: They are no longer heroes, but they act as heroes.³⁶ With this, the hero becomes a work of art rather than of morality. By making himself aloof and indifferent, he puts himself at a distance to society. Coolness as a "habitus of withdrawal of the self from society" creates an antipole to social commitment and courage. The self-referentiality of the hero – he creates himself and maintains himself – also leads to inner disruption and fragmentation. The philosopher Joseph Früchtl attributes two aspects to coolness. Firstly, to be cool is an aesthetic style modifying and mollifying social coldness. Secondly, a cool style is expressed in the quality of media signs and staging. According to Früchtl, coolness is an act of aesthetics.³⁷

The aspect of aestheticism can be studied in detail when looking closely at media representations of heroic figures. The hypothesis that everyday heroes are no longer put on a pedestal, but come from our midst, can be exemplarily illustrated by the changes within sports photography, as Christine Walter has shown in her detailed study of photographs of winners in sport journals since the late 19ᵗʰ century.³⁸ Whereas in the early days of sports photography there was no clear distinction between a winner and a runner-up, an iconography of winning was established alongside the technical improvement of photography. When outdoor photography was made possible, pictures of winners could include the added drama of the winning moment: The crossing of the finish line, or the triumphant pose of raised arms in the seconds after the victory. The snapshot, according to Walter Benjamin, was to become the definition of modern seeing, an exemplary expression of an acceleration of life. Photography guidebooks promoted the snapshot as "the real sport picture." With a bigger aperture, however, the background became blurred, and because photographers wanted to give the blur as little room as possible, they zoomed in on their object, causing a visual language of close-ups to be born as the sujet of winner's images. In contrast to portraits, where the person took up about a third of the whole area, the sports heroes filled the

---

36 Benjamin, "Charles Baudelaire," 600.
37 Joseph Früchl, *Das Unverschämte Ich. Eine Heldengeschichte der Moderne* (Frankfurt am Main: Suhrkamp, 2004), 295. Immer and van Marwyck also trace the line of thought that the heroic as an aesthetic experience is a quality of the civic or, in Münkler's words, the post-heroic age. See Nikolas Immer and Mareen van Marwyck, *Ästhetischer Heroismus. Konzeptionelle und figurative Paradigmen des Helden* (Bielefeld: Transcript, 2009).
38 Christine Walther, *Siegertypen. Zur fotografischen Vermittlung eines gesellschaftlichen Selbstbildes um 1900* (Würzburg: Königshausen & Neumann, 2007).

entire picture. Thus, the close-up became an iconographic indicator for portraying the sports hero – and not only in sports. In addition, the reduced distance to the athlete suggests that his gestures and facial expressions are aimed at the individual viewer, which is then interpreted as an invitation to enter into his world. Beginning around 1910, this development was enhanced with the advent of home stories, in which the illustrated magazines depicted sports heroes in their living rooms, or with their spouses and children.[39] By coming closer, and by letting the audience into their private lives, athletes were partaking in one of the ambivalences of everyday heroism: mixing exceptional talent and skills with an authentic, i.e. normal, personality. Put another way, they became extraordinary in the ordinary. With Western society being founded on ideals like commitment, individual freedom, democracy, and social mobility, this elevates ideas of diligence, fair play, loyalty, and decency. To illustrate this point further, Fredrik Schoug compares the media representations of sporting heroes to those of rock stars and comes to the conclusion that, "whereas the rock star as *agent provocateur* appear [sic] hyper-individuated, the sporting star is hyper-socialized."[40]

Heroes have also become closer in the spectator's imagination. Florian, a sixteen-year-old high school student talks about a close-up of Michael Ballack that he has stuck into his schoolbook for good luck, saying that, "when I see that picture, I feel really close to him. He looks such a nice guy there, really, I talk to him and stuff. And I always see his image in *Kicker* and in other magazines and on TV, with his family and his kids. He is so real and close." Two aspects are important here: Florian translates the everyday scenes of soccer star Ballack with his family and in his home into authenticity, and he sees this interpretation confirmed by the intimacy of the close-up. The first aspect speaks to the omnipresence of stars in contemporary media. We encounter them on a regular basis; not only doing what they are famous for, such as playing soccer or singing on stage, but in their daily lives at their homes, or while they shop, dine in a restaurant, walk on the beach, etc. And they act "just like us," thereby elevating the quality of authenticity and fostering identification. As Johannes says about his "hero" Sebastian Schweinsteiger: "I love it when I see him in his normal clothes; he is just like everybody else. My favorite

---

39 Walther, *Siegertypen*, 101–102.
40 Fredrik Schoug, "Transformations of Heroism. Fame, Celebrities, and Public Performances," *Ethnologia Europaea. Journal of European Ethnology* 27, no. 2 (1997): 107.

picture of him is from the story when he plays on the computer with Poldi [Lukas Podolski, fellow German national soccer player], when he is out or with his girlfriend. They go to Burger King and to McDonald's and then he says that some things stress him. He admits that sometimes he does not feel like practicing and that it is difficult, sometimes. And that he is sad when he loses or does not play well. But then he keeps going, that is like when we lose, then I feel bad, too, and then I think of that."

Johannes emphasizes that his hero shows weakness but then overcomes it – a central element of the hero narrative in which the hero has to pass through trials and tribulations. For Johannes, the combination of exceptional talent, endurance, and capacity for everyday challenges are qualities he admires in his hero, who is not beyond criticism. In Florian's words: "He is so real and close." The authentic quality as part of the heroic is therefore linked to the nature of information we received about public figures. A home story shows its protagonists in everyday life and surroundings with a "heroic unaffectedness," a term Schoug coined for the "ordinariness" that is a "precondition"[41] of the hero's role.

As with Walther's study of photographic conventions in illustrated magazines, the second aspect is linked to media techniques, since close-ups allow insights into highly emotional moments. When a camera zooms in, we witness tears and triumph, rage and jubilation at close range, and thereby identify with the heroic experience. Florian speaks about an image of Michael Ballack after his team lost in the semi-finals of the World Cup in 2006: "Of course, it was terrible when they lost. But I thought it was great how brave he was. When we lose, I look at the picture and then I feel better." Schoug refers to this when he writes: "Because of his propensity to present the spectator with images of ordinariness, that is, of the spectator himself, the unaffected hero seems authentic."[42] Thus, we can infer that a precondition for everyday heroism is the institutionalized and discursive search for identity. Accordingly, only modernity could have yielded everyday heroism.[43]

When close-ups overcome the distance between image and spectator, the image takes on an aesthetic quality which the performance scholar

---

41 Schoug, "Transformations," 109.
42 Ibid.
43 Ibid.

Philip Auslander has called "co-presence."⁴⁴ Florian reinforces the co-presence of the Ballack portrait by sticking it into a schoolbook and by talking to the image – a practice we can compare to worshipping saints' images. Auslander proposes to no longer distinguish between the aesthetics of a live performance and a media presence because the intimacy of the close-up conveys an authenticity which is lacking in the distance of a live performance, such as a big rock concert. Close-ups of tears and laughter which are accompanied with interviews on how the sporting heroes felt when they scored the winning goal or when they lost the game further contribute to overcoming the distance between the sports heroes and their audience. This atmosphere of "public privacy" is, again, maintained and managed by a notion of authenticity.⁴⁵

Electronic media leave very little room to cover up mistakes and bloopers. Within seconds, every slip is broadcasted and preserved for the future, thereby closing the gap between the heroic and the ordinary. Leo Braudy has called this process the "democratization of fame."⁴⁶ Judith Williamson describes how representations of the British royal family have changed over decades, moving from an accentuation of the status of aristocracy to projecting an image of a "normal family."⁴⁷ In addition, Joshua Meyrowitz has analyzed a similar phenomenon for American presidents and politicians.⁴⁸ He argues that President Lincoln could only go down in history as a charismatic speaker because there are no recordings of his unusually high-pitched voice. Jefferson's speech impediment is hardly ever mentioned. But Gerald Ford tripping over when leaving Airforce One in Austria, and Ronald Reagan falling asleep during a sermon by Pope John Paul II have become part of public memory. Dixon Wecter describes this change in journalistic coverage, stating that, "when the world was young and there were men like gods, no reporters were present ... only poets."⁴⁹

---

44 Philip Auslander, *Liveness. Performance in a Mediatized Culture* (London and New York: Taylor & Francis, 1999).
45 Schoug, "Transformations," 122.
46 Leo Braudy, *The Frenzy of Renown. Fame and its History* (New York and Oxford: Vintage, 1986).
47 Judith Williamson, *Consuming Passions. The Dynamics of Popular Culture* (London and New York: Marion Boyars Publishers, 1988), 75–89.
48 Joshua Meyrowitz, *No sense of Place. The Impact of the Electronic Media on Social Behavior* (New York and Oxford: Oxford University Press, 1985), 268–304.
49 Dixon Wecter, *The Hero in America. A chronicle of Hero-Worship* (New York: Scribner, 1972), 4.

Conclusion

Heroism is not a universal or static category. The contemporary use of the term "hero" in its everyday context is the result of a social change with regard to heroism. When young people become heroes by applying for job trainings, then the battle arena is the labor market and the shield is made of endurance and willpower. When the heroic and the ordinary merge, closeness and distance, coolness and care are qualities of the heroic that coincide: Heroic actors apply and elude themselves simultaneously and construct themselves through a fragmentized self by merging the ordinary and the extraordinary. Their concurrence is made possible in the mediated quality of authenticity.

The sociologist Mike Featherstone has described post-modernity as a counterrevolution: popular culture, small traditions, sensual aesthetics, immediate experience, and the everyday have been revalued by postmodern society. From this he derives a heightened attention for ambivalence, complexity, syncretism, and heterogeneous practices within daily routines.[50] Postmodern heroes are everyday heroes ready to face ambivalence and pluralism, and they re-evaluate the mundane with their significance. The blueprint of the everyday hero is derived from an elevation of everyday challenges and a pluralism of answers to those challenges. In Clifford Geertz's "World in Pieces," he states that we must "content ourselves with diverging tales in irreconcilable idioms, and not attempt to enfold them into synoptic visions. Such visions (this vision has it) are not to be had."[51] And when heroes are manifestations of the culturally and historically specific needs, ambitions, and aspirations of a society, then the diverse and ambivalent features of everyday heroes provide answers to questions of mobility, reflexivity, pluralism, and their co-existence.

---

50 Featherstone, "Heroic Life," 160–164.
51 Geertz, "The World in Pieces," 222.

After Watergate and Vietnam: Politics, Community, and the Ordinary American Hero, 1975–2015

William Graebner

The defining moment in the history of the ordinary hero came on a cold night in January of 1982, when Air Florida flight 900, descending into Washington's National Airport, struck the 14th Street bridge and plunged into the icy waters of the Potomac River. Of the 79 people on board, 74 died, most of them on impact, with the rest drowning as most of the plane disappeared below the surface. Remarkably, the tail section remained afloat for a time, and clinging to it were six passengers, of whom five would survive. The sixth, later identified as Arland Williams, perished while passing a lifeline and flotation devices to the others.[1]

Williams would become the decade's most vivid symbol of the ordinary hero. Media reports disregarded his not-so-ordinary occupation – he was a senior examiner with the Atlanta Federal Reserve Bank – to focus on his ordinariness: for *Reader's Digest*, Claire Safran described him as a "balding, middle-aged, 'average' man." What he was *not* also took on importance: he was neither a police officer nor a firefighter nor part of an official rescue team – that is, not expected to be regularly in the midst of danger, and not paid to risk his life. "Only minutes before his character was tested," wrote Roger Rosenblatt for *Time*, "he was sitting in the ordinary plane among the ordinary passengers …. For a while, he was Everyman, and thus proof (as if one needed it) that no man is ordinary." Concluding her essay, Safran wrote, "Isn't it, in times of danger, the 'average' man who saves us all?"[2]

---

1 "Death on the Potomac," *Newsweek*, January 25, 1982, 26–28.
2 Roger Rosenblatt, "The Man in the Water," *Time*, January 25, 1982, 86, Claire Safran, "Hero of the Frozen River," *Reader's Digest*, September 1982, 49–53. It is usually assumed that firefighters and police officers have exceptionally dangerous jobs. But in the twenty-first century, a variety of occupations have much higher fatality rates: logging workers, aircraft pilots and flight engineers, refuse collectors, truck transport workers, and electrical power line repairers and installers, among others. Noam Scheiber, "New Labor Rules for Public Sector Workers Don't Apply to All," *New York Times*, March 20, 2015, B1–B2.

Without diminishing what Williams did, it is important to reflect on the historical context in which the media – and Americans, generally – elevated him to heroic status and indulged in the cult of the ordinary hero. In 1982, when Williams made his sacrifice, the latest incarnation of the cult of the ordinary hero was already well developed, more than a decade old. The idea surfaced in the early 1970s, when brief accounts of the extraordinary deeds of ordinary people began to appear in the *Congressional Record*, and it was solidly established by the late 1970s, when the ordinary-hero concept was widely accepted in the popular press. In this period, ordinary heroes were welcomed and celebrated in part because "standard" heroes – generals, presidents, war heroes on the order of World War I's Sergeant Alvin York– were in short supply, having succumbed to a disastrous war in Vietnam; the seedy, corrupt politics of Watergate; globalization and economic decline; the Iranian hostage crisis; a widespread suspicion of authority; and a wave of multicultural pluralism whose adulation was likely to be bestowed not on the out-of-favor white men of the American meta-narrative, but on ethnics, people of color, minorities, women, the working class, even celebrities. Although there were people to admire, and heroes to be had – Muhammad Ali, the Reverend Martin Luther King Jr., Gloria Steinem, Cesar Chavez, Karen Silkwood, Curt Flood, and Farah Fawcett-Majors – the journalists, politicians, cultural critics, and pundits could see only loss: "The End of the American Hero."[3]

In this "disappearing heroes" lament, and in the celebration of ordinary heroes like Arland Williams that came in its wake, one can hear concern – understandable, legitimate, and often bipartisan concern – about the decline of the American nation and the degradation of American culture; alarm that the "American Century" might be over after a mere thirty years. But one can also hear the ring of politics, with partisan voices on the right using these discourses – elements of a larger phenomenon that would become known as the "culture wars" – to attack and blame liberalism and the left. One purpose of this political critique was to link the decline of traditional heroism with liberal values (including permissiveness, ethical relativism, the idea of the victim, and the primacy of the group), movements of the "sixties," and the "malaise" of the 1970s. By doing so, they hoped to encourage Americans to turn away from liberalism, the

---

3 For a fuller treatment of the crisis of heroism and the politics of heroism in the 15 years after 1970, see my essay, "'The Man in the Water': The Politics of the American Hero, 1970–1985," *Historian* 75 (Fall 2013): 517–543.

Democratic Party, and an emerging multicultural, feminist America and to embrace a Republican conservatism that privileged the white male, the cult of the individual, absolute values, and the militarized nation-state. For example, writing in *U.S. News & World Report* in 1991 in the aftermath of the Gulf War, M. Barone rejoiced that the conflict had given the nation "heroes, not victims." "A country that focuses on victims," he added, "takes on an air of being beaten. Ronald Reagan, understanding this, tried to shine a light on heroes who were doers. Now we have the troops of the gulf."[4] While a logical response to the sorry state of traditional heroism, the vogue of "ordinary" hero was, as I have argued at length elsewhere, also part of the right's effort to bring the white working class into the Republican Party. Hence, Ronald Reagan, eager to woo those who would come to be labeled "Reagan Democrats," made the ordinary hero a prominent feature of his 1982, 1984, and 1985 messages.[5]

Today, the mania of the ordinary hero, now in its fifth decade, remains as strong as ever, bolstered by the events of 9/11 and by deep cultural and social concerns. The movement has by-and-large shed its hard, white-male, political edge, slowly embracing women, minorities, socially conscious do-gooders, those whose actions were not life-threatening, police officers and fire-fighters, and others once excluded from the category, mostly for political reasons. As the discourse of ordinary heroism embraced these changes, it articulated – and in its own way, analyzed – a profound unease over social fragmentation, over Americans' weakening obligations to one another. This emerging concern, more liberal than conservative, and more attuned to the voices of women and minorities than to the plight of men, was, at its core, about the decline of community. The discourse of the ordinary hero was a way of understanding this problem of decline. And the ordinary hero was, as odd as it may seem, one part of a solution.

---

4 M. Barone, "This Time, They're Heroes," *U.S. News & World Report*, March 18, 1991, 14. For a critique of 1960s relativism, see Joseph C. Keeley, "Hail the Hero," *American Legion Magazine*, June 1985, 24.

5 The Reagan State of the Union addresses are available online at www.thisnation.com/library/sotu/1988rr.html (1982); http://www.reagan.webteamone.com/speeches/reagan_sotu_1983.cfm (the 1983 address, which contains a reference to "ordinary' Americans"); http://www.reagan.webteamone.com/speeches/reagan_sotu_1984.cfm (1984); and www.presidency.ucsb.edu/docs/sou/reagan4.htm (1985). Carter took a stab at appealing to the populist sentiment that underlay the idea of the ordinary hero, staying at the homes of ordinary people and wearing a sweater when he presented his energy plan. Leonard Quart and Albert Auster, *American Film and Society since 1945*, 2nd edition, revised (New York: Praeger, 1991), 106.

A survey of the popular literature on ordinary heroes – stories appearing in magazines such as *Good Housekeeping, Newsweek,* and *American Legion* – produces a general, though not always consistent, portrait of the ordinary hero in the late twentieth and early twenty-first century. The range of ordinary heroes was broad and often depended on the magazine or organization making the claim. For example, *Overdrive,* a magazine for truckers, praised truckers who had engaged in rescue efforts after road accidents.[6] Similarly, *Trains Magazine* profiled an assistant conductor who had shown leadership and presence of mind – though apparently without risking his life – after an Amtrak train had derailed into a Louisiana bayou in 1993. In this case, a member of the safety board noted that, "We find that it's often the cabin attendants and the on-board-service crew that make the difference between life and death."[7] And the Pension Rights Center paid tribute to "retirement security hero" Robert E. Nagle, who had played an important role in the drafting and passage of the Employment Retirement Income Security Act of 1974.[8] Although some publications pointedly excluded military figures from the category "ordinary heroes," *American Legion Magazine,* intended for veterans, just as pointedly emphasized recipients of the Medal of Honor in an article entitled "Ordinary Heroes."[9] The Carnegie Commission which, since its founding in 1904, had been naming an average of 85 heroes per year, excluded "professional guardians," including armed forces personnel, firefighters, police officers, paramedics, and even lifeguards. "Particularly sought out by the Commission are ordinary folk who responded to the plight of a total stranger (the majority of cases) and those who 'walked into hell *full knowing* the danger involved.'"[10] Of course, the exclusion of professionals from the ranks of ordinary heroes became unthinkable after 9/11; an October 1 editorial in *Business Week* announced that "Big, beefy working-class guys became heroes once again."[11]

---

6 "Goodyear Hails Heroic Truckers," *Overdrive* 25, February 1985, 60–61.
7 Don Phillips, "Amtrak's Unsung Hero," *Trains Magazine,* March 1994, 18.
8 "A tribute to retirement security hero Bob Nagle," Pension Rights Center Press Release, August 18, 2014, at http://www.pensionrights.org/newsroom/releases/tribute-retirement-security-hero-bob-nagle.
9 "Ordinary Heroes," *American Legion Magazine,* May 2002, 42, 44. See also Norman Vincent Peale, "A Different Breed of Hero," *Good Housekeeping,* July 1989, 66, which begins with the following tease: "These three Americans haven't won any medals."
10 "Unknown Brigade of Civilian Heroes," *American Legion,* May 1981, 12.
11 Bruce Nussbaum, "Real Masters of the Universe," *Newsweek,* October 1, 2001, 55.

The preference for working-class and male heroes – ordinary and otherwise – was especially marked in the first decade of the crisis of the American hero: the 1970s. Soldiers from World Wars I and II (but not Vietnam) were favorites,[12] while, in a reaction to the feminist movement, women were usually excluded. In a notable 1979 essay on the decline of the hero in *Newsweek*, writer Pete Axthelm hurled insults at Jane Fonda, Vanessa Redgrave, and Margaret Trudeau while waxing eloquently over the men who had defended the Alamo and fought at Guadalcanal.[13] Almost two decades later, neo-conservative Norman Podhoretz blamed the feminist movement for feminizing American society and damaging men, leaving the nation with cinematic heroes such as Clint Eastwood and Mel Gibson, but without real ones.[14]

Nonetheless, women were increasingly brought under the rubric of ordinary heroes – again, especially after 9/11, when the contribution of women to rescue efforts was impossible to ignore. An article in *Good Housekeeping* began with the contributions of several women to 9/11 rescue efforts, but then moved on to praise the "unsung heroism" of women helping those with severe handicaps, women working two or three jobs, or women – like Karen Silkwood and Erin Brockovich – who spoke up to confront injustice.[15] *Redbook*, a women's magazine, did the same, highlighting the actions of a fifth-grade teacher in the immediate aftermath of 9/11, and then telling the stories of courageous women who had protected and saved children in a variety of other contexts and situations.[16] In 1986, when *McCall's* highlighted the actions of young people in a "21-hero salute," 10 were female.[17]

"Ordinary heroes" was a flexible – and contested – concept; one that could encompass a variety of different heroic types. At one extreme were the Medal of Honor recipients and 9/11 responders, many of whom had willingly and selflessly risked their lives in acts of extraordinary courage. At the other extreme were ordinary heroes who were, one might say, ordinary

---

12 "Heroes: To Hell and Not Quite Back," *Time*, June 14, 1971, 27.
13 Pete Axthelm, "Where Have All the Heroes Gone?" *Newsweek*, August 6, 1979, 44–50.
14 Norman Podhoretz, "Heroism in a Politically Correct Age," *National Review*, January 1998, 45.
15 Elise O'Shaughnessy, "Finding the Hero in You," *Good Housekeeping*, January 2002, 112.
16 "Save One Life, and You Save the Entire World," Redbook Report, *Redbook*, February 2002, 100. See also "2004 Heroes for Health Awards," *Good Housekeeping*, December 2004.
17 Anne Cassidy, "21 Kids Who Have Made a Difference," *McCall's*, July 1986, 44, 49–51.

to a fault. According to *Grit* magazine, parents could be heroes: "It's heroic to bring a child into the world, sacrifice and agonize over that child and her future then let go to allow the child the freedom to find her own way."[18] Businessman John Mariotti had four heroes when he was growing up: Sam Walton, destined to make billions with his superstores, Vince Lombardi, the pro-football coach – and his parents. His father was a professional musician, his mother a successful businesswoman.[19] "It's corny," said newswoman Cokie Roberts, "but my hero is my mother, Lindy Boggs. Mom has the ability to keep learning and laughing and loving and making the world better for everyone else."[20] In 1999, *Insight on the News* put former president Ronald Reagan on its cover, and a writer for the magazine who knew one of Reagan's sons, had this to say: "Mike Reagan is lucky to be able to call his hero 'Dad.' The older I get, the more I feel that way about my own father. And my mother. They are heroes to me on the smaller playing field of life where you get to look at character up close and personal."[21] Even more insular was the response given by 8 of 20 eight- and nine-year-old children when asked the question "What do you want to be?" Their response was "Me."[22]

Only a decade after one cultural critic after another lamented the disappearance of the American hero, heroes – that is, ordinary heroes – were ubiquitous; or at least the critics said they were. "They are single mothers struggling to provide for their families," wrote Ryan Mathews in the trade journal *Grocery Marketing*. "They are older Americans trying to preserve their dignity in a society that worships youth. They are your neighbors, your customers, and your employees."[23] An essay in *The Humanist*, featuring whistleblowers as heroes, made the same point: "The whistleblower could be your neighbor, your coworker, your spouse – or

---

18 Jean Teller, "Finding Heroes" (Editor's note), *Grit*, September 15, 2002, 2.
19 John Mariotti, "Where Have All the Heroes Gone?" *Industry Week*, January 8, 1996, 25.
20 O'Shaughnessy, "Finding the Hero in You," 112; On Moms and Dads as heroes, see also James P. Comer, "Ideology Formation and Hero Worship," *Parents* 56 (April 1981): 98.
21 Paul M. Rodriguez, "Just Who Qualifies as a 'Hero' Today?," *Insight on the News*, November 29, 1999, 48.
22 Ralph Schoenstein, "A New Generation of Heroes?" *50 Plus*, July 1985, 26–28.
23 Ryan Mathews, "A Moment of Silence for an Act of Courage," *Grocery Marketing*, May 1994, 5.

perhaps you."[24] Addressing the 1986 graduating class of Boston University, president Joel Silber concluded a weighty speech with the example of Arthur Miller's Willy Loman and his son Biff, not as tragic figures but as heroic ones – "a dime a dozen," as Biff put it, but also, as Willy recognized, "magnificent."[25] Reflecting on the tenth anniversary of the end of the Cold War, a Reagan admirer praised the heroism of the "average American who remains faithful to our country's values, does the work and earns the wage, cares for his and her own family with just enough left over to help a neighbor, and pours out the sweat and blood and tears that protect the peace."[26] An academic psychologist summed it up: "You may not realize it, but heroes are everywhere."[27]

Ordinary and not so ordinary heroes were not only everywhere, but modest. A mother of two who had stopped and helped a badly injured mother and her four children, confused and bleeding, avoid further injury after a car accident, "shakes off any 'hero' labels," claiming, "I didn't run into a burning building. I just ran into a situation where people needed some help and applied the resources that I had."[28] The assistant conductor at Amtrak's Alabama bayou disaster refused to talk to the media, making an exception for his hometown newspaper.[29] Even the extraordinary heroes, recipients of the Congressional Medal of Honor, reportedly "feel they didn't deserve" the award. "They just helped their buddies or someone else."[30] And modest heroism was "quiet heroism," a heroism of the "quiet, ordinary person," the guy at the gas station or at the supermarket checkout, "quietly leading lives by example, even with the

---

24 James R. Bennett, "Trading Cards, Heroes, and Whistleblowers," *The Humanist* 57 (March–April 1997): 23. On spousal heroism – a man saving his wife from a cougar in the back yard–see "Real-life Superheroes," *Maclean's*, September 23, 2013, 8.
25 Joel R. Silber, "Of Mermaids and Magnificence: Heroism," *Vital Speeches of the Day*, July 1986, 589–593.
26 Rodriguez, "Just Who Qualifies as a 'Hero' Today?," 48.
27 Tamra B. Orr, "To the Rescue: Our Real Life Heroes," *Current Health 2: A Weekly Reader Publication*, March 2000, 18. See also Denise Foley, "The Hero in All of US," *Prevention*, August 1985, 72–74.
28 "Save One Life, and You Save the Entire World," *Redbook*, February 2002, 100.
29 Phillips, "Amtrak's Unsung Hero," 18.
30 "Don't Call Them Heroes," *50 Plus*, July 1986, 9–10. On the modesty of military heroes, see also Reid Andrews, "Washington Report," *Guns & Ammo*, November 1984, 6.

burden of their own faults."[31] In this discourse about modest, quiet, and ordinary heroes, one can hear echoes of Franklin Roosevelt's "Forgotten Americans" and, especially, Richard Nixon's "silent majority," a term first used by Nixon in 1969 as his Republican Party began a decades-long campaign to attract white, working-class voters.[32] So here, amidst all this ordinariness, we have a glimpse into the politics of heroes.

The admiration for modesty had its parallel in another aspect of the discourse of heroism: an intense hostility to celebrity and to the idea of celebrity heroism. The problem was real. In the 1970s, when traditional heroes – presidents, politicians, and military leaders among them – became harder to accept as heroic, celebrity heroes emerged to fill the gap, especially among youth. In poll after poll, young people filled the void with celebrities: model and actress Farah Fawcett-Majors, Paul Michael Glaser, star of the television drama *Starsky & Hutch*, O. J. Simpson, Elton John, Jerry Lewis, John Wayne, and so on. Even in 1985, when *U.S. News & World Report* optimistically titled its survey of heroes "Heroes are Back," young adults picked Clint Eastwood and Eddie Murphy before turning to a political figure, Ronald Reagan. This turn of events was widely seen as unfortunate, even sad. Most pundits and critics blamed the media, both for revealing so much about the traditional heroes that they could no longer be appreciated, and for creating the celebrities that took their place. "Today's heroes," opined a former editor of *American Legion Magazine*, "are more likely to be the creations of smart press agents than individuals striving for true greatness."[33] Writing in *Seventeen*, a magazine for late teens, Ron Powers wrote that "we have put heroism on the mass market and got it all confused and intertwined with celebrityhood."[34] *The Nation* summoned the testimony of artist – and celebrity – Andy Warhol: "If … everyone in the 1960s was entitled to fifteen minutes of celebrity, everyone today is eligible for a brief fling with heroism: the astronaut-of-the-month, the latest artificial-heart recipient, the freed hostage, the megabucks lottery winner ….

---

31 O'Shaughnessy, "Finding the Hero in You," 112; Teller, "Finding Heroes"; Chris Katterjohn, "Casalini Book Shines Bright Light on Heroism," *Indianapolis Business Journal*, February 12, 2001, 15.
32 Jefferson Cowie, *Stayin' Alive: The 1970s and the Last Days of the Working Class* (New York: The New Press, 2010), 129.
33 Joseph C. Keeley, "Hail the Hero!" *American Legion Magazine*, June 1985, 24.
34 Ron Powers, "Do Teens Hunger for Heroes?" *Seventeen*, July 1981, 108.

Win a basketball game and get a locker-room call from Ronald Reagan and a Rose Garden reception the next day."[35]

The quiet, humble, ordinary hero offered a way out. One could worship hockey superstar Wayne Gretzky because "he doesn't call himself a hero .... Real heroes are ordinary people." Acknowledging the "lure of celebrity culture" in the aftermath of the killing of Osama bin Laden, *Newsweek* editor Tina Brown described genuine heroism as "about submerging the ego in the service of the group, and the country. Fortunately," she concluded, "the narcissists are truly vastly outnumbered by those who prefer to say, 'Don't call me a hero.'"[36]

Consistent with, and related to, this critique of celebrity, writers determined that the decline of traditional heroism was related to the seductions of a narcissistic, selfish, decadent, materialistic, consumer culture that overvalued money and career success – athletes with their big contracts are often mentioned in the literature – and undervalued the idealism and altruism that had characterized heroes of another age, such as scientist Marie Curie and Civil War nurse Clara Barton. The legendary Yankee centerfielder Joe DiMaggio, now "just Mr. Coffee"; the heroic pantheon of Mt. Rushmore, "replaced by a mirror."[37] Such sentiments were especially common in religious publications and those catering to veterans of the military,[38] but they were by no means limited to those venues. Boston University's president went so far as to describe modern people as "in thrall to hedonism, cut off from past and future," living in a "disconnected present."[39] Even business journals commented on the

---

35 "Heroes are Made," *Nation*, September 28, 1985, 267.
36 Anthony Wilson Smith, "Remembering True Heroes," *Maclean's*, January 1, 2000, 26; Tina Brown, "Profiles in Courage," *Newsweek*, November 12, 2012, editorial.
37 Schoenstein, "New Generation of Heroes?" 26, 28 (Curie, Barton, Rushmore); Robert Bell, "Heroes: Are We Better Off Without Them?" *Boston Magazine*, August 1985, 110 (DiMaggio). On the relationship between the narcissistic personality and celebrity worship, see Christopher Lasch, *The Culture of Narcissism: American Life in an Age of Diminishing Expectations* (New York: W. W. Norton, 1978), 84–86.
38 Dick Keyes, "Lite Champions: Has Heroism Become a Trivial Pursuit?" *Christianity Today*, May 1988, 32; Todd Hertz, "Capeless Crusaders," *Campus Life Ignites Your Faith*, January–February 2008, 30; Kenneth S. Kantzer, "In Search of Heroes," *Christianity Today*, November 8, 1985, 16, 17; Al J. Stump, "Unknown Brigade of Civilian Heroes," *American Legion Magazine*, May 1981, 12.
39 Silber, "Of Mermaids and Magnificence," 592; Nussbaum, "Real Masters of the Universe," 55. See also Barry Van Lenten, "In Search of Today's Male Icons," *Daily News Record*, April 17, 1998, 56; "How to Be Great! What Does it Take to Be a Hero?,"

excessive materialism, selfishness, and insularity of American society. After 9/11, the editorial page editor of *Business Week* asked: "Have we stripped too much away in recent years in order to make us lean and mean for the race to riches?"[40]

At the center of the discourse on heroes, encompassing most of its elements, was the concept of community. Community appears regularly, and in a variety of forms and expressions, in this literature. One important perception was that the country was coming apart; socially fragmented by what would become known as multi-culturalism and by what many argued was a spreading ethical relativism. For distinguished psychologist Kenneth E. Clark, heroes were the solution, or part of one. "We do need heroes," he said in 1982, unifying figures that would help us "resolve conflicts" and "pull various segments of our country together."[41] Emphasizing the critical role of heroes in any society, and especially one socially fragmented and in ethical disarray, *Christianity Today* promoted "public heroes" who "provide coherence at a deep level to the society."[42] At the local level, the celebration of heroes – ordinary and extraordinary – was a plea for a return to face-to-face community, to people helping people, to neighbors helping neighbors, to strangers helping strangers. "Carnegie Commission heroes," wrote Al J. Stump in *American Legion*, "prove that some of us still care enough for our neighbor to die for him." The Commission, Stump explained, favored "ordinary folk who responded to the plight of a total stranger."[43] "Heroes remind us," echoed Susan Littwin in the magazine *Los Angeles*, "that we are not so bad, so fearful, so indifferent after all. They reassure us that out there in the dark and when the chips are down, we can still count on one another."[44]

The tragedy of the twin towers evoked a profound longing for forms of community seen to be in decline. One brief essay in *Business Week* contained several expressions of this longing: "The rush to church,

---

Psychology Today, November–December 1995, 46; Katterjohn, "Casalini Book," 15; Mariotti, "Where Have All the Heroes Gone," 25.

40 Nussbaum, "Real Masters of the Universe," 55.

41 "America Needs Heroes to 'Pull the Country Together,'" *U.S. News & World Report*, June 7, 1982, 68. On value fragmentation and relativism, see also Robert Bell, "Heroes: Are We Better off without Them?," *Boston Magazine*, August 1985, 112; and Powers, "Do Teens Hunger for Heroes?," 108.

42 Keyes, "Lite Champions," 29.

43 Stump, "Unknown Brigade of Civilian Heroes," 12.

44 Littwin, "Heroes," 142. On heroes as strangers, see also Orr, "To the Rescue," 18.

synagogue, and, yes, mosque"; the "quick return to family, community, church and patriotism"; surprised New York residents observing their city becoming a "small-town community"; neighbors joining neighbors in mourning; a new appreciation for "public service"; people suddenly "polite and generous."[45] For *Good Housekeeping*, the lesson of 9/11 was that heroism "is not a matter of talent or physical ability or fame .... It is about acting in service of others and, many times, making sacrifices for them."[46]

This deep desire for community, for a renewed social solidarity, helps explain why heroes had to be ordinary, why they had to be the guy next door, the woman down the street, the local pharmacist, a customer, an employee, a clerk, a co-worker. It explains why the veneer of commonality represented in celebrity culture was so often and thoroughly rejected. It explains why so many of those ordinary heroes were celebrated for their altruism: the volunteer mentoring inner-city students, the mother creating a foundation to fight cardiomyopathy, the white man who saved two black toddlers from drowning, the ophthalmologist who one day a week treated poor patients for free, the young man who ran an inter-racial basketball program in Brooklyn.[47] Cindy Schweich used two events, both touchstones in the history of altruism, in her brief essay on good Samaritans in *Right Now*, a newsletter for women. One was the story of Kitty Genovese, who was stabbed to death outside her apartment in Kew Gardens, a part of New York City, in 1964. Though the incident was witnessed by many people, no one – as the urban legend has it – intervened or called the police. The second incident, nearly two decades later, featured the heroic actions of Arland Williams, an ordinary man giving his life to save his fellow passengers in Washington's Potomac River.[48]

---

45 Nussbaum, "Real Masters of the Universe," 55.
46 O'Shaughnessy, "Finding the Hero in You."
47 Hertz, "Campus Life Ignites Your Faith," 30; "2004 Heroes for Health Awards," 51; "White Florida Man Pulls Twin Toddlers from Car Plunged in Roadside Canal," *Jet*, July 12, 1999, 24; Peale, "Different Breed of Hero," 66; Foley, "The Hero in All of Us," 72; Michael Daley, "Heroes for Today," *New York*, January 18, 1982, 32. On the interracial community in the heroism discourse, see "Ordinary Heroes," *American Legion Magazine*, 42. George Gilder argues that profits were a form of public service in "The Real American Heroes," *Chief Executive*, January–February 1989, 8.
48 Cindy Schweich, "Good Samaritans: Why Do They Do It?," *Right Now*, December 1982, 49. The story of what happened to Kitty Genovese, and what observers did or did not do at the time, is more complex than the brief description here. What became known as the "bystander effect" or the "Genovese Syndrome" began with Martin Gansberg's story in the *New York Times*, published two weeks after the murder and rape. Gansberg,

Schweich's hope, that the nation had turned a corner toward a new sense of community and self-sacrifice, proved to be wishful thinking. The decline of community was no fiction of the American imagination. It was real and profound, and it continues to this day, bringing new fuel to the celebration of ordinary heroes. We know this from three excellent studies of community, appearing fifteen years apart. The first was sociologist Robert Bellah's *Habits of the Heart: Individualism and Commitment in American Life*, published in 1985, in the middle of Ronald Reagan's two-term presidency. Based on over 200 interviews, this team effort – like the heroism discourse – found Americans overly materialistic and lacking firmly grounded moral values. They were insufficiently committed to the public good and collective action and, especially, overly given to the ideal of the "autonomous individual." "The modern American hero," wrote Bellah, is the "hard-boiled detective," "a loner." Following Alexis De Toqueville, Bellah and his team found Americans involved in an "astounding variety of voluntary associations," yet they also revealed that this voluntarism was not accompanied by a commitment to "social responsibility."[49]

Next up was Robert D. Putnam's bestseller, *Bowling Alone: The Collapse and Revival of American Community*, published in 2000. Putnam covered some of the same ground as Bellah, finding individualism, materialism, and distrust of institutions excessive and on the rise – issues also raised in the ordinary heroes discourse. But what he had to say about Americans'

"Thirty-Eight Who Saw Murder Didn't Call the Police," *New York Times*, March 27, 1964, at http://ww2.southeastern.edu/Academics/Faculty/scraig/gansberg.html. It seems likely that the interest in altruism in the ordinary hero discourse is part of a broader inquiry into the nature of altruism among social scientists in the same period. A recent example is David Sloan Wilson, *Does Altruism Exist? Culture, Genes, and the Welfare of Others* (New Haven: Yale University Press, 2015), in which Wilson seeks to demonstrate that altruism exists for some other reason than genetics. See H. Allen Orr, "The Biology of Being Good to Others," a review of Wilson's book, in the *New York Review of Books*, March 1915, 27–29.

In *Becoming Freud: The Making of a Psychoanalyst* (New Haven: Yale University Press, 2014), Adam Phillips argues that for Freud, heroism, or more precisely "the idea of heroism," "was an attempted self-cure for our flagrant vulnerability." Quoted in Vivian Gornick, "The Interpretation of Freud," *New York Review of Books*, August 10, 2014, 10. The idea has relevance not only for vulnerable individuals such as accident victims, but to the American nation in the 1980s, shaken and humbled by recent events.

49 Robert Bellah, Richard Madsen, William M. Sullivan, Ann Swidler, and Steven M. Tipton, *Habits of the Heart: Individualism and Commitment in American Life* (New York: Harper & Row, 1985), vii, 47, 79–80, 143–145, 167, 177, 295.

participation in groups and organizations was new and would have had Toqueville turning in his grave. According to Putnam, participation had been declining since 1965, and precipitously. By 2000 – indeed, long before then – there were fewer card parties, fewer union and church groups, fewer fraternal organizations, fewer people who participated in Parent Teacher Association (PTA) activities or civil rights organizations such as the National Association for the Advancement of Colored people (NAACP), lower rates of church membership and attendance, less volunteering in community projects, less participation in club meetings, less interest in current events, less reading of daily newspapers, less political participation of all kinds, less trust of others, less philanthropy – and fewer bowling leagues. Two factors were responsible. One was generational: an older generation that had experienced World War II and had very high levels of social interaction and participation was being replaced, first by boomers and then by Generation Xers; groups with much less interest in such networks. The second factor explains the first. Boomers and Gen Xers were raised on television entertainment – essentially, a heavy dose of celebrity culture (frequently mentioned in the heroes discourse) – a vacuous and home-centered activity and, according to Putnam, the most important predictor of civic disengagement.[50]

The latest entry is Marc J. Dunkelman's *The Vanishing Neighbor: The Transformation of American Community*, which was published in 2014. Some of the complaints that surfaced in the heroes discourse and found their way into the books by Bellah and Putnam – especially individualism and narcissism (though not materialism and not affluence) – are also present in Dunkelman's account. Indeed, he credits late-twentieth century prosperity with having enlarged the possibilities and choices open to Americans and, by doing so, encouraging various forms of social balkanization and insularity. Like Putnam, Dunkelman is concerned about the obvious decline of what he calls "middle-ring" relationships (such as fraternal associations and older neighborhoods) that fostered interaction among diverse people. He is concerned, too, about the replacement of those

---

50 Putnam, *Bowling Alone: The Collapse and Revival of American Community* (New York: Simon & Schuster, 2000). Older Americans were not only more likely to participate and belong, they were also more likely to select traditional figures – presidents and military figures – than young people. See the responses of 15 (famous) people to the question, "What is Your Favorite American hero – and why?" in the article by that title in *Good Housekeeping*, July 1986, 108–09.

relationships with intimate "inner-ring" ties (parent/child, close friends, life in the home) or casual "outer-ring" links (networking with like-minded people, often strangers on the internet, for which he uses the term "communal narcissism"). Even so, the book lacks the apocalyptic tone of its predecessors. As the subtitle suggests, community is not in decline; it is undergoing an inevitable transformation. The key, Dunkelman suggests, is to "adjust" our institutions to the new forms of community.[51]

Whether community was in decline or being transformed, the changes were real and, to many Americans, deeply disturbing. Among those interrogating the problem, albeit indirectly and for the most part unconsciously, were the writers and editors who collectively told the story of the decline of the American hero and, alongside it, the story of the ordinary hero. The discourse to which they contributed was about heroes, of course. But it was also, as we have seen, about community. The negative side of the discourse was about the things that damaged community, that prevented people from coming together in genuine solidarity, whether as a nation or on the local level: celebrity, the media, narcissism, materialism, affluence, hedonism, a surfeit of individualism, ethical relativism and, to some extent, multiculturalism and feminism. The positive side of the discourse featured words and images that evoked the social solidarity that was so much desired. Heroes were "everywhere": neighbors, employers, customers, the "guy at the gas station," truckers and train conductors, the white man rescuing the black child, women engaged in social service, strangers helping strangers, people doing what was right, people "pulling the country together." At the center of the discourse, doing the heavy lifting in this work of collective imagination, was the ordinary hero, whose every act stood for what America was not, but wanted to be.

---

51 Marc J. Dunkelman, *The Vanishing Neighbor: The Transformation of American Community* (New York: W.W. Norton, 2014).

"It Must Have Been Cold There In My Shadow": Everyday Heroism in Superhero Narratives[1]

Michael Goodrum

Saruman believes it is only great power that can hold evil in check. But that is not what I have found. I've found it is the small things, everyday deeds of ordinary folk that keeps the darkness at bay. Simple acts of kindness and love.

Gandalf in J. R. R. Tolkien's, *The Hobbit*.

"Everyday heroism" seems oxymoronic. By its very nature, a heroic act is something that transcends the everyday, elevating the individual responsible for it in the eyes of those around them – eyes through which the act and actor are imbued with their heroic status. To understand "everyday heroes," we must therefore understand the context of "everyday heroism." It is a term that emerged in the nineteenth century in an explicitly political context, offering an alternative to the "false heroes of barbarous man ... who can only boast of the destruction of their fellows" that, in the eyes of people such as Andrew Carnegie, was being promoted by the militaristic culture of imperial Britain at the time.[2] "Everyday heroism" was actively mobilized by critics of this culture as an alternative; a means of serving rather than subjecting humanity. There are points of continuity between the two, though, as both forms clearly draw on the same threads of muscular Christianity; of a heroic, self-sacrificing man who performs such deeds out of a sense of moral and religious duty. That

---

[1] I would like to thank Simon Wendt for organizing the conference at the Goethe-University of Frankfurt in March 2015 that formed the basis of this edited collection. I would also like to thank John Haynes (Essex) & Gavan Lennon (CCCU) for some useful pointers on this piece, and my old comrades John Price and Craig Barclay, without whom I might never have got into or out of that Eintracht Frankfurt Ultras bar.

[2] The "false heroes" reference is to the inscription on a tomb in Dunfermline, erected in 1886, and funded by Andrew Carnegie, which reads: "The false heroes of barbarous man are those who can only boast of the destruction of their fellows. The true heroes of civilization are those alone who save or greatly serve them." See also John Price, *Everyday Heroism: Victorian Constructions of the Heroic Civilian* (London: Bloomsbury, 2014), 159–165.

tensions and continuities existed demonstrate that definitions of heroism offer an insight into the conflicts at play in constructions of "worthy" behavior at precise points in time. Heroism is in the eye of the definer, and is socially constructed, meaning that heroes operate, as Max Jones states, as "sites within which we can find evidence of the cultural beliefs, social practices, political structures, and economic systems of the past."[3] Cultural products are therefore excellent vehicles for analysis, granting an insight into processes of creation and reception that show how intentions and interpretations were at play in the moment of creation. Analysis of everyday heroism in superhero narratives deepens understanding of these tensions through the co-existence of multiple layers of heroism and active fan communities who debate the meaning of characters and stories. Superhero narratives also offer a means of analyzing the ways in which culture was mobilized in order to build support for definitions – and, indeed, to position them as models capable of replication in the real world.

In order to appreciate everyday heroism in the very specific context of superhero narratives, it is first necessary to consider the experience of heroism in the USA. American history has offered excellent opportunities for the development of everyday heroism – and for its mythologizing. From the midnight ride of Paul Revere to the tales of heroic slave resistance, from Civil Rights campaigners to those who sought to help during the attack on the World Trade Center in 2001, the US is awash with tales of "everyday" heroes.[4] After all, it was Revere who sought a better life for all the colonists; the slaves who sought a better life for themselves and their fellows; the Civil Rights campaigners who tried to make the U.S. live up to its ideals; and the firefighters, police, and others who went to the Twin Towers to serve New York and set an example of everyday heroism for the rest of the world. It is in this context that superhero narratives take place. Those narratives have sometimes complemented or reinforced the work of "real" heroes and, sometimes, as with the attacks of September 11,

---

3 Max Jones, "What Should Historians do with Heroes? Reflections on Nineteenth and Twentieth Century Britain," *History Compass* 5, no. 2 (2007): 440.

4 Paul Revere is an excellent example of the role of myth in shaping a heroic identity. For a demythologizing of the Revere story, see Patrick M. Leehey, "The Real Story of Paul Revere's Ride," http://www.biography.com/news/paul-reveres-ride-facts. For the shaping of a heroic slave tradition, see Celeste-Marie Bernier, "From Fugitive Slave to Fugitive Abolitionist: The Oratory of Frederick Douglass and the Emerging Heroic Slave Tradition," *Atlantic Studies* 3, no. 2 (2006): 201–224.

2001, the narratives themselves have broken down in order to show appreciation for the acts that superheroes cannot do.

Although superheroes cannot exist in reality, everyday heroes can exist in superhero narratives. However, before considering their role, it is necessary to consider the ways in which these stories function. Superhero narratives are largely defined through the ability of an individual or group, such as Superman or the Justice League of America, to save humanity from peril. In the course of their actions, they routinely endanger themselves, providing narrative drama and readily accessible definitions of heroism. Although this could be seen to meet the remit of everyday heroism, there are clear differences between these narratives and Carnegie's vision. First, superheroes can hardly be said to be "everyday," despite their often humble beginnings, whether on a farm in Smallville or in a poor neighborhood in New York. Their very definition as "super" – the abilities that lift them from man to superman – take them out of the everyday, even as many superhero origin stories attest to their everyday status. Second, it is also possible to interpret superheroes as proxies for American military power; as cultural products that work towards the justification of American military intervention overseas.[5] This might be positioned as serving humanity but, all too often, such expeditions benefit political and social elites, not humanity as a whole. Besides this, the militaristic nature of their "heroic" interventions takes them out of Carnegie's vision of non-military heroism. However, superhero narratives are not just about superheroes: they have friends and family; they meet and inspire people. All of these individuals are capable of acts of heroism that can match, if not exceed, those of superheroes, and their presence requires a more nuanced approach to everyday heroism than that so far offered. Before advancing further, it is worth considering both superhero narratives and their relationship with Carnegie's definitions of heroism more closely.

In *Dr. Horrible's Sing-Along Blog* (2008), the superhero Captain Hammer asserts that "everyone's a hero in their own way," though he rather undermines his position by completing the verse he is singing with the lines "everyone's got villains they must face, they're not as cool as mine,

---

[5] For a persuasive account of this idea in relation to *Agents of S.H.I.E.L.D.* (2013–), see Samira Nadkarni, "'I Believe in Something Greater than Myself': What Authority, Terrorism, and Resistance Have Come to Mean in the Whedonverses," *Slayage: The Journal of Whedon Studies* 13, no. 2 (2015), http://www.whedonstudies.tv/uploads/2/6/2/8/26288593/nadkarni.pdf.

but folks you know it's fine to know your place."[6] Thus, a clear hierarchy of heroism is established, with Hammer at its pinnacle. This is the orthodox interpretation of heroism in superhero narratives – a transcendent hero and the people who must be saved, served, and defeated. It is, though, worth considering the villains in this series. Captain Hammer is opposed by the protagonist, Dr. Horrible, who plans to impress the object of his affection, Penny, by securing membership to the Evil League of Evil. The interactions between hero and villain are therefore not a space for the testing of oppositional ideologies as in so many superhero narratives. Instead, they are reduced to little more than the clashing of male egos. Although marginalized and objectified, Penny is capable of securing her desired ends, if only indirectly: through her relationship with Captain Hammer, Penny is able to bring about the creation of a homeless shelter for which she has long campaigned. Penny's actions are therefore the "everyday deeds of ordinary folk" mentioned in the epigraph, but they are mediated; dependent on the intervention of a superhero for their success. Penny's cause serves humanity, but she does not risk her life to secure it (though – spoiler alert – she does lose it). Consequently, Penny's actions do not fit within the definition of everyday heroism offered by the Carnegie Fund Hero Trust: "an action which has as its object the saving of human life cannot be regarded as one of heroism, unless the rescuer incurs serious personal risk in doing it."[7] It is therefore essential to consider whether this definition of heroism is suitable, or whether alterations are necessary in order to make it workable.

Such a definition, where heroism involves serious personal risk, focuses on the conduct rather than the goal. This conduct/conclusion division raises the philosophical quandary of whether value lies in the action – the fulfilment of one's moral duty regardless of consequence – or whether the result of an action is more important than the way it happened. Had Penny battled Dr. Horrible on a slippery rope bridge over an icy ravine in order to obtain the council's permission for the homeless shelter, her actions would be deemed heroic in Carnegie's terms, even though the outcome was the same. The necessity of risk means that many superhero narratives would also instantly be struck off as "unheroic" since, while superheroes serve humanity, they quite often do so without placing themselves in particularly

---

6 "Everyone's A Hero," *Dr. Horrible's Sing-Along Blog* (2008), dir. Joss Whedon.
7 Carnegie Hero Fund Trust, Report September 1908 to December 1908, 30, as cited in Price, *Everyday Heroism*, 129.

great jeopardy. It may therefore be necessary to draw a distinction between behavior that is deemed to be "heroic" and that which is just "worthy." Alternatively, other types of risk, or sacrifice, could be considered. Penny does not risk her life when collecting signatures, but her life on screen is shown as revolving around laundry and working with the homeless, meaning that, in a more modern sense, she does sacrifice her "life" – her social life – in order to pursue her chosen goal. Her relationship with Captain Hammer could be offered as a rebuttal to this, but it is a relationship of which she soon tires. This is unsurprising given Captain Hammer's lack of emotional investment and his treatment of her as an instrument; as a means rather than an end. Penny's example suggests that "everyday heroism" could be broadened to include elements outside bodily risk – a long, slow sacrifice of potential rather than a quick, bodily action. This would drive a wedge between the morality and the modes of behavior privileged in enacting it. Jude Akudinobi brings us closer to such a definition when remarking that everyday heroism "brings together the familiar, regular and even the banal with the 'remarkably exceptional, [which] emerges from a deep-seated, pro-active well-spring ... defined by ideals.'"[8] This suggests that, to some extent, everyday heroism is the active embodiment of familiar socio-political values; the acting out of abstract ideas. Such a broad definition of everyday heroism concentrates on the ability of individuals to realize, through deliberate action, ends identified in generally accepted moral codes.

Despite essentially representing these moral codes, superheroes raise serious questions about everyday heroism within their narratives. Stories about superheroes are full of actions that many would unproblematically deem heroic but, as already discussed, these are generally undertaken by extraordinary individuals. However, there are other points to consider. First, whether it is possible for anyone to commit an act of everyday heroism, in any of the suggested senses, in a world populated by superheroes. Second, whether the nature of the superheroes involved creates a space for everyday heroism. Third, whether the narrative is used as a vehicle to encourage acts of everyday heroism in the world outside it – either through the explicit promotion of a moral code that emphasizes

---

8 Jude Akudinobi, "Durable Dreams: Dissent, Critique and Creativity in *Faat Kiné* and *Moolaade*," *Meridians: Feminism, Race, Transnationalism* 6 (2006): 181, as cited in Karen Lindo, "Ousmane Sembene's Hall of Men: (En)Gendering Everyday Heroism," *Research in African Literatures* 41, no. 4 (2010): 110.

such actions or implicitly through the depiction of everyday heroism. Through engaging with these questions, answers to other questions such as who created heroes and why, how did those heroes change over time and why, and what functions were served by these pop culture figures, become clearer.

Roger R. Rollin states that "of all the fictional heroes, from those of folk culture to those of elite culture, popular culture heroes may have the best claim to divinity: they are the most widely known, the most unreservedly celebrated, and they offer the greatest potential good for the greatest number."[9] In Rollin's terms, superheroes "bring about a kind of community, one whose citizens are the fans and whose popularly supported leaders are the heroes' creators."[10] This provides a straightforward model that implies an uncontested mode of reading. Fans of superhero comic-books, however, are a rather unruly bunch: they might all agree that the protagonist of the series is a superhero, but there could well be major disagreement as to the significance or meanings of their actions and the ultimate goal of the character. Creative teams are also generally subject to far more criticism than Rollin suggests, with changes in art or writing eliciting debates in the letters pages about the respective qualities of the past and present team. Rather than a fixed point around which debate can revolve, superheroes are seen as serving a range of functions by readers from across the political spectrum, establishing the primacy of reception rather than intention in this remarkably negotiated terrain. Attitudes to heroism can differ substantially among the readers of a particular character. For instance, Iron Man began life in 1963 as an arms manufacturer supplying weapons to the U.S. military in Vietnam. In 1963, this was generally embraced – at least according to letters pages – as a suitably heroic activity. However, by 1967, there was rather more dissent as attitudes to the war began to shift and Stark's role as an arms manufacturer eroded his heroic position in the eyes of some readers. By 1972, it was a toxic political past from which Iron Man was deliberately distanced by a new creative team who shared the left-leaning views of a significant number of readers (to the chagrin of the right who had embraced Iron

---

9 Roger R. Rollin, "The Lone Ranger and Lenny Skutnik: The Hero as Popular Culture," in *The Hero in Transition*, ed. Ray B. Browne and Marshall W. Fishwick (Bowling Green, OH: Popular Press, 1983), 24.
10 Ibid.

Man as one of their own).[11] Similarly, a lengthy debate with regard to the nature of patriotism emerged in the letters pages of *Captain America* towards the end of the 1960s. People *usually* agreed Captain America was a hero – though not always – but there was disagreement on issues such as whether he should intervene in the war in Vietnam, or whether his entire moral code was outmoded; simply a relic of a bygone era that was ill-suited to an increasingly complex situation.[12] The world of superheroes is therefore marked by just as much disagreement as our own on the nature of heroism, and it is with an awareness of this variance that analysis of "everyday heroism" within it must take place.

A more straightforward point is that the presence of superheroes complicates the undertaking of any heroic act in that universe. Any act committed with the expectation of superhero support or assistance is more problematic than one pursued without the possibility of such support. For instance, in a Superman radio serial narrative of 1946, the *Daily Planet* cub reporter and friend of Superman, Jimmy Olsen, goes undercover in a criminal organization in an attempt to bring it down. When Stetson Kennedy went undercover in the Ku Klux Klan, also in 1946, he did so without the expectation that Superman would be there to save him if things went wrong.[13] It is therefore far easier to regard Kennedy's actions as heroic, despite both Kennedy and Olsen essentially doing the same thing. The connections between the two events are furthered by the fact that Olsen is effectively being instrumentalized to reproduce Kennedy's

---

11 For Iron Man's embrace by the right, see David Nolan, "Bigger than Batman," *The New Guard* (Washington, DC: Young Americans for Freedom, Inc., June 1966), as retrieved from <http://comicscomicsmag.com/?p=5471>. *The New Guard* was the magazine of Young Americans for Freedom, part of the New Right movement that emerged in the aftermath of Barry Goldwater's crushing defeat in the 1964 presidential election. David Nolan went on to cofound the Libertarian Party.

12 The debate on Captain America and patriotism, known at the time as the "patriotism-centered controversy," ran in the letters pages from *Captain America* #110 (New York: Marvel Comics, 1969) until at least *Captain America and the Falcon* #130 (New York: Marvel Comics, 1970). Notable letters include Albert Rodriquez in #110, who defined Captain America as "a defender of the Establishment"; Kenneth Burke in #113 (New York: Marvel Comics, 1969) who blamed "apathists, not patriots" for contemporary American problems; and J. Glenn Bevans in #115 (New York: Marvel Comics, 1969) who argued that Captain America needed to fight in Vietnam.

13 For a full discussion of this, see Michael Goodrum, "'His Greatest Enemy – Intolerance!' The Superman Radio Show in 1946," *Scan* 5, no. 2 (2008), and Rick Bowers, *Superman Versus the Ku Klux Klan: The True Story of How the Iconic Superhero Battled the Men of Hate* (New York: National Geographic Society, 2011).

own actions, based on information fed to the writers of the series by Kennedy himself as part of his project to undermine the Klan. Olsen and Kennedy both pursue worthy causes, and both involve risk: Jimmy Olsen is knocked unconscious and thrown from a bridge, while a pine grove close to Kennedy's house was set alight with the intention of causing his house to catch fire once his true identity had been discovered. The difference is that Jimmy is saved by Superman,[14] whereas Kennedy had to rely on himself, his wife, and some friends to put out the fire – a deed that reinforces, rather than undermines, his earlier acts of heroism.[15] Although both Olsen and Kennedy endanger their lives in the course of a worthy goal, the question of conduct and consequence must once again be addressed. Both courses of action bring about desirable ends – the erosion of support for a radical group advocating racial hatred – but everyday heroism in its classical form focuses on the conduct as well as its result. In this interpretation, Olsen's heroism is problematic as he acts under a more than reasonable expectation that no serious harm will come to him. He does not, therefore, "incur *serious* personal risk" but, at the same time, his actions clearly are "driven by ideals" and are "pro-active" in their approach to securing the ends implicit in those ideals. The series therefore offers a space for everyday heroism, both that of Kennedy and Olsen, but it is problematic: Olsen is not successful, Superman is; Olsen, despite his relationship to Kennedy, can hardly be a model for direct listener emulation as it would be too dangerous without superpowered support; Olsen could actually be seen as a pawn in Superman's game rather than as an agent in his own right, thereby reducing the extent to which he is responsible for his actions.

Less problematic, at least in terms of incurring personal risk, is the idea of ordinary people taking on the mantle of heroism in the absence of a superhero. Perhaps the most prominent example of this is in the *Death of Superman* story arc. Early on in the narrative, Superman sacrifices himself to defeat a monster referred to as Doomsday, saving Metropolis and potentially the world in the process. During the fight, Bo "Bibbo" Bibowski, a bar owner and friend of Superman, attempts to assist those fighting against Doomsday, even though the monster has made short work

---

14 "Hate Monger's Organization," *Adventures of Superman*, Mutual Broadcast Network, May 17, 1946.
15 For a description of this, see Stetson Kennedy, *I Rode with the Ku Klux Klan* (London: Arco, 1954), 267–272.

of many superpowered members of the Justice League: after Superman dies, Bibbo dons a version of his costume and states that "I'm gonna help everybody I can ... an' I'm gonna do it all in yer memory!"[16] Among the other heroes that emerge claiming to be Superman, the most engaging is a steelworker (and former military ballistics expert) named Henry Johnson, who never claims to be Superman, but was told by the superhero to "make [your life] count for something."[17] In Superman's absence, Johnson turns himself into a literal Man of Steel, using his metalworking skills and physical prowess to fashion himself a metal suit to protect him while he protects Metropolis and its people. The Man of Steel is just one of four "Supermen" who emerge after the death of Superman, but it is only Johnson who seems to embody the true spirit of moral heroism that Superman possessed – to the point that he challenges one of the other "Supermen" to live up to the example set by Superman rather than just engage in theatrical heroics.

It is therefore possible to identify multiple flows of everyday heroism in superhero narratives and culture more generally. There is an in-flow, where examples from the real world are fed into narratives, such as Stetson Kennedy, and an out-flow, where models of heroism from narratives feed into the real world. An example of the latter is found in the case of Riquelme Maciel, a five-year-old Brazilian boy who, while dressed as Spider-Man, ran into a burning building to save a one-year-old girl.[18] Flows of heroism in and out of superhero narratives are connected, as both establish explicit relations between the real world and superheroes. However, it is more likely that superhero narratives are intended to inspire moral, rather than heroic, engagement. Few members of the audience are likely to fashion their own metal suits and fight crime in order to make amends for past actions or to fulfil a promise, or go undercover to gather information to incriminate a violent group, but these actions can be partially accomplished through "worthy" actions alone. This could be as simple as giving to charity, challenging racist rhetoric when they hear it, or encouraging others to think more critically about their tolerance of, or

---

16 Roger Stern, Jackson Guice, and Denis Rodier, et al., *The Return of Superman* (New York: DC Comics, 1993).
17 Louise Simonson and Jon Bogdanove, et al., *The Return of Superman* (New York: DC Comics, 1993).
18 "Boy's Daring Superhero Rescue," *CBBC Newsround,* November 13, 2007, http://news.bbc.co.uk/cbbcnews/hi/newsid_7090000/newsid_7092000/7092039.stm.

ideological investment in, questionable groups. The example of superheroes can, occasionally, spark truly heroic behavior, such as that of Maciel. But, here, the way in which it is reported is of interest: it seems unlikely this story would have made it to the U.K. from Brazil had Maciel not been dressed as Spider-Man. It is therefore the out-flow from superhero narratives, the connection to superheroism, which makes this everyday heroism a global commodity as a news story. Everyday heroism might be the story, but superheroism forms the context that makes it a *global* news story.

The difficulty so far has been to define everyday heroism. It may well be easier to pin the concept to a more difficult one. Everyday heroism could be understood as a more diffuse entity akin to Deleuze and Guattari's use of the term *rhizome*: a non-hierarchical network with multiple entry and exit points that does not privilege one form over another.[19] Deleuze and Guattari also state that "any point of a rhizome can be connected to anything other, and must be" – a process that forges connections across all ongoing projects of defining heroism, both fictional and real.[20] As such, the discussions in superhero narratives have equal validity with those elsewhere in delineating contemporary constructions of heroism. Rhizome is contrasted with *arborescent,* a hierarchical form with clear lines of privilege. Rhizome is also a useful concept as it keeps in play the question of movement, of constant redefinition where "good and bad are only the products of an active and temporary selection, which must be renewed," – such terms, indeed, being constantly renewed and reinterpreted through cultural artefacts.[21] For instance, in the absence of Superman, who constitutes the privileged node of heroism in the *Death of Superman*, multiplicity is made possible and through it, space lost to superheroism can be reclaimed by everyday heroism –itself a multifaceted, dynamic process rather than a monolithic institution, as individual superheroes have the potential to become. However, the absence of Superman is presented as A Bad Thing, as is to be expected in a comic-book devoted to him, and the space made vacant by his demise is soon reconquered upon his (inevitable) return.

---

19 Gilles Deleuze and Felix Guattari, *A Thousand Plateaus: Capitalism and Schizophrenia* (London: Continuum, 2003), 3–25.
20 Ibid., 7.
21 Ibid., 10.

Before moving on from Deleuze and Guattari, it is worth considering another of their concepts in relation to superhero narratives: the Body without Organs (BwO).[22] The BwO draws attention to the fact that just as bodies are conceived of as a whole rather than a composite of distinct parts, so is society – an understandable body politic with clearly defined organs undertaking clearly defined functions. Deleuze and Guattari seek to overhaul this, showing how the BwO exists in a constant state of becoming, and that organs such as those in the body cannot be seen to exist in society – and that the body itself is in fact devoid of a single uniting principle that drives it forward. Instead, society exists as a space in which events can occur. Such a definition is potentially more accurate, hinting at the plurality – of ideology, of desire – inherent in any assembly, while making plain the contested nature of everything. Rather than superheroes and their allies operating as clearly defined agents of order in a clearly defined body, both the superheroes as "organs" and society as a "body" are in a constant state of flux along trajectories of development. Instead of defending a clear idea of society and its morals, superhero narratives, through authorial intention and ongoing reader debate, contribute to the definition of both. Everyday heroism in these narratives complicates the idea of superheroes serving a clear function since, through its existence, it problematizes the idea of superheroes (why do they not just do it themselves? why leave it to a non-powered individual?), by echoing or disrupting patterns established by superheroes. Instead of an organ operating as part of an organism, superhero narratives exist as constantly renegotiated bodies of practice. Although intimately connected to the society in which they surface, superhero narratives do not just mediate the values and aims of the elite, despite initial appearances to the contrary, since their function, and the interpretation of it, are never fully fixed.

Superman narratives have, so far in our discussion, made space for different models of heroism in two ways. First, through allowing a normal person, Jimmy Olsen, to pursue heroic aims, however problematically; second, as a result of Superman's death, through allowing others to lay claim to his heroic mantle – again, however problematically. Both allow everyday heroes to engage with the bodies of practice that construct superhero narratives and establish their own intervention in them. However, superhero narratives can also serve to limit the types of heroism

---

22 Ibid., 149–166.

available. This is partly through their construction of, and interaction with, villains and the ideological confines this creates. For instance, Firebrand, a Marxist ideologue, made his first appearance in 1970 in *The Invincible Iron Man* #27. Despite the cogency of his critique of the U.S. and the occasionally sympathetic portrayal of it, Firebrand is always positioned as a villain. Most importantly for this piece, he is essentially an ordinary man who comes to do extraordinary things to further what he regards as the good of society as a whole. It is this focus on the abstract, rather than the personal, that causes difficulties in regarding Firebrand as a hero in the conventional sense imagined by the definitions offered so far. In *The Invincible Iron Man* #27, Firebrand offers a persuasive account of the state of the Civil Rights movement and the U.S.:

> I'm just an all-American boy, Iron Man, one of those wide-eyed innocents who started out to make this nation a better place. I sat in for Civil Rights, marched for peace, demonstrated on campus, and got chased by vicious dogs, spat on by bigots, beat on by "patriots", choked by tear gas, and blinded by mace until I finally caught on. This country doesn't want to be changed! The only way to build anything decent is to tear down what's here and start over.[23]

In this speech, Firebrand raises a crucial point with regard to heroism: its relationship to the social order. The military heroism decried in the initial construction of everyday heroism was clearly designed to reinforce state apparatus and was in fact mobilized to this effect. The idea that a quick military victory will prop up a government is evident throughout history. Yet everyday heroism did not necessarily criticize the state – in fact, John Price states that the commemoration of everyday heroism in Victorian and Edwardian Britain by private, middle-class individuals was designed "as a mechanism to promote and encourage more "respectable" behavior among the working classes as a whole."[24] We can take "respectable" to mean "behavior in accordance with dominant values as defined by the socio-political elite." This is evident in that the state sought to equate "heroic acts with loyalty to the Crown or the nation-state," mobilizing acts of everyday heroism as a means of securing continued ideological investment in governing elites and the system that guaranteed their position of privilege.[25] But Firebrand refuses to serve this function. Having

---

23 Archie Goodwin and Don Heck, et al., *The Invincible Iron Man* #27 (New York: Marvel Comics, 1970).
24 Price, *Everyday Heroism*, 64.
25 Ibid.

pursued tactics of accommodation without result, he turns to confrontation, asserting that there is nothing of value left in the system if it treats peaceful reformers with violence – essentially laying bare the coercive nature of power.

It is Firebrand's absolutism that marks him as a villain in the terms of the narrative. That he is prepared to let people die in order to secure his political ends is a direct contravention of many, but not all, superhero moral codes (for instance, Batman states in *Batman Begins* [2005] that he cannot kill Ra's Al Ghul but he does not *have to* save him). It is this absolutism that ultimately costs Firebrand his heroic position, having briefly been elevated to it within the narrative by the group of demonstrators whose cause he adopts. Firebrand's failure here, his appeal to abstract political goals rather than individuals, recalls the lack of success enjoyed by Soviet cinema of the 1920s, where "films structured around the active intellectual engagement of the audience" demonstrated, as John Haynes points out, "the need to engage spectators in emotional as well as rational dialogue."[26] Firebrand's ideologically-infused rhetoric fires enthusiasm among the demonstrators until its basis is laid bare – the individual can be sacrificed for the good of the collective. The internal critique of Firebrand is, however, limited to him, and not his cause – his failure is that of over-commitment and inability to convince others to invest in his vision of a new Reconstruction. Firebrand's defeat is made into a personal one when the position of the demonstrators is actually strengthened by a subplot. The fight between Iron Man and Firebrand causes a riot and Eddie March, a friend of Iron Man, intervenes in it to pull a young woman to safety. She then escorts March around the area occupied by the demonstrators to show how the city's plans for the area do not take into account local concerns. Multiple heroic narratives are therefore created within the same text: even as Iron Man defeats Firebrand, his friend Eddie March ultimately demonstrates the soundness of Firebrand's argument. March, having seen the deprivation in the area occupied by the demonstrators, states that "when a good idea can't make it through the system, maybe it's time to get out of that system."[27] Thus, the "heroes" and "villains" are arguing the same point in slightly different words, while establishing the points of continuity expected in a rhizomatic

---

[26] John Haynes, *New Soviet Man: Gender and Masculinity in Stalinist Soviet Cinema* (Manchester: Manchester University Press, 2003), 11.
[27] Goodwin and Heck, *The Invincible Iron Man* #27.

system of values. Given his ideological investment in the state apparatus, it is hardly surprising that Iron Man did not come round to the demonstrators' way of thinking until Firebrand's next appearance, two years later. In his renewed confrontation with the villain, Iron Man thinks, "Could it be you're afraid he's right, and by power you wish to force him into falsity?"[28] In this single thought, Iron Man acknowledges the role mechanisms of containment play in reducing the chances alternative models have to establish themselves. Heroism, and in some respects everyday heroism, could therefore be seen as a conservative force – though one riven with tensions and conflicts – and at the service of the state in policing acceptable definitions of "worthy" behavior.

The very theatricality of superhero actions poses further questions about their relationship to everyday heroism and the position of both in relation to the social order. In assuming an audience for superhero conflict within the narrative, as well as those who actually engage with the stories through reading comic-books or watching films, superhero actions can be seen as serving a range of functions. In one way, superhero battles are instructive in that they offer emulative models for everyday heroism. This approach has the potential to align everyday individuals, such as Henry Johnson and Bibbo Bibowski from *The Death of Superman*, with the morality and political outlook of their inspirational role models. It is not necessarily a given fact that the inspired will stay true to the vision of the inspiration, and this is the driving factor behind the narrative in *The Death of Superman*. In this way, superheroes exercise a regulatory function akin to Michel Foucault's interpretation of public execution.[29] Criminal acts are a threat to the socio-political order. By resisting them, and inspiring others to resist, superheroes, through their actions and influence, are able to exercise a degree of control over levels of ideological investment in the governing principles of their society. However, this is not always straightforward, as demonstrated in the case of Firebrand and, indeed, Eddie March. Here, Iron Man's victory in battle does not necessarily win the argument, but it does suggest that the point in question can be brought back within the confines of the system. This is replicated at both the superhero and everyday hero level: Iron Man considers Firebrand's words rather than

---

28 Mike Friedrich and George Tuska, et al., *The Invincible Iron Man* #48 (New York: Marvel Comics, 1972).

29 Michel Foucault, *Discipline and Punish: The Birth of the Prison* (London: Penguin, 1991).

writing them off out of hand, and Eddie March adopts the position of the demonstrators in subsequent negotiations.

As superheroes are only violent to the degree necessary (with some exceptions such as the Punisher), the idea of them as regulatory bodies in a network of power could offer a persuasive account of their socio-political function. The violence they use is carefully measured; it is just enough to bring the criminal under control and usually to deliver them to the authorities where they will be subject to the same process of law as anyone else. However, this assumes a preferred, or dominant, reading of the narrative where authorial intention is clearly received by the reader; a reading where the audience want the superhero to win, and to win in a certain way for certain reasons. Therefore, it is worth returning to the concept of the rhizome and the idea of the unruly body of superhero readers. Instead of a more conventional binary approach to heroes and villains, superhero narratives often position the villain as a reflection of the hero, or an exaggerated part of their psyche. For instance, Batman represents order and rationality, Joker chaos and disorder, yet both share an obsessive personality type.[30] Established points of continuity between the characters demonstrate that every point in the narrative and characterization is connected to every other.

It is also apparent that superheroes depend on villains and that, rather than having a hierarchical relationship where one is better than the other, they exist in something far more akin to a rhizomatic state. Both offer points of entry into the story, both invite reader engagement, both offer philosophies on how society should function. Competing visions are clear in the relationship between Superman and Lex Luthor, as demonstrated in *Superman Returns* (2006) when Lex Luthor, while discussing the myth of Prometheus, states that, "Gods are selfish beings who fly around in little red capes and don't share their power with mankind. No, I don't want to be a god. I just want to bring fire to the people. And ... I want my cut."[31] Superman might not share his power with the world, but he also does not seek to profit from it. Indeed, it is Luthor's desire for profit, instead of all his pretended ideals, that marks him as a villain. Similar connections were

---

30 For a more complete discussion of the relationship between Joker and Batman, see Michael Goodrum, "'You Complete Me': The Joker as Symptom," in *The Joker: A Serious Study of the Clown Prince of Crime*, ed. Robert Moses Peaslee & Robert G. Weiner (Jackson: University Press of Mississippi, 2015).
31 *Superman Returns* (2006), dir. Bryan Singer.

explored in the alternate universe miniseries, *Superman: Red Son*, where instead of crash-landing in Kansas, the infant Superman landed in Soviet Russia, eventually becoming the leader of the Soviet Union and ultimately being defeated by Lex Luthor, who is President of the United States. In *Red Son*, as in the case of Iron Man and Firebrand, agreement is found which problematizes the apparent opposition between the characters. Where Iron Man fears that Firebrand's critique of the U.S. is correct, Superman ultimately comes to see the logic of Lex Luthor's argument, with his totalitarian Soviet Union constituting an abuse of his power. Such agreement makes heroism a more contested concept; one that can be used to reinforce or criticize the status quo, or even both simultaneously. Even though Superman takes the USSR to the very brink of success in the Cold War, the U.S. still wins because its argument, the cause of freedom, is the most persuasive. Once Superman has abandoned his post as leader of the Soviet Union, the government is taken over by a radical coalition of democrats styling themselves on an alternative version of Batman – again, demonstrating the influence of superhero forms on everyday heroism and its ability to reconfigure dominant values. Thus, the role of everyday heroes, however defined, accentuates points of connection, but also problematizes them, thereby establishing other points of entry into the narrative that work towards the uncoupling of a monolithic definition of heroism from its superhero mooring.

Soviet heroes have already been touched upon in this piece, but they are worth reconsidering. Haynes reports that in the mid-1930s, Soviet culture deliberately moved away from the idea of a "fractured consciousness" and that socialist realism "sought to bridge the gaps between rhetoric and literature … [and] also operated to efface the distance between the subjective and the objective, that is, between the individual and society."[32] The Soviets were keen to do this in order to create the notion of a collective of submerged individuals. Superheroes, on the other hand, are essentially the logical extreme of the American ideal of the self-made man: the self-made superman. Evidence of individuality can be found in their powers, and in their superhero costumes, both of which mark them as unique, as well as in their origin stories, which craft a single narrative explanation that can be used to account for all their subsequent acts. Everyday heroes are not necessarily subject to the same processes of

---

32 Haynes, *New Soviet Man*, 45.

attempted containment, as they are not always bound by an origin story. This is another point where a comparison to Soviet heroes is worthwhile. The nature of Soviet heroes was dictated by ideology, and this led to a hero being characterized by a set of values and characteristics: a figure "so deindividualized that he could be transplanted wholesale from book to book, regardless of the subject matter."[33] This is a far cry from the highly individual origin stories of superheroes and the fan communities constructed around them. Both served the ideological needs of their societies by offering Soviet citizens narratives and characters intended to reinforce ideas about constructing a socialist future where the sacrifice of individuals is encouraged, and Americans ones that promoted a pluralistic democracy of free individuals pursuing their own interests. The everyday hero could therefore be seen as the very epitome of the Soviet hero: the ordinary person who demonstrates their "party-mindedness" and transcends their own limitations to take the collective one step closer to the "shining future" to be enjoyed by workers under the triumph of communism.

To posit the everyday hero in this way, however, is to overlook the complexity inherent in the character. In fact, it falls at the first hurdle, as the everyday hero found among superheroes does not point the way to socialist victory. Firebrand might suggest the desirability of such an end, but his critique is problematized by the narrative. Firebrand's commitment to abstract ideological goals makes him seem heartless in comparison to Iron Man, especially once Iron Man accepts the major points of Firebrand's argument. Jimmy Olsen's acts of heroism, discussed earlier, simultaneously call their own heroic status into question and reinforce that of Superman as, ultimately, Superman must have the "last word" on any issue to provide a satisfactory superhero story. This, then, is an arborescent heroic model – the hierarchical approach outlined by Deleuze and Guattari in opposition to the non-hierarchical rhizome – since Superman's heroism outstrips that of Olsen which, as mentioned earlier, is even problematic in terms of its heroic status if we use the classical definition of "everyday heroism". In contrast, the hero in Soviet culture of the 1930s was rhizomatic, with the heroic individual effectively being dissolved into multiple manifestations of the same character that connected disparate elements of Soviet culture together into a more uniform collective with a

---

33 Katerina Clark, *The Soviet Novel: History as Ritual* (Indianapolis: Indiana University Press, 2000), 47, as cited in Haynes, *New Soviet Man*, 44.

single purpose. It is a slightly different story in *The Death of Superman* since the everyday heroism of Steel (Henry Johnson) takes place in a world without Superman when the very idea of what it is to be a hero is contested – although Superman remains the dominant form of heroism even in his absence. It is, however, questionable whether Steel actually incurs any personal risk as a result of the apparent impenetrability of his metal suit. The fact that he is positioned as the successor to Superman, even though he never claims to be Superman like his three rivals, also works towards the reinforcement of a monolithic definition of heroism, even as multiple claimants contest that concept. *The Death of Superman* therefore positions Superman as someone capable of sparking emulation for the "right" reasons in narrative terms (the purity of the heroic concept), and the "wrong" reasons (the fame and trappings that come with that status in the capitalist West). The reason for the division is clear, as heroes should always work for the good of society, not the "laying up of treasures here on earth."[34] Those superheroes who are rich, such as Batman, tend to use that wealth for good, partially following the philanthropic logic of Carnegie, though never taking it to the extreme of one of his favorite maxims: "the man who dies rich, dies disgraced." For Bruce Wayne, it is well and good to give some money away, but all that bat-tech is expensive. Several superheroes benefit from their scientific prowess, but selflessness is also evident with some scientist superheroes, such as Spider-Man, who continue to live in straitened circumstances while using their highly marketable scientific skills as part of their superheroic altruism.

One figure from science in the Marvel universe provides another way of looking at everyday heroism in superhero narratives. Bill Foster is a biochemist introduced in *The Avengers* #32 (1966) when he is recommended to Hank Pym by Tony Stark – high praise indeed, as both rank among Marvel's greatest scientific minds. However, Foster's introduction comes as part of a storyline to introduce a group calling themselves the Sons of the Serpent, a racist organization who attack the African American Foster. Foster is therefore the victim, someone who "kept fighting till we beat him senseless,"[35] which is heroic in its own way but must ultimately be seen as conferring victimhood rather than heroic status. It is the Avengers, not Foster, who then tackle the Sons of the Serpent. Foster's heroic status effectively exists in a state of becoming.

---

34 Matthew 6:19.
35 Stan Lee and Don Heck, et al., *The Avengers* #32 (New York: Marvel Comics, 1966).

While he is "everyday," Foster is only a hero by association. But, as is so often the case with superhero narratives, Foster eventually acquires the same abilities as Pym, thereby ceasing to be ordinary as a result. This is a common trope, with Lois Lane, Jimmy Olsen, and other support characters in Superman narratives often acquiring temporary superpowers and seeking equality with Superman on that basis. Therefore, everyday heroism is, to some extent, presented as a step on the journey towards superheroism; a way of proving oneself worthy of "proper" heroism.

It is worth returning to Rollin's piece on cultural heroes to reflect on everyday heroism as a state of becoming. In his title, Rollin refers to Lenny Skutnik and the Lone Ranger. Skutnik was briefly famous in 1982 when he was caught on camera committing an act of classic everyday heroism, diving into "the freezing waters of the Potomac River in order to rescue an injured and drowning crash survivor."[36] Skutnik is perhaps now best known as the name given to the tradition of inviting notable "ordinary" people to attend a joint session of Congress – usually so they can be commended for their actions. For many people in the U.S., and certainly the majority of people outside it, however, Skutnik would require a quick Internet search to determine his identity. As Rollin notes, in contrast, the Lone Ranger is just known. Heroes of popular culture are "greater than the sum of their parts," and have a symbolic meaning beyond that of the everyday hero, whose heroism is so often confined to one instance and one interpretation: an individual who acted to save someone. Cultural heroes are open to far greater debate, and their heroism is often the constant that drives a serial narrative – a constant that remains open to interpretation. With superheroes, the very nature of that heroism, its superlative status, creates issues around the notion of the everyday hero, questioning whether it exists as a step toward "proper" heroism, which is to say superheroism, or whether it can even be said to exist at all.

Questions of circulation also problematize the everyday amid the extraordinary. By virtue of being better known, and being on their own territory as it were, superheroes dictate the terms of heroism – a reason why everyday heroism is so often simply a stage on the way to "true" heroism in superhero narratives. This did break down after the terrorist attacks of September 11, 2001, when ordinary Americans rushed to help others trapped in the World Trade Center. The comparison between the

---

36 Rollin, "The Lone Ranger and Lenny Skutnik," 44.

ordinary and extraordinary was made explicit in a tribute volume, *Heroes*, which stated:

"And there came a day, a day unlike any other ... when Earth's mightiest heroes found themselves united against a common threat." Those words were originally written about the Avengers, a band of fictional heroes battling fictional foes. But they apply as well to the harrowing events of September 11, 2001, and to the men and women who responded to those events.[37]

Everyday heroes were explicitly connected to superheroes, and were in fact positioned as superior since, while they were able to act, superheroes merely stood and watched – as in *The Amazing Spider-Man* #36 (2001), which opened with Spider-Man staring at the devastation of Ground Zero.[38] Yet the way in which many of the ordinary heroes were coded *as* heroes was through their adoption of superheroic iconography – firefighters with a Superman tattoo, for instance. The cover of *9-11: The World's Finest Comic-book Writers and Artists Tell Stories to Remember* (New York, 2002) worked against this by recycling and inverting an image from 1944 to have Superman and his dog, Krypto, looking up at a group of firefighters, policemen, and nurses and saying "wow," but the connection is still there –superheroes are still used to acknowledge and validate everyday heroism.[39]

9/11 therefore caused some disruption to conventional relationships between superheroes and everyday heroism. The everyday, if such an event and responses to it could be deemed "everyday," was elevated above the superhero, while the latter was still held up as a model for emulation; an ideal to which people could aspire. This suggests an alignment of sociopolitical goals between fictional superhero narratives and rhetoric around the deeds of everyday heroes. For instance, Susan Faludi reports that Peggy Noonan, a Republican speechwriter, would not have thought it out of place if President Bush tore open his shirt to reveal "the big 'S' on his chest," while Bush's rhetoric reminded United Press International's

---

[37] Carlos Pacheco, Jesus Merino, Tom Smith, & Kurt Busiek, *Heroes: the World's Greatest Super Hero Creators Honor the World's Greatest Heroes 9-11-2001* (New York: Marvel Comics, 2001), 14.

[38] J. Michael Straczynski & John Romita Jr., et al., *The Amazing Spider-Man* vol. 2 #36 (New York: Marvel Comics, 2001).

[39] *9-11: The World's Finest Comic-book Writers and Artists Tell Stories to Remember* (New York: DC Comics, 2002), cover by Alex Ross; and cover of *The Big All American Comic Book* (New York: DC Comics, 1944), artist unknown.

national political analyst, Peter Roff, of the "'Whams,' 'Pows,' 'Biffs,' and 'Whaps,'" of comic-book heroes.[40] Just as many of those witnessing the attacks could only compare it to watching a film, the only way of understanding the actions of leaders and everyday heroes, and deeming them heroic, was through recourse to fictional frameworks.

It is appropriate to return to the title of this piece to think in more detail about the relationship between the superhero and the everyday. "It must have been cold there in my shadow" is a line from the song "Wind Beneath My Wings" sung by Bette Midler, and describes a relationship between a public icon and the "beautiful face without a name" who supports and enables her success. A similar relationship can be seen to exist between superheroes and everyday heroes. Everyday heroes inevitably exist in the shadow of superheroes, even when they star in their own ongoing series such as *Superman's Girl Friend, Lois Lane* or *Superman's Pal, Jimmy Olsen*. Even the title emphasizes that the ordinary character only has value as a result of their connection to Superman. However, questions remain as to whether Superman gets anything out of the relationship: whether Lois and Jimmy are the "wind beneath his wings," where their endorsement of his actions and attempts at emulation create a space in which, and through which, Superman can occupy a heroic identity; or whether they constitute turbulence – a potentially disruptive force that complicates the smooth trajectory of Superman's heroism. This also returns us to the epigraph: Superman undoubtedly does keep evil in check through grand gestures, but there are different ways of measuring the efficacy of this. First, Superman has been doing this, several times a month and in high profile films, since 1938 and, yet, there seems to be no sign of grand gestures creating a better society on anything but the most temporary basis. By this standard, Superman is not particularly effective. Second, there is the extent to which superheroes inspire everyday heroes to achieve the "small things" and "everyday deeds" that hold great power and evil in check. These emulative deeds sometimes serve a restorative function, shoring up the society Superman saves. Sometimes, as in the encounter between Iron Man, Firebrand, and Eddie March, "simple acts of kindness and love," like pulling a girl out of a riot, lead to a subtly dissonant note – as when March loses faith in the system in which Iron Man is so invested. In the wake of 9/11, however, as the ordinary became

---

40 Susan Faludi, *The Terror Dream: What 9/11 Revealed about America* (London: Macmillan, 2008), 47.

extraordinary, the superheroic was more straightforwardly translated into reality as everyday heroes ran into a towering inferno to help others they had never met. What was more problematic was the way that this heroism was used as a means of obscuring and legitimizing subsequent policy decisions in the War on Terror; a campaign which, at least initially, superheroes were quick to join.[41]

Everyday heroes occupy a difficult position in superhero narratives. The oxymoronic nature of their status – the extraordinary manifestation of the ordinary – is rendered especially obvious when superheroes are an everyday occurrence. The continued presence of everyday heroes, however, attests to the fact that superheroism alone is not enough, either to reinforce or reform the existing socio-political order. Everyday heroes echo and disrupt the resonances of superheroes, highlighting their successes and failures simultaneously. When inspiring everyday heroes, superheroes are encouraging others to invest ideologically in the values they espouse and the system they support. When messages of reform are presented, they are often brought about by a deviation from "American" principles as enshrined in the Constitution – most clearly evident in Superman and Jimmy Olsen's campaign against the Clan of the Fiery Cross. Everyday heroism does not, however, have to exist in conjunction with superhero narratives – it does not have to be arborescent, in the terms of Deleuze and Guattari; it can be rhizomatic, offering greater equality in terms of points of entry and exit. In doing so, it also opens up heroism, demonstrating how multiple forms can co-exist in the same narrative and, indeed, in the society mediated through that narrative. In apparently offering a monopolar account of heroism, superhero narratives actually open up a space in which, and through which, multiple forms of heroism can be acknowledged and debated. Superheroes may well be an agent of narrative closure, but this does not mean they have the final word on heroism.

---

41 For a detailed discussion of this, see Michael Goodrum, "Superhero Films and American National Identity," in *Histories on Screen: The Past and Present in Anglo-American Cinema and Television*, Sam Edwards, Michael Dolski, and Faye Sayer (London: Bloomsbury, 2016).

After the Working-Class Hero: Popular Music and Everyday Heroism in the United States in the Twenty-First Century

Martin Lüthe

In a collaborative article that was published in 1977 in the *Antioch Review*, Marian J. Morton and William P. Conway established a meaningful, if slightly obvious connection between heroism and popular music:

> Popular figures – one hesitates to call them "heroes" – emerged instead from the underside of American culture: rock musicians – scruffy, bearded, young, and ostentatiously anti-Establishment, and black and Indian rebels, insurgents with non-white skins captured the imagination of youth. Tonto, bearded, long-haired, and dark-hued, rode the range triumphant, and Tonto's gain has been the Lone Ranger's loss.[1]

In this weird and exoticist, yet striking, passage, Morton and Conway reproduce one of the essential and intuitive ways of engaging pop music through the prism of heroism and, vice versa, heroism through pop music; namely in the conflation of two figures: the pop music performer and the hero. The hero, here, functions both as a social and narrative agent and, typically, as someone who decisively transcends the ordinary and "the everyday." This idea we find, for example, in Bon Jovi's chart-breaking song from 1986, "Wanted Dead or Alive," in which Jon Bongiovi and Richie Sambora sing the famous lines of the chorus: "I'm a cowboy, on a

---

1 William J. Morton and William P. Conway, "Cowboy Without a Cause: His Image in Today's Popular Music," *Antioch Review* 35, no. 2/3 (1977): 195. For a more general discussion of how popular culture has engaged with heroism and – to a lesser extent – everyday heroism, see, for example, Lance Strate, "Heroes: a Communication Perspective," in *American Heroes in a Media Age*, ed. Susan J. Drucker and Robert S. Cathcart (Creskill, N.J.: Hampton Press, 1994), 15–23; Robert S. Cathcart, "From Hero to Celebrity: The Media Connection," in *American Heroes in a Media Age*, 36–46; Ray B. Browne, "Hero with 2000 Faces," in *The Hero in Transition*, ed. Ray B. Browne and Marshall W. Fishwick (Bowling Green, OH: Bowling Green University Popular Press, 1983), 91–106. On Hard Rock and heroism, see Jan Mohr, "Männer mit Äxten: Heroismus in der Populärkultur, das Imaginäre und Hard Rock. Ein Versuch," *KulturPoetik* 12, no. 2 (2012): 208–232.

steal horse I ride, I'm wanted, dead or alive" (1986). The song produces an impressive conflation of the metaphoric West with the life reality of the travelling musician, which brings about the logical conclusion and climax of the song: "I've seen a million faces and I have rocked them all!"[2] Pop music's first entanglement with heroism, then, can be found in the artist/performer (as the voice of a given pop song) assuming the role of hero.

We often take for granted that one of pop music's powerful narrative engines can be found precisely in the ways in which the embodied singer's voice and the (heroic) narrative voice of the song merge, often times made visually explicit in a corresponding music video clip release. The embodied and narrative voice once again merge with the voice of the audience, as they appropriate the song, in music and narration for their own meaning-making and simultaneous identity-generating purposes: in our own, more or less private, renditions of the song – in the shower, the car, or a karaoke bar – we are, both the million faces rocked and the heroic singer rocking them. Thus, and here I follow Steven Shaviro's insights in *Post-Cinematic Affect*, I read the examples from contemporary pop music that follow as "expressive," as "both *symptomatic* and *productive*."[3] In Shaviro's

---

[2] The official music video of the song in its performance of what I term "visual choreography" – a complex and meaning-making relationship between the lyrical and musical quality of a recorded piece of music with the visual narrative of its corresponding music video clip – really drives the analogy between cowboy and travelling man home. Not only, but most obviously, in the continuing visual representation of the lead guitarist, Richie Sambora, with what appears to be a cowboy hat and the multiple shots and scenes that involve a variety of "steel horses" for the cowboy-musician to travel the world on/in. Cholly Atkins, Motown's long-time choreographer invented the practice and also made-use of the term "vocal choreography" to describe what he was aspiring to achieve as part of the physical performances of Motown artists (on TV and live). "Vocal choreography" typically was used to underline the crucial ideas, sentiments, emotions, or lyrical lines of the performed songs, most frequently through danced gestures audiences could easily decipher as performed instances of embodiment of the lyrics. In the music video clip era, and from the beginning of the success of the genre with MTV, the music video has similarly been used to – in more complex and different ways – enter a meaningful relationship with the recorded musical track and to add to, perform, embody, complicate, or re-imagine the cultural meaning making potential of the song it is used for. Again, this I call "video choreography." Martin Lüthe, *Color-Line and Crossing-Over: Motown and Performances of Blackness in 1960s American Culture* (Trier: WVT, 2011); Jacqui Malone & Cholly Atkins, *Class Act: The Jazz Life of Choreographer Cholly Atkins* (New York: Columbia University Press, 2001).

[3] Steven Shaviro *Post-Cinematic Affect* (Winchester UK: Zero Books, 2010), 3.

conceptualization, a cultural artifact's affective potentialities are mani- but at least twofold. He writes:

These works are symptomatic in that they provide indices of complex social processes, which they transduce, condense, and rearticulate in the form of what can be called after Deleuze and Guattari, "blocs of affect." But they are also productive, in the sense that they do not represent social processes, so much as they participate actively in these processes and help to constitute them.[4]

The following examples I read indeed as "machines for generating affect," and as means of "extracting value from" that very process of generating affect."[5] Setting out to transcend a mere genealogy of everyday heroism in pop music forms, I argue that the archetype of the "Working Class Hero" of folk and folk-inspired pop musical forms of the second half of the twentieth century reemerges, yet is drastically remodeled and remade into the "everyday hero" to serve different affective, gendered, and economic purposes in pop musical production in the first decade of the twenty-first century on the levels of music, lyrics, and the staged choreography of music videos and filmed live performances. This holds true because of an overall renegotiation of everyday heroism within pop-cultural formations in response to the challenges posed by the matrix of the "war on terror," the changing realities of pop music production and consumption, and the broader implications of global, neoliberal late-capitalism. Here, I argue, it is decisively this historical conjuncture of (1) late capitalism in its neoliberal form, (2) the pop music apparatus in the age of digital webs, and (3) the post-9/11 homeland, in which pop music's own traumatic technological crisis coincides with a renewed cultural contemplation and narrative proliferation of "heroism" in response to 9/11 – something, I trust, that

---

4 Shaviro, *Post-Cinematic Affect*, 3; and, because this analysis puts pop culture center stage, I also consider it a contribution to counter the ambiguous and skeptical stance the European humanities have displayed when engaging popular culture. Often times we consider the study of pop culture, much like its object of inquiry, as "either too lightweight or exceptionally pretentious," as Jaap Kooijman reminds us in *Fabricating the Absolute Fake: America in Contemporary Pop Culture* (Amsterdam: Amsterdam University Press, 2013), 22; for the complex and uneasy relationship between popular culture studies and history, see Jürgen Danyel, Alexa Geishövel, and Bodo Mrozek, "Pop als Zeitgeschichte," in *Popgeschichte Band 2: Zeithistorische Fallstudien 1958–1988*, ed. Bodo Mrozek (et al.) (Bielefeld: transcript, 2014), 7–18.
5 Shaviro, *Post-Cinematic Affect*, 2–3.

thoroughly complicates, among other things, broad assertions of a "post heroic age" in "Western" and late modern societies.[6]

In a nutshell, my conceptualization of the relevance of everyday heroism in popular music history is based on two main observations: firstly, in the somewhat crude observation following Morton & Conway that pop music performers enact, make tangible, and embrace crucial characteristics of what we typically deem heroic according to, and in relationship with, the logics of their time. Secondly, I argue that U.S. pop music history has produced a specific discourse of "everyday heroism" in the lyrical contents and musical style in the blueprint of the genre of guitar-based political folk music, which I will refer to as the apparatus of the "working class hero," in obvious reference to John Lennon's self-referential pop musical piece from 1970. This discourse, I argue, becomes powerfully re-invoked in the pop-musical rediscovery of a new kind of "everyday heroism" following the events of September 11 in 2001.

The following segment further explores the specific historical conjuncture alluded to above, before I turn to two interrelated readings of specific instances of pop-musical productions after and – to some degree – in response to the events that have productively entered the cultural imaginary of the twenty-first century as "9/11."[7] The first of these engages

---

[6] The notion of a post-heroic age in the "Western World" itself provides an interesting and crucial element in the broader cultural and discursive formations of our post-9/11 world and speaks to the subtle and not-so-subtle Islamophobia produced within and as an essential part of them. For a discussion of the notion of post-heroism, see Nikolaus Immer and Mareen van Marwyck, "Helden gestalten: Zur Präsenz und Performanz des Heroischen," in *Ästhetischer Heroismus: Konzeptionelle und figurative Paradigmen des Helden*, ed. Nikolaus Immer and Mareeenvan Marwyck (Bielefeld: transcript, 2013), 11–28; for a brief critical analysis of the idea of the post-heroic age, see also Dorothea Flothow, "Unheroic and yet Charming – Alternative Heroes in Nineteenth-Century Historical Plays" in *helden.heroes.héros. E-Journal zu Kulturen des Heroischen: Populärkultur*, ed. Carla Gebauer and Christiane Hadamitzky, Vol. 2, 2014: 5; for a thorough discussion of how race and racism intersect with heroism in North American culture, see William L. Van Deburg, *Black Camelot: African-American Culture Heroes in their Times, 1960–1980* (Chicago: University of Chicago Press, 1997).

[7] Among the abounding literature on the events of September 11, Amy Kaplan's published 2013 presidential address to the American Studies Associations stands out in terms of its scope and impact. She carefully analyzes the meaning of the semantics of the very term "homeland," which I take as a point of departure for my deployment of the term. She writes: "In the idea of America as the homeland we can see the violence of belonging." Amy Kaplan, "Violent Belongings and the Question of Empire Today:

Bruce Springsteen's album "The Rising," which was released in 2002 and was instantaneously conceived of as "the Boss'" immediate response to the events of "9/11." The second reads the complexities that emerged around two very successful female recording artists, who articulated their criticism and disillusionment with the political realities following "9/11"; namely, the country-pop group Dixie Chicks and the pop-rock solo artist P!nk. My argument unfolds on two interrelated spheres: firstly, I attempt to contribute to an ongoing critical analysis of the "homeland" formation following the events of September 11 and the complex developments taking shape within it, with the specific prism of popular culture studies. Secondly, by tackling the notion of everyday heroism, this contribution grounds the theoretical reflections in a reading of a contested and decisively intersectional discursive trope which became increasingly meaningful in "the homeland": the pop musical hero, whose genealogy and current expressive potential both brings together and complicates some of the macro-theoretical claims of recent debates on pop cultural production in the late twentieth and early twenty-first centuries, especially through its distinctively gendered expression.

Framing Pop Music Heroism Today

The discourses and practices that pop music in the United States displays when it engages with heroism today speaks, not surprisingly, to a brief, yet meaningful history of pop-musical forms that utilized heroism to make meaning. As hinted at above, I identify "the working class" hero formation of the social protest and/or folk song as the defining field of reference for any self-reflective engagement with popular music heroism today. Even the early scholarship on folk music, most notably Jerome L. Rodnitzky in *Minstrels of the Dawn: The Folk-Protest Singer as a Cultural Hero* (1976), assigned heroic qualities to the music and the actors (or performers) of folk music, and argued for its thorough embeddedness in the political protest movements that began to penetrate into the imaginary of white middle class America during the 1960s. While I share the skepticism of reviewers of the piece, I maintain that the fact that heroism and popular music

---

Presidential Address to the American Studies Association, October 17, 2013," *American Quarterly* 56, no. 1 (2014): 8.

conflate in the folk song and protest song, which culminates in the notion of a working class hero, is by no means coincidental. Woody Guthrie, Pete Seeger, and later Bob Dylan began to simultaneously, and self-consciously, embody and narrate the politically invested qualities of the working classes in the United States. More crucially still, the entire critical and scholarly discourse ascribed heroic qualities to the performers and the qualities of their music, thus making them the pervasive point of reference for pop music heroism they are to this day. This, I maintain, additionally points to the overall processes of generational meaning-making and cultural gate keeping of the so-called baby boomer generation, and to the pivotal role they played in making what we now consider popular music in the first place – specifically in terms of dissemination and reception.[8]

There are, naturally, a variety of ways to approach pop music heroism today. One of the more obvious choices one has to make is whether or not to utilize the performative, media-technological contexts of pop musical production and their logics as a contextual prism for an analysis of the cultural work of the recorded music (and its subsequent dissemination). After all, the pop-musical performances of everyday heroism are thoroughly embedded in an entire media apparatus that frames pop music and everyday heroism (and their interrelation). More specifically, the rise (and recent fall) of the pop music casting show format in the United States and the world itself drives a notion of heroism that we, as scholars and thinkers, might disagree with or feel uneasy about, but that is nonetheless discursively productive. There are three interconnected ways in which the pop music casting show performs culturally meaningful notions of everyday heroism for/in the pop-musical world. Firstly, and most obviously, the very narrative mechanics and the performative engine of these shows can be found in a notion of everyday heroism. In other words, what the casting show seemingly makes visible and graspable to an audience is how everyday Americans – neighbors, friends, and family members – become "American Idols." While an idol is not quite the same as a hero, the journey we are made to witness in terms of narrative is essentially a heroic one: seemingly chosen by fortune, we get to know the

---

[8] The monograph is Jerome L. Rodnitzky, *Minstrels of the Dawn: The Folk-Protest Singer as a Cultural Hero* (Chicago: Burnham, 1976). Already in early reviews we find a critical assessment of the ascription of the heroic onto the singer. See R. Serge Denisoff, "Minstrels of the Dawn, Review," *Contemporary Sociology: A Journal of Reviews* 6, no. 2 (1977): 269–270.

protagonists and their often unlikely discovery of their own talent as the shows proceed, obligatory and overbearing mentors, and then a culmination (a showdown) with one of the contestants succeeding to take the price.

Secondly, of course, the everyday heroism these shows produce generally follows the logics of the cultural-industrial complex itself, in that the very premise of all of these shows is that there is something meaningful about the endeavor and thus the contestants' journey towards "stardom." In other words, the casting shows disseminate the idea that the quest for becoming famous provides U.S. culture with one crucial source of everyday heroism: those that try are deemed heroic by us/them. Throughout cultural history, and in the narrative form and cultural practice of the "epic," narratives of the heroic and narratives of celebrity have been closely interrelated and, more often than not, conflated. In our age of post-industrial media landscapes, the two are more difficult than ever to keep distinct. Thus, these shows visualize and reiterate a version of the American Dream that simultaneously continues the legacy of the rags-to-riches story, often in segments that obsess over the humble beginnings of contestants, while it also updates it to this moment in media-cultural and entertainment history, where being famous seems to have replaced being heroic, or possibly functions as both the means to become heroic and the result of the quest. However, as I argue below, in response to the events of September 11, 2001, the notion of the individual heroic deed forcefully returned into the cultural imaginary and enabled a re-interrogation and further complication of heroism in U.S. popular culture in the early twenty-first century.[9]

Thirdly, in our post-Network-TV era, these shows enter an interesting and meaningful relationship with the aesthetics and logics of what is called reality television and the way this televised form has begun to complicate the meaning of stardom, celebrity, and heroism, as they re-purpose the very notion of the "everyday" for television – or, better yet, of the German *Alltag* – and revolve around the small "heroic" deeds we all perform to get

---

9 For a brief depiction of the role of media in complicating the already complex interrelationship between celebrity and heroism, see Robert S. Cathcart, "From Hero to Celebrity: The Media Connection," in *American Heroes in a Media Age*, 36–46; Silke Meyer, „Helden des Alltags: Von der Transformation des Besonderen," in *Die Helden-Maschine: Zur Aktualität und Tradition von Heldenbildern*, ed. LWL-Industriemuseum (Essen: Klartext-Verlag, 2010), 28–40.

by.[10] The heroes and heroines of reality television seem to indeed point to a possible age of "post-heroism," or at least of a very real change – an emptying out of the signifier "heroism" – in the meaning of the concept of everyday heroism itself.[11] And, Simon Wendt in his introduction to this volume rightfully reminds us to not fall into this very trap or to broaden the term unnecessarily so as to make it almost universally applicable. These changes in the production and the contexts of the dissemination and reception of popular music then enter yet another interesting relationship with the musico-lyrical responses to and as part of the post-9/11 cultural apparatus.

The Rising: The New Working-Class Hero and "Affirmative Reaction"

I want to point to two specific instances of musico-lyrical responses to 9/11 and the post-9/11 period respectively and the ways in which they renegotiate the powerful pop-musical trope of the "working class hero," which I would consider the defining one for the discourse of everyday heroism in twentieth-century popular music.[12] My first reading foregrounds the most obvious and conclusive lyrico-musical response to 9/11– namely, Bruce Springsteen's 2002-record *The Rising*. *The Rising*,

---

10 While reality TV shows more often than not, of course, maintain the distinction between them ("celebrities") and us ("audience") at the same time.
11 Also, as I imply here, everyday heroism has thus produced a discourse of power and placement similar to the one of old vs. new money – legitimate stardom vs. incidental stardom. What is more, unlike the pop music casting show, which in its obsession over talent beautifully upholds the notion of a meritocracy, at least in accordance with a meritocracy of the culture industries, reality television has simultaneously hyper-accelerated celebrity culture and deconstructed its premises in a way that indeed makes it hard to keep up with the Kardashians and their peers. Thus, when it comes to the fairly recent changes in the institutional and media frameworks of the contemporary pop musical world, the casting show embodies a certain notion of everyday heroism based in a meritocratic notion of the concept that enters a complex and tension-laden relationship with its Other, which can be found in the narrowest conception of "reality TV." Also, as far as production costs are concerned, this kind of heroism comes cheap.
12 And, of course, I bracket here the romantic hero, a figure that also often engages the "everyday," even though it also and necessarily transcends it; which is exactly what makes the romantic hero a hero.

Springsteen's first studio album after a 6-year hiatus and his first with the E Street Band since 1986, was immediately conceived of as the All-American rocker's response to the events of 9/11. The marketing of the album centered on the frequently reiterated anecdote of the stranger urging Springsteen to come back now, captured in the stranger's alleged roadside appeal, "we need you now."[13] Additionally, Springsteen's oeuvre of socially conscious songs, as well as the album title, naturally generated the privileged reading of the album as a record about 9/11 and its effects on everyday Americans. All of that is to say that it made sense and seemed almost inevitable that the New Jersey-native Springsteen would musically respond to what was going on at the time.

In a way, then, the album began to embody mainstream America's popmusical response to 9/11 – the album rose to the top of the Billboard charts, the Canadian charts, and the UK charts – and became emblematic of the larger pop-cultural response to the events of the day and the period that followed it. Consequently, public discourse marginalized various other possible responses to 9/11 that were produced in a variety of segments of popular music – rap musicians, many of them, of course, native New Yorkers, also by and large responded musically to 9/11. Still, *The Rising* became the quintessence of responses to the events. In his insightful analysis of what he calls an "Affirmative Reaction," Hamilton Carroll, as one of the few scholars who has zoomed in on the changing faces of everyday heroism after the events now remembered as 9/11, specifically analyzes the production of "new formations of white masculinity" in discourses and assemblages vehemently generated by the event.[14] Carroll

---

13 We find the anecdote discussed repetitively, for example, as late as 2009 in an interview with Springsteen for his then-upcoming release of *Life Itself* with Mark Hagen for the *Guardian*: "Springsteen has seldom shied away from big themes – think back to 1975 and the way a worried post-Vietnam, post-Watergate America responded to *Born to Run*'s romantic vision of escape, or how the small-town dramas of 1984's *Born in the USA* found resonance as the Reagan era deepened the divide between have and have not. In recent years that has continued to be the case; he famously began to make 2002's *The Rising* in the wake of 9/11 after a passing stranger wound down his car window and told the singer: 'We need you now.'" Hagen, Mark, "Meet the New Boss," in *The Guardian*, January 18, 2009: http://www.theguardian.com/music/2009/jan/18/bruce-springsteen-interview.

14 The monograph is entitled *Affirmative Reaction: New Formations of White Masculinity* and it prominently features a chapter dedicated to "'Everyday Heroes' and the New Exceptionalism" that I will take as a point of departure for my own analysis here;

rightfully analyzes how in "the wake of the September 11 attacks a narrative discourse was produced in which the emergency worker as everyday hero became both victim and survivor of the attacks, and thus the exemplary U.S. citizen." However, as he is careful to point out, the many cultural re-imaginings and the overall cultural engagement with what had happened and how, also incited a productive discourse following "a reactionary national logic of gender and ethnic identity that coalesced around the production of an exemplary white ethnic, working-class hero, figured most completely in the image of the New York City fireman."[15]

Not surprisingly then, Bruce Springsteen's *The Rising* epitomizes this notion in at least a twofold manner: firstly, because it came to be immediately understood as the emblematic and representative American response to the events of September 11 on musical record, it reproduced or doubled the very idea of heroic white working-class masculinity as crucial since, after all, Springsteen embodies that very concept. Secondly, the songs – their lyrics and music – became instantly perceived as expressing and speaking intimately to the white-working class heroism that became meaningful on the day of and the days following September 11. Here, it is necessary to take the analysis a step further than Carroll's undoubtedly helpful and insightful one, specifically with regard to the more complex mechanics of discursive production and the inherent expressive dimensions of cultural artifacts that came to generate meaning and affect following 9/11. It is simply not enough to pose and analyze an incitement to discourse on the side of cultural production, but one must take the complicated and manifold processes of secondary, paratextual production and reception into account.

The Rising serves as a case in point, as it is only as much an album about the events and effects of 9/11 as it has been made such through the reading (or production) of it as a 9/11-album on the reception side and the sphere of in-between, of a journalistic public. What makes the album really the "quintessential album" about 9/11 is that it must be about 9/11 in the eye and ear of the receiver – cannot really be about anything else – and thus epitomizes our own cultural reflex to read 9/11 as to the degree culturally productive as we have since made it out to be – rather

---

Hamilton Carroll, *Affirmative Reaction: New Formations of White Masculinity*. (Durham: Duke University Press, 2011).

15 Carroll, *Affirmative Reaction*, 50.

independent of intention and authorship. As Kurt Loder in his five-star review in *Rolling Stone* so memorably put it:

> The heart sags at the prospect of pop stars weighing in on the subject of September 11th. Which of them could possibly transmute the fiery horror of that day with the force of their art, or offer up anything beyond a dismal trivialization? The answer, it turns out, is Bruce Springsteen. With his new album, *The Rising*, Springsteen wades into the wreckage and pain of that horrendous event and emerges bearing fifteen songs that genuflect with enormous grace before the sorrows that drift in its wake.[16]

It is noteworthy how Loder alludes to the possible danger for an artist to respond to the events of September 11, while he simultaneously underlines Bruce Springsteen's outstanding accomplishment, even though, of course, much of the album had been recorded prior to the events. Additionally, Loder describes Springsteen explicitly in terms of the specific qualities of the everyday heroism of the Firemen and other emergency helpers of that day, as well as keeping in line with the album's own religious topic and tone, when he writes that Springsteen "wades into the wreckage and pain of that horrendous event and emerges."[17] This expansion of the circle of everyday heroism, having Springsteen, the white working-class' rock musical representative, and the Firemen symbolically aligned, indicates not only how the reception of the album became so powerfully about September 11 and, consequently, about the white "working-class" subjects of everyday heroism in the United States, but furthermore indicates how the political notion of "the homeland" came to be co-produced by, and through pop culture. Specifically, here, in the legitimacy of belonging ascribed to the white rock hero Bruce Springsteen, which contributes to the clear demarcation of those that belong and those who intrude. As Kaplan writes, "the notion of homeland itself" makes certain lives "terribly insecure" in that it

> polices the boundaries between the domestic and the foreign not simply by stopping aliens at the borders, but by continually redrawing those boundaries everywhere throughout the nation, between Americans who can somehow claim the United States as their native land, their birthright, and immigrants and those who look to homelands elsewhere, who can be rendered inexorably foreign. This

---

16 Kurt Loder, "The Rising: Album Review," *Rolling Stone*, July 2002; http://www.rollingstone.com/music/albumreviews/the-rising-20020730.
17 Ibid.

distinction takes on a decidedly racialized cast through the identification of homeland with a sense of racial purity and ethnic homogeneity that even naturalization and citizenship cannot erase.[18]

To the journalistic critics and the audience, "Lonesome Day," the album's first song and first released single, sets the tone for what much of the album came to be understood to be about, both in terms of lyrical and musical themes. It also evidences the specific cultural articulation of a sense of overall insecurity, which operated pivotally in the homeland formation.[19] Even though the lyrics of the song in the beginning revolve around the typical romantic longing caused by romantic loss of the Western pop musical canon, the second verse produces a more abstract and monumental imagery of a looming end of the narrative voice's environment and circumstance driven by images taken from nature, such as the storm and dark skies. What is more, the chorus following the verse culminates in the bridge of the song, which is played again very much towards the end of the song.

Musically, the bridge is set apart through the change of tone and its simple two/two-and-a-half words lyrical repetition of the emblematic motivational mantra, "it's alright" that Springsteen and a background vocal section repeat three x three times – each time Springsteen concluding it with an emphatic "yeah" and then twice, with the second "it's alright" vocally extended into the next bar to round off the musical bridge. The second time Springsteen and the background section repeat it six times simultaneously, before Springsteen sets himself apart as the solo vocalist of the song to reinterpret the bridge "it's alright" in terms of tempo and tonality in call-and-response with the background section. This alternative bridge continues with the structure and rhythm of the original bridge in the back, as Springsteen "improvises" on the front of the recorded track – in the rather typical and conventional style of these vocal performances of pop music as they have come to be recorded at least since the 1960s. However, here, the seemingly individual narrative of romantic loss of the first verse and the individual need to leave that sense behind and to deal with the title-giving "lonesome day" head on, becomes powerfully collectivized through the call-and-response pattern of the musical bridge as such, and the second bridge specifically. In the context of the release of the

---

18 Kaplan, "Violent Belongings," 8.
19 See Kaplan, "Violent Belongings," 8.

album and of the already established prism of the album responding to 9/11, naturally, it encapsulates the cliché of U.S. working class trials and tribulations and how these actually provide the U.S. working class with a crucial sense of identity: that they keep on living, that they will make it through, and that everything will be or is alright.

Additionally, Carroll reminds us that, in these clichés of everyday heroism and the everyday hero himself: "the United States found a powerful figure through which the nation could flatten the complex terrain of the post-September 11 world into a prelapsarian state of exception."[20] Springsteen's "it's alright" then could almost be perceived as the stubborn, but solemn musical response and chorus of post-9/11 working class and everyday heroism in the United States. Still, I maintain that the album's own telos – its logical point of culmination – is its last song, "My City of Ruins," which Springsteen then also played as the opening song for the Telethon "America: a Tribute to Heroes," which was broadcast on more than thirty media outlets – among them all the major networks – on September 21. It was in this moment, at the latest, that the notion of heroism, and everyday heroism, as put forth on *The Rising* became thoroughly inscribed into the cultural discourse of how the U.S. tried to make sense of and come to terms with the events of September 11 in 2001.

This acoustic version performed on *America: A Tribute to Heroes* sounds a little different than the version we find on the record. Also, the music of the song becomes thoroughly embedded in the performative and visual frame of the Telethon. Expanding on the idea of "vocal choreography," which ascribes the performing bodies an agency in its meaningful and meaning-making relationship with the piece of recorded music they embody on stage or in a TV studio, we have, since the success story of the music video clip entered a period of pop music video choreography. Thus, the previously recorded pop song becomes thoroughly embedded and re-purposed in the music video clip, typically deployed as a marketing tool for the single releases of any given pop music album. Also, with TV broadcasts like the telethon, the performance of songs can be recontextualized and can thus acquire an entirely different or additional set of meanings. Bruce Springsteen's performance of "My City of Ruins" provides a powerful example of the potential and complexities inherent in the performance of pop music songs on television. What follows is a close description and

---

20 Carroll, *Affirmative Reaction*, 72.

reading of how the performance unfolds and is framed, and to what intended effect.

After the camera has panned along a dark New York City skyline, without the Twin Towers, but with Lady Liberty standing its ground, to the simple backbeat of a percussion drum, we enter the dark studio with candles in the background and we see the silhouettes of Springsteen and a choir section. The lights go on to the sound of the harmonica. Springsteen then describes the song as "a prayer for our fallen brothers and sisters," and thereby already introduces the most important tropes of the song: that of a collectivity, of a family of Americans with a strong sense – and a need – for spatial, communal, and spiritual belonging.[21] In the context of the telethon's *mise-en-scène* and as a result of the framing of the album as a 9/11 response, the audience's reception of the song and the song's lyrics becomes exclusively about 9/11. Thus, the telethon and the album in a reciprocal feedback loop powerfully reinforced the sense that the song – and by extension the album – are essentially about the events of that day and firmly embedded in the U.S. American cultural response to them. In fact, the obvious religious overtones of both the song and the *mise-en-scène*, with its numerous candles in the dark, simple TV studio made the song the natural opener of the telethon and in a powerful way appealed to and tapped the collective spiritual belief in the U.S. American project and the specific U.S. branch of civil religion.

However, as the song unfolds, two performative inscriptions become evident and simultaneously powerful: firstly, the "folksy" appeal of this acoustic version of the song that, in terms of vocal performance, melody, and rhythmic section, self-consciously performs its own embeddedness in the quintessential American song-writing tradition of the folk song, or the "white man's blues". This, of course, Springsteen had effectively utilized at different moments in his recording career in order to place himself in that tradition, but it becomes especially meaningful in the context of the album and the telethon. The working-class song, then already signifies a specific nostalgia for the times and cultural/social/or historical formation, in which these songs allegedly became America's music – during the dustbowl years of the 1930s and then, even more pervasively, as part of the social, political, and media contexts of the 1960s. This is typical of Springsteen: he is a nostalgic futurist, who – in style and content – looks to and conjures a

---

21 In addition, the notion of the fallen powerfully merges the figure of the rescuers with the figure of the soldier in a war.

mythic past for a promising future. The song, in much of its imagery and style, then appears to be nostalgic in this specific sense, most notably exemplified in the extensive use of the harmonica and acoustic guitar as a stylistic departure from the album version. "My City of Ruins," as performed for the telethon, expresses a sense of nostalgia for "simpler times" that became progressively emblematic of many responses across the spectrum of U.S. culture (and politics) following 9/11.

Additionally, the aforementioned obvious religious overtones of the song and the album's central trope, "The Rising," add an entire layer to this vision and one that is just as effective and affective. The church holds a prominent place in the city that becomes one of the addressees of the song and the chapel-like appeal of the performance setting is all too obvious. Springsteen sings, "The church door is thrown open, I can hear the organ sound, but the congregation is gone, My city of ruins."[22] Strikingly, the narrative and imagery of the song, even though not straight forward and linear, move from a sense of collective desolation symbolized by the title-giving city of ruins which Springsteen, for example, conjures with the imagery of the emptied out church, towards the sense of personal loss and longing. The second verse essentially reroutes the song towards the conventionalized pop musical narrative and imagery of love lost, when Springsteen sings, "Now, there's tears on the pillow, darling, where we slept, and you took my heart when you left; without your sweet kiss my soul is lost, my friend, tell me how do I begin again; my city is in ruins." Generally, then, the song repurposes the city of ruins as a metaphor in the second verse aligning the individual lover's pain and heartbreak of the narrative voice of the song with the broader expression of general despair and crisis in the city of ruins. In the context of the telethon, however, the second verse strongly invites a reading of a permanent loss through the death of a lover, husband, or wife. It is through the tone and performance of mourning that the song re-collectivizes the individual feeling of loss in the telethon version of "My City of Ruins" and thus produces the double sentiments of violent belonging and an urgent longing for security. Additionally, and very obviously, through the introductory shot of the Statue of Liberty and the dark, solemn New York City skyline behind it, "My City of Ruins" becomes absolutely about this specific city at the very historic moment of the taping of *America: A Tribute to Heroes*.

---

22 Bruce Springsteen (2001), "My City of Ruins," on: *America: A Tribute to Heroes*; https://www.youtube.com/watch?v=zld2cSIVUO4.

As the song progresses, the pan-racial choir and the call-and-response structure of the song's climax further emphasize the thorough spiritual message of the song as it evolves from a folk song towards an all-out gospel song. The final segment and climax of the song accordingly express a distinctive religious longing in this time of crisis and even have the narrative voice plead for the faith to remain faithful: "I pray for the faith Lord," Springsteen sings. In a way, then, Springsteen's heroes are more than "the scattered young men" in the city of ruins. Rather, it really is the mythical place of "the city of ruins" itself: the collective, the quasi-religious community of an American society bound by civil religion that the song's voice then also belongs to, and almost paradoxically, lays claim to. It is, after all, "my" city of ruins. *The Rising* situates everyday heroism firmly in its own musical traditions, while it simultaneously – in contents and musical style – reinvokes the powerful notion of collective and communal spiritual belonging, in a nostalgic past and mythic future, as the best heroic practice to honor the ("everyday") heroes of the post-9/11 world. Honoring everyday heroes itself becomes a heroic deed of "responsible" and "patriotic" citizens in this post-September 11 formation of the homeland. While this state of political exception probably lasts until today, the cultural and the pop-musical response to it has become decisively more contradictory and their reception more controversial.

"Dear Mr. President": Gender, Heroism, and Protest in Popular Music Today

One of the undeniable achievements of Springsteen's lyrical response to the events of September 11 on *The Rising* can certainly be found in the more abstract allusions to U.S. American spirituality and civil religion that the album puts center stage rather than a more aggressively political or more aggressively partisan reaction. While I still conceive of *The Rising* as an embodiment of, and a pop musical engine for, the politico-cultural formation of the homeland, which made the notion of a homeland a new political and cultural obsession and consequently put "homeland security" first in response to the events of September 11, it nevertheless powerfully put the lost lives and the mourning first. However, as the political climate changed in the years following 2001 and especially as a consequence of the

U.S. military endeavors in Afghanistan and Iraq, mainstream pop culture and pop music became visibly and audibly politicized. Now, it seemed, pop music's own investment with everyday heroes and with heroes of the everyday had abated, as pop cultural meaning-making took a turn towards a more explicitly political critique and stance.

The ongoing media attention targeting the Dixie Chicks and the controversy emerging from a statement Natalie Maines had uttered at a concert in London in 2003, regarding the fact that she felt ashamed sharing her home state with then-President George W. Bush became essential during the years of production and for the marketing of their album *Taking the Long Way*. The subsequent release of the album to unprecedented success in 2006 signifies two crucial aspects of the evolving pop musical performances of everyday heroism in the homeland formation: firstly, as a consequence of one of the crucial aspects of "affirmative reaction," namely the prominent and ideologically pivotal place white masculinity occupied within it, the political investment of pop music became simultaneously powerfully informed by gender. Secondly, as the deeds of firemen, police, and first-aiders became a less immediate element in the cultural memory, the notion and location of everyday heroism also underwent a noticeable change, even as it built upon one of the pervasive tropes and performative effects of Springsteen's *The Rising* which ascribed everyday heroism onto the pop music performer him- or herself. As "affirmative reaction" and the discourse of everyday heroism embedded in it was and is decisively gendered, pop musical performances began to become progressively more explicit in their criticism of the homeland formation and began to reflect the cultural complexities of gendered violent belongings or the violence of gendered belonging in the homeland.

Unlike *The Rising* and *Taking the Long Way*, P!nk's 2006 album *I'm Not Dead* was arguably neither intended nor received to be in its entirety, or conceptually, responding to the immediate political context it came to be released in. However, the album featured the song, "Dear Mr. President" which, like the version of "My City of Ruins" discussed above, references the past of a specific song-writing and pop musical tradition: namely, that of the political protest song. Even though the song received a lot of attention, the artist and record company never released it as a single and stated that they did not want the song to be perceived as merely a publicity stunt.[23]

The song's addressee is then-President George W. Bush and the imagined community produced by the song is an American public disillusioned by the political apparatus and the political elites in the U.S. government. Consequently, in terms of the song's positionality within the homeland formation, the song foregrounds the everyday heroism of said community as the opposite other of the Anti-Hero Bush, whose own performances of All-American "folksy groundedness" become the target of the straight-forward attack of him as a person and politician. What the song performs is essentially a double inversion of the two components of everyday heroism, the everyday and the heroic, in the person of the president. Bush himself, in his presidential rhetoric and practice, tapped both discursive fields in a very productive manner at the beginning of his presidency and in his response to the sense of urgency and crisis following September 11. After all, his ordinariness and folksiness paired with his infamous communicated determination to "hunt these folks down" arguably brought the ordinary and the heroic together in George W. Bush as president and leader for a period of time. However, in 2006, the public mood and the cultural response to the president had already undergone a notable shift. P!nk's "Dear Mr. President" not only exemplifies said mood, but articulates and performs the specific anger that Bush's appropriation of the everyday hero brought about.

Accordingly, the song's climax brings back one of the central tropes of everyday heroism in American popular music of the twentieth century and before September 11: work, and specifically, hard work. The narrative voice of the song, a version of P!nk, in the simultaneous bridge and climax of the song, addresses the President, saying, "let me tell you about hard work: minimum wage with a baby on the way, let me tell you about hard work, rebuilding your house after the bombs took it away," before she concludes the passage with the accusation, "you don't know nothing 'bout

---

23 Such a statement on the side of P!nk's team is meaningful for two reasons: firstly, it expresses a sense of a changing political climate in which a protest song against then-President George W. Bush might be read as a publicity stunt, as an all-too obvious, cheesy way to cater to an abounding affect of disillusionment. Secondly, though, it furthermore expresses the meta-reflected and self-reflective state of some elements of contemporary pop culture, in which specific performative gestures are already treated carefully because of an anticipated, seemingly inherent, response by an audience of current pop music audiences.

hard work, hard work, hard work."²⁴ In making the president the addressee of the song, P!nk – much like Springsteen – establishes a feeling of collectivity: here, of an us versus him. The collective now is that of the disillusioned population of the "Homeland" and of the post-9/11 activation of "Homeland" as a political apparatus, as discussed by Amy Kaplan. But also, and more specifically, it is the honest, hard-working "folks" that Bush had originally identified as the backbone of his campaigns and as the ordinary heroes of an America to come and who thus in many ways functioned as the imagined audience for much of his political rhetoric and as the blueprint of much of his public performance and practice. P!nk here, secondly, resurrects hard work and the (hard-) working-class hero as the epitome of a betrayed American – betrayed by a fraud.

The climactic accusation, "You don't know nothing 'bout hard work!" establishes Bush not only as the ultimate political impostor but simultaneously, especially in the deployment of the double negation as stylistic device, places P!nk in the quote-unquote authentic, blue collar, folksy working-class environment of her own upbringing, which provides a cornerstone to her star text.²⁵ More importantly still, it firmly grounds P!nk's song in the pop musical tradition of the protest song. This, in addition to P!nk's frequent self-conscious and sometimes self-ironic performative gestures, especially with regard to celebrity culture and life, serve as a means for P!nk to play the game of working-class "authenticity" in a media-cultural environment that seems so acutely aware – even obsessed – with its own "fabricatedness," and strikingly hostile to these performances of distinct belonging, especially by a young female pop singer.

---

24 P!nk (2006), *I'm Not Dead*. LaFace Records.
25 In his crucial contribution to studying music television, Andrew Goodwin put forth the idea of a star text, as the trans-medial and repetitive performances of the identity of a performer, for example in live shows, music videos, interviews, photos, and so on. Andrew Goodwin, *Dancing in the Distraction Factory: Music, Television, and Popular Culture* (Minneapolis: University of Minnesota Press, 1992); the aforementioned album by the Dixie Chicks foregrounds a re-fashioned, politicized, and decisively feminist star text for the band; Dixie Chicks (2006), *Taking the Long Way. Open Wide*/Columbia Nashville.

Conclusion

In its thorough embeddedness in the network of (1) late (late) capitalism, (2) pop music in the age of digital webs, and (3) the post-9/11 homeland analyzed above, P!nk's attempt at rooting herself – both in terms of her class and musical belongings – in contrast to and opposite the presidential impostor of the time thus marks her very own heroic (or anti-heroic) quest as it aims at interrogating and opening up the semantic and discursive space of violent belonging in the popular and political cultures of the 21st century. More recently, and arguably as a consequence of popular cultures' engine to always produce and present itself as new – one of its obvious, if complex, serial qualities – the knee-jerk reaction of producing a homeland of gendered, violent belonging in the popular cultures and its inherent and, at times, seemingly paradoxical responses, have lost its discursive and performative fervor: somewhere in between the everyday heroes, the firemen responding to the events and those affirmatively reacting to them, and Green Day's "American Idiots" of a "redneck agenda", the dust of the intensification of pop music through and by a "new working class" hero has seemingly settled. In its place, it appears, pop culture's self-reflective celebration of itself has taken center stage again, partly – I assume – because the drastic media technological changes have now been accommodated to the needs of those producing and disseminating pop music as we listen to today. However, the performative complexities revolving around questions of gender and sexualities persist to drive popular music even as it slowly but surely seems to be leaving behind its own "City of Ruins" and the homeland these ruins co-produced.

Notes on Contributors

Craig Barclay is Head of Museums at Durham University in the U.K., with responsibility for major collections of European and Asian art, social history, archaeology, and natural history. He has written extensively on heroism and medallic art, authoring *The Medals of the Royal Humane Society* (1998) and *Acts of Gallantry Volume 3* (with Bill Fevyer, 2001). He co-edited *Treasures of the Oriental Museum, Durham University* (2010) and has published journal articles on topics including studio pottery; nineteenth-century silversmiths; the medallic work of Nicholas Hilliard; and the engravers William Wyon and G. W. de Saulles. Craig is the Secretary of the Life Saving Awards Research Society and represents the Commonwealth Association of Museums at the Commonwealth Consortium for Education.

Michael Goodrum is a Senior Lecturer in Modern History at Canterbury Christ Church University. His research interests include representations of heroism, gender, and national identity in American history. He is the author of *Superheroes and American Self Image* (2016) and co-editor of *Firefly Revisited* (2015), and his articles have appeared in the journals *Social History*, *Literature Compass*, and *Studies in Comics*, as well as in a number of edited collections. Michael Goodrum is currently in the process of co-editing another volume on representations of gender in superhero narratives, and articles on a range of topics in American and Anglo-American history.

Matthias Grotkopp is a researcher (post-doc) at the Center for Advanced Film Studies "Cinepoetics – Poetologien audiovisueller Bilder" at Freie Universität Berlin. He wrote his dissertation at the Cluster of Excellence "Languages of Emotion," investigating the cinematic evocation of guilt feelings as a mode of experiencing history and community (expected to be published in 2017 by De Gruyter). His research interests include genre theory, audiovisual expressivity, film theory and political philosophy, audiovisual constructions of climate change, the so-called Berlin School and French post-war cinema. He is currently working on a poetology of the heist film genre.

William Graebner is Emeritus Professor of History, State University of New York at Fredonia. His books include *Coal Mining Safety in the Progressive Period* (1976), winner of the Frederick Jackson Turner Prize by the Organization of American Historians; *A History of Retirement* (1980); *The Age of Doubt: American Thought and Culture in the 1940s* (1991); *Patty's Got a Gun: Patricia Hearst in 1970s America* (2008); and, with Dianne Bennett, *Rome the Second Time: Fifteen Itineraries that Don't Go to the Coliseum* (2009). He currently serves on the editorial board of *American Studies*, writes a blog on alternative Rome (romethesecondtime.com), and is studying the relationship between film zombies and the Holocaust.

Christiane Hadamitzky is a research associate at the Collaborative Research Center 948 "Heroes – Heroizations – Heroisms" at the University of Freiburg, Germany. Her research interests revolve around popular culture, the Victorian publishing industry, representations of the heroic, and concepts of the individual and the collective. She has recently completed her dissertation on negotiations of the heroic in Victorian magazines between 1850 and 1900.

Wolfgang Hochbruck is Professor of North American Philology and Cultural Studies at the University of Freiburg, Germany. His research interests are Disaster and Security Studies, Syndicalism, and Atlantic Canada. His most recent books are *Geschichtstheater* (2013), a typology of living history interpretation, and a cultural history of the American Civil War, *Die Geschöpfe des Epimetheus* (2011). He is working on a book about the culture of Firefighting.

Janice Hume is Professor of Journalism and Carter Chair in Journalism Excellence in the Grady College of Journalism and Mass Communication, University of Georgia in Athens, Georgia. Her research considers journalism history, public memory, and media coverage of death. She is the author of *Obituaries in American Culture* (2000) and *Popular Media and the American Revolution: Shaping Collective Memory* (2014), and co-author of *Journalism in a Culture of Grief* (2008). She has published numerous articles on media history in *Journalism & Mass Communication Quarterly*, *Journalism History*, *American Journalism*, and *Journal of Popular Culture*. Hume serves as head of the Department of Journalism at UGA and is working on a project about uses of history in twentieth-century American electronic media.

Barbara Korte is Professor of English Literature at the University of Freiburg, Germany. She works on British literature and culture since the nineteenth century and is currently a member of the Freiburg Collaborative Research Center "Heroes, Heroizations, and Heroisms" (SFB 948). Her book publications include *English Travel Writing: From Pilgrimages to Post-colonial Explorations* (2000), *The Penguin Book of First World War Stories* (2007), and *Poverty in Literature* (2014). A co-edited collection of essays on *Heroes and Heroism in British Fiction* is forthcoming.

Silke Meyer is Associate Professor in the Department of History and European Ethnology at Innsbruck University, Austria. Her research interests are economic anthropology, the culture of debt and credit, processes of nation building, visual anthropology, as well as social and cultural aspects of heroism. Her books include *The Iconography of Nations: Stereotypes in 18th-Century English Prints* (2003) and *The Debt Complex: The Making of Economic Subjects* (forthcoming). In addition, she has co-edited *Historicity* (2007), *The Disciplines of Anthropology* (2011), *The Power of Things: Symbolic Communication and Culture* (2011), and *Money Matters: Dealing with Money as a Social and Cultural Practice* (2014). Her current research focus lies on remittances as social practice in the migration-nexus Turkey and Austria. Here, Meyer studies economic practices as strategies of transnational participation and identity markers.

Martin Lüthe is Assistant Professor of American Culture at the John F. Kennedy Institute of Free University of Berlin, Germany. His research interests revolve around African American studies, gender and cultural theories, popular culture studies, and media history. He is the author of *Color-Line and Crossing Over: Motown and Performances of Blackness in 1960s American Culture* (2011) and *"We Missed a Lot of Church, so the Music Is Our Confessional": Rap and Religion* (2007), and the co-editor of the forthcoming *Unpopular Culture: A Reader* (2016). Lüthe is currently working on a study on actor-networks of media and technological change in the Progressive Era.

John Price is a Senior Lecturer in Modern British History at Goldsmiths, University of London. His primary area of research is nineteenth and twentieth century heroism, specifically civilian heroism, and he is the author of *Everyday Heroism: Victorian Constructions of the Heroic Civilian* (2014). John has written extensively on the Watts Memorial to Heroic Self-Sacrifice in Postman's Park, London, including the official history of the monument, *Postman's Park: G. F. Watts' Memorial to Heroic Self-Sacrifice* (2008) and *Heroes of Postman's Park: Heroic Self-Sacrifice in Victorian London* (2015), which documents the lives and deaths of the people com-memorated. In addition to heroism, John also researches social movements and popular protest; in particular, how popular manifestations of con-tentious politics can be better understood and analyzed by historians. He also works on public memory, memorialization, and commemoration, with a particular emphasis on the reception of commemoration and popular memory.

Sylka Scholz is Professor of Qualitative Methods and Micro Sociology at the Friedrich Schiller University in Jena, Germany. Her research interests circuit around gender sociology, especially research on masculinities, family sociology, sociology of film, and qualitative methods like discourse analysis and audio-visual methods. She is the author of *Männlichkeitssoziologie* (2015) and *Männlichkeit Erzählen: Identitätskonstruktionen ostdeutscher Männer* (2004), and co-editor of a number of books, including *Wissen – Methode – Geschlecht* (2014) and *Postsozialistische Männlichkeiten in einer globalisierten Welt* (2008).

Simon Wendt is Assistant Professor of American Studies at the University of Frankfurt in Frankfurt, Germany. His research interests revolve around African American history, American gender history, memory, nationalism, and the history of heroism. He is the author of *The Spirit and the Shotgun: Armed Resistance and the Struggle for Civil Rights* (2007) and co-editor of a number of books, including *Globalizing Lynching History: Vigilantism and Extralegal Punishment from an International Perspective* (2011) and *Masculinities and the Nation in the Modern World: Between Hegemony and Marginalization* (2015). Simon Wendt is currently completing a book manuscript on the history of the Daughters of the American Revolution.